ACTING IN DOCUMENTARY THEATRE
Tom Cantrell

'Tom Cantrell's fascinating book breaks new ground in exploring the role of the actor in documentary theatre. What emerges is a richly detailed picture of the physical discipline and moral responsibility that the representation of living people requires. By frequently invoking Brecht and Stanisl..... h   ʃund questions about the way acting is c   in   to   orms, I learned a lot.' – **Michael Billington**

'Refreshing and innovative, it is an exceptionally accessible text that rigorously engages with the mechanisms of making a piece of documentary theatre from a variety of perspectives.' – **Alison Forsyth**, *Aberystwyth University, UK*

'*Acting in Documentary Theatre* deals with a very interesting aspect of theatre, but what distinguishes it is the constant questioning of every phase of it, probing it, never taking anything for granted. Cantrell has allowed himself to be surprised by it, which is a wonderful quality in a theatre book. Bravo.' – **Simon Callow**

Drawing on interview material with over thirty actors, directors and writers, Tom Cantrell explores the challenges of performing documentary theatre. By analysing key contemporary productions in light of acting theory, he exposes the complex processes of character creation and makes a significant contribution to our understanding of stage performance.

Tom Cantrell is Lecturer in Drama at the University of York, UK.

Also by Tom Cantrell

PLAYING FOR REAL: Actors on Playing Real People
(*co-edited with Mary Luckhurst*)

Acting in Documentary Theatre

TOM CANTRELL

palgrave
macmillan

First published 2013 by
PALGRAVE MACMILLAN

Palgrave Macmillan in the UK is an imprint of Macmillan Publishers Limited,
registered in England, company number 785998, of Houndmills, Basingstoke,
Hampshire RG21 6XS.

Palgrave Macmillan in the US is a division of St Martin's Press LLC,
175 Fifth Avenue, New York, NY 10010.

Palgrave Macmillan is the global academic imprint of the above companies
and has companies and representatives throughout the world.

Palgrave® and Macmillan® are registered trademarks in the United States,
the United Kingdom, Europe and other countries

ISBN 978–1-137–01972–1 hardback
ISBN 978–1-137–01971–4 paperback

This book is printed on paper suitable for recycling and made from fully
managed and sustained forest sources. Logging, pulping and manufacturing
processes are expected to conform to the environmental regulations of the
country of origin.

A catalogue record for this book is available from the British Library.

A catalog record for this book is available from the Library of Congress.

For Michael Cordner and Mary Luckhurst, the most supportive and inspiring of colleagues

Contents

List of Illustrations

Acknowledgements

I would like to thank Professor Mary Luckhurst and Professor Michael Cordner and all the staff in the Department of Theatre, Film and Television at the University of York for their support and encouragement. Dr Derek Paget and Dr Chris Megson have both provided many fascinating events, papers and conversations and have been invaluable to my work. I would also like to thank the staff at the British Library and at the University libraries of York and Cambridge.

Personal thanks go out to the following people: Robert Waiting, Angharad Hughes, Rachel Alexander-Medhurst, Lilly Henley, Tom Adams, Alan Stewart, Richard and Caroline Waiting, Richard Moss, Alastair Ross, Michael Lightfoot, Kate Lovell, Nik Miller, Michael Billington and Simon Callow. Academic colleagues Dr Christopher Hogg, Dr Nik Morris, Douglas Kern, Mark Smith and Ollie Jones have constantly inspired me. Jenna Steventon and Jenni Burnell at Palgrave Macmillan have offered words of wisdom and advice throughout, and to them I am most grateful.

My study would have been impossible without the time and commitment of the actors, directors and writers whom I interviewed, and who generously gave their time and allowed their words to be published. All were enthusiastic and encouraging and without them there would be no book. All quotations in the text without references are taken from these interviews, for which full details are given in the bibliography.

Finally, I would like to thank my family: Richard, Rosie and Rachel Cantrell for their support, and Anna Pinkstone for being wonderful.

TOM CANTRELL

Introduction

This book places actors centre stage in debates surrounding performance, and demonstrates both their creative tenacity in the rehearsal
room and on stage, and their reflective capacity to articulate these
often private processes in interview. Playing real individuals on stage,
and speaking a text created solely from those individuals' own words,
presents actors with numerous challenges. By analysing these actors'
processes in relation to the teaching and theories of actor trainers, we are
able to identify the ways in which they adapt current rehearsal and performance techniques and invent new strategies in the service of playing
a real person. Academic studies have tended to overlook actors when
using first-hand interview material, preferring instead to talk to directors and writers. It is this imbalance that this book aims to redress.

Documentary Theatre

The popularity of documentary theatre shows little sign of abating.
In the arsenal of political theatre, documentary forms have become
the weapon of choice. Only 25 years ago, when Derek Paget first
wrote of the use of tape recorders to make documentary theatre,
he noted that documentary forms were situated at the 'edges of the
professional theatre' (1987: 317). Now, however, documentary theatre is firmly established as a mainstream British theatre tradition.
Many leading news stories or international controversies have been
swiftly followed by documentary responses on some of Britain's most
high-profile stages. Take, for example, the Iraq war; the invasion of
Iraq in 2003 was arguably the most contentious political decision of
the first decade of the twenty-first century. Artistic responses to the
invasion took many forms, but on the British stage few were as immediate and powerful as the stories of those directly affected by the
events. Documentary productions were numerous: director Nicolas
Kent and the *Guardian* journalist Richard Norton-Taylor staged
Justifying War (Tricycle Theatre, 2003), constructed of scenes from

the Hutton Inquiry which investigated events surrounding the scape-goating and subsequent suicide of Dr David Kelly in the lead-up to the war. This was followed in 2004 by David Hare's research into the background of the war in the pseudo-documentary, *Stuff Happens* (National Theatre, 2004). Further questions were asked in 2007, when the Tricycle staged *Called to Account*, a mock-court hearing to establish whether Blair could be tried as a war criminal over his actions in Iraq (this production is analysed in Chapter 3 of this book). However, the exploration of the Iraq war did not end there. In the same year, the newly formed National Theatre of Scotland staged Gregory Burke's enormously successful *Black Watch*, which followed the Scottish regiment on its tour of duty in Iraq, and explored the psychological impact of the death of servicemen on their colleagues. Following the theme of British army deaths in Iraq, Steve Gilroy's play *Motherland* (2008) was composed of interviews with mothers who had lost children fighting in the campaign. Most recently, the Tricycle has returned to the events in Iraq with their staging of *Tactical Questioning* (2011), which comprises scenes from the Baha Mousa Inquiry into the death of the Iraqi national, after being beaten by British army soldiers whilst held in custody in Basra. It is clear from the example of the Iraq war alone that documentary productions are seen as an immediate theatrical response, and that theatre companies are drawn to the stories of real people when staging issues of current political debate.

Documentary theatre: definitions

There are a number of terms which researchers use in attempting to distinguish the use of found material from plays that are solely the playwright's own invention. In addition to 'documentary theatre', these include 'verbatim theatre', 'fact-based theatre', 'faction' and 'theatre of actuality'. 'Verbatim theatre' warrants special mention here as it is, in Britain at least, the principal term currently used to describe these plays. According to Derek Paget, the term was coined by Clive Barker, and first appeared in print in Paget's article '"Verbatim Theatre": Oral History and Documentary Techniques' (1987). The phrase has been contested and problematised ever since. The actual definition in Paget's article was offered by playwright Rony Robinson, in relation to a particular set of working processes:

> It is a form of theatre firmly predicated upon the taping and subsequent transcription of interviews with 'ordinary' people, done in the context of research into a particular region, subject area, issue, event, or combination

of these things. This primary source is then transformed into a text which is acted, usually by the performers who collected the material in the first place. (Robinson, quoted in Paget 1987: 317)

Since this first definition was offered, researchers have attempted to rework and rephrase Robinson's description to adequately embrace the multifarious forms of verbatim theatre that have been developed in the intervening 25 years. The debate has centred on the question as to whether Robinson's description of verbatim theatre as 'predicated upon... taping' should be taken to mean 'exclusively based on taping', or if, in fact, the definition should encompass productions which are merely based on recorded interviews. In their study of contemporary Russian verbatim theatre, Mark Lipovetsky and Birgit Beumers state that although this is a key distinction, at the moment both approaches fall under the umbrella term 'verbatim'. They identify the looser definition of a verbatim play as 'constructed on the basis of interviews conducted by the playwright (or by the creative team) with real people' (2008: 296). However, they also recognise 'verbatim in the more strict sense of the term – that is, directly using recorded or reported speech on stage' (2008: 297). Similarly, Mary Luckhurst highlights the importance of the ability of documentary theatre-makers to prove their findings. She notes that 'verbatim theatre, in its purest sense, is understood as a theatre whose practitioners, if called to account, could provide interviewed sources for its dialogue' (2008: 213).

Despite these disagreements with regard to the specifics of the definition, it is clear that verbatim theatre is understood to be based on the *spoken* words of real people. We shall see that *My Name is Rachel Corrie* was based entirely on written rather than spoken testimony, and as such falls within the wider field of documentary theatre, rather than verbatim. I also agree with Janelle Reinelt that '"verbatim" needlessly ups the ante on the promise of documentary... "verbatim" as a category over-extends what was a sufficiently rich and proximate archive in all these cases' (Forsyth and Megson 2009: 13–14). In addition, American scholarship does not use the term 'verbatim'. Hence, 'documentary' is the most useful term to categorise and unite the productions analysed here, though naturally some commentators who are quoted prefer to use the term 'verbatim'.

The absence of the actor's voice

With the rise in popularity of documentary theatre has come an intensification of publications on the subject. The body of literature has tended to focus on questions of authenticity and, particularly, the complex and problematic relationship between the testimony from which these plays were derived and the productions themselves. Despite these interventions, the analysis of acting processes in documentary theatre has been almost entirely overlooked. The two most significant recent publications on documentary theatre are notable for their lack of focus on acting. Will Hammond and Dan Steward's *Verbatim: Verbatim* (2009) featured seven new interviews with documentary theatre-makers. Although in the blurb for the book the authors stated that they would 'discuss frankly the unique opportunities and ethical dilemmas that arise when portraying real people on stage' (2009: back cover), the collection omitted actors entirely and Hammond and Steward only interviewed writers and directors. Finally, although Alison Forsyth and Chris Megson's excellent edited collection *Get Real: Documentary Theatre Past and Present* (2009) was ambitious in scope, there were no essays dedicated to questions of performance, and none of the contributors interviewed actors.

This lack of focus on acting is curious since Derek Paget's aforementioned research into the first wave of British documentary productions featured interviews with performers. However, the absence of actors' narratives has begun to be addressed in research into documentary theatre. For example, Bella Merlin, who appeared in Max Stafford-Clark's production of David Hare's play, *The Permanent Way* (2003), has written about her experiences in an article in *Contemporary Theatre Review* (2007c) and in a chapter in *The Cambridge Companion to David Hare* (2007a). Her work is an attempt to analyse the ways in which her Stanislavskian approach was challenged when playing a real person in Hare's play, and her experiences will be considered in Chapter 1.

In addition to Merlin's research, from 2007 to 2010 a research team under the leadership of Derek Paget at the University of Reading conducted a project entitled 'Acting with Facts: Actors performing the real in British theatre and television since 1990'. Though not limited to theatre or to documentary forms, this project began to involve actors in the analysis of performance. At the conclusion of the project, Paget guest-edited editions of *Studies in Theatre and Performance* (31.1, 2011) and *Studies in Documentary Film* (4.3, 2010), and both make useful new contributions to this field.

In response to the lack of material from actors, I co-edited *Playing for Real* (2010) with Mary Luckhurst, which is the first study to draw together testimony from actors on portraying real people across theatre, film and television. The book did not focus on documentary performance, but it was clear that the majority of the actors in *Playing for Real* felt that portraying a real person is qualitatively different from playing a fictional character. Although the actors' experiences were heterogeneous, certain preoccupations arose recurrently, and signalled that specific issues come to the fore when actors portray real people. For example, whilst careful research for a role was unanimously understood to be vital – Henry Goodman stated that it 'liberates the creative instincts' (Cantrell and Luckhurst 2010: 74) – many actors noted the tensions between their research into the real-life individual and the role as it appears in the play. Goodman noted that 'it's a fatal mistake to try and act your research' (2010: 74). Playing a real-life figure also incurred a sense of responsibility towards the representation of that figure which is wholly different from playing a fictional character. Ian McKellen found that 'you want to do the right thing by them' (2010: 104), whilst Siân Phillips observed that 'When you are playing real people who have died recently, or who are still alive, it is a nightmare. It is a ghastly responsibility for a start, because of families and descendants' (2010: 136). Also prevalent were questions of physical similarity, issues which were particularly pronounced when an individual was widely recognised. Whilst the sixteen interviews in *Playing for Real* are not definitive, they strongly indicate that actors' testimony can contribute significantly to discourses surrounding theatre practice, and that the particular exigencies of playing real people is a fertile new area of research that has been puzzlingly overlooked. As we shall see, the study of acting in documentary theatre raises different issues again. This book will analyse innovative and previously unexplored rehearsal and performance strategies.

The lack of actors' narratives or examination of acting processes has led to particular problems in the current body of literature on documentary theatre. The most prevalent issue is that the experiences of writers and directors have been privileged by researchers, and they have ventriloquised for actors in their accounts of documentary practices, leading to them making claims about the actors' processes. This appears to be a product of academic prejudices which presume that writers and directors are more authoritative than actors. I offer these claims up for scrutiny throughout my case-studies. This in turn has meant that researchers have made assumptions about the way in which actors approach these roles. We shall see that non-actors who speak on behalf of actors have considerably misrepresented the issue.

There are also considerable misunderstandings about the lineage of documentary theatre, and researchers have frequently made erroneous statements about the practitioners and acting processes I examine here. This may be partly attributable to Derek Paget's identification of the 'broken tradition' of documentary theatre (Forsyth and Megson 2009: 224). Locating it firmly as an oppositional theatre movement, he has suggested that 'generation after generation, oppositional modes of theatrical address tend to fade from the collective cultural memory' (Forsyth and Megson 2009: 225). Paget thus notes the 'resultant discontinuity' of documentary theatre, suggesting that the lineage is complex, sporadic and lacks a clear linear progression (Forsyth and Megson 2009: 224). In order to locate these case-studies within particular traditions, the analysis of the actor's processes on each production will be contextualised by an investigation into both the lineage of the specific forms analysed here, and a detailed examination of the working methods. A certain amount of 'setting the record straight' is thus required. As we shall see, placing the actors' testimony in these contexts is imperative to our understanding of their work.

The case-study productions

The four case-studies that comprise this study are: Robin Soans' *Talking to Terrorists* (Theatre Royal, Bury St. Edmunds, 2005), directed by Max Stafford-Clark for Out of Joint; Alan Rickman and Katharine Viner's *My Name is Rachel Corrie* (Royal Court Theatre, 2005), directed by Alan Rickman; Richard Norton-Taylor's *Called to Account* (Tricycle Theatre, 2007), directed by Nicolas Kent; and Alecky Blythe's *The Girlfriend Experience* (Royal Court Theatre, 2008), directed by Joe Hill-Gibbins for Recorded Delivery. For each of my four case-study productions I have interviewed the actors, writer and director. Using new interview material, this book will uncover and analyse processes of acting, and interrogate the particular demands of playing a real person in documentary theatre.

These four productions represent the widest range of working methods for actors in contemporary documentary theatre. In *Talking to Terrorists* the actors often met the individuals they played and to some extent were responsible for creating the material through these meetings as well as performing the testimony. Megan Dodds, who played Rachel Corrie, had the difficult task of performing written testimony that was never designed to be spoken. In addition, Dodds had the challenge of being alone on stage throughout, and had to portray a woman who had died. In *Called to Account*, Kent's cast received a DVD of the interview they were tasked with recreating, and were told to stick closely to what they observed. Finally, the cast of *The Girlfriend Experience* worked in a very unusual way – there was no script, rather the actors had to listen to interview material played through headphones and simultaneously repeat it as accurately as they could in performance. The differences in the casts' involvement in research, rehearsal and performance challenged these actors to develop new strategies and processes.

These four productions were also very high-profile, and were staged by practitioners who are heralded as being at the forefront of the resurgence of British documentary theatre. For example, Michael Billington has stated that: 'it was Nicolas Kent at Kilburn's Tricycle Theatre who led the way with some assistance from Max Stafford-Clark at Out of Joint' (2007b: 385). Kent deploys documentary theatre strategically to make interventions on matters of national importance, and Stafford-Clark has used it to investigate topical issues. Both are generally acknowledged as among the most important directors working in British documentary theatre. *My Name is Rachel Corrie* was also a critically important production. When the play's transfer to New York was cancelled, it provoked an international debate in the arts – according to Houchin, an 'outrage exploded with a force rarely seen in New York theatre' (2008: 17). The allegations of censorship and the storm that developed around the play transformed *My Name is Rachel Corrie* into a highly contentious political event, leading to demonstrations both outside and inside the theatre. Finally, within the canon of documentary work, Blythe's headphone technique has repeatedly been called 'cutting edge' and 'innovative', and she has been credited with bringing a new and unusual performance practice to the stage.

A British study within an international context

This study focuses on contemporary documentary plays which originated in Britain. However, it is important to note that documentary theatre is not a solely British phenomenon, and where relevant to the exploration of the working processes on my case-study productions, I will refer to international examples. Documentary theatre-makers in Australia, New Zealand and America in particular demonstrate and articulate a keen sense of inheritance from, and cross-fertilisation with, the productions I investigate here. Publications such as

Forsyth and Megson's *Get Real*, and Carol Martin's edited collection *Dramaturgy of the Real on the World Stage* (2010) provide the interested reader with essays from various other international perspectives.

Despite its relative infancy, Australian documentary theatre practitioners have developed a similarly diverse range of working methods to those we shall find in this book. Arguably the most celebrated Australian documentary production was Paul Brown's *Aftershocks* (1993), exploring the aftermath of the earthquake in Newcastle, New South Wales, which killed 13 people in 1989. According to Brown, this was the first Australian documentary production. It had many similarities with the early British tradition that Paget identifies above, in that the play was performed back to the community who provided the material, and sought to bring these under-represented voices to the stage. Brown called the production an example of 'pure verbatim theatre', by which he referred to the exclusive use of taped interview material in the play (Brown 2009). As in the work of Max Stafford-Clark which will be analysed in Chapter 1, the majority of researchers who conducted the tape-recorded interviews then appeared in the play. Brown has also edited *Verbatim: Staging Memory and Community* (2010) in which he explores his own documentary projects and overviews Australian documentary theatre, and I refer the reader to this work.

Alana Valentine has also raised the profile of documentary forms within Australian theatre. Like Brown, her work places an emphasis on the community from which the material is gathered. She states that 'the playwright continues to have a relationship with the community that they are drawing the story from' (2008). One of the ways in which she achieves this is by inviting those depicted to watch the play, so that they can see themselves performed. The actor's response to the presence of the person they are playing in the audience is a factor I will explore in the case-studies in this book. One of Valentine's most successful productions was *Parramatta Girls* (2004). The play was based on interviews with women who attended the Parramatta School, a Girls' Training School for young women, at which many were abused and lived in appalling conditions. Valentine states that staging these marginalised voices is a critical concern in her work: 'I have a serious belief that the people who don't get their voices on the Australian stage have the same human right that we all have to see themselves in that dimension' (2011). She thus identifies that her productions 'become in a very real way a continuing part of the life and narrative of the community represented' (2008). She describes *Parramatta Girls* as an example of 'massaged verbatim', as Paul Brown notes:

> On this project she explores a form she terms 'massaged verbatim' as opposed to the 'pure verbatim' style she employed on her previous work, *Run Rabbit Run* (2004), in which interviewee's stories are faithfully transcribed and presented as they were told by real people. In *Parramatta Girls*, Valentine shapes her collected interviews around an invented narrative structure. (2010: 60)

Valentine is the sole-researcher on her projects, and the actors are deployed in a more recognisable way; they rehearse with the script once it has been edited, but are not part of the process of generating the material.

Many documentary theatre projects in Australia have been performed under the auspices of the Urban Theatre Projects, a Sydney-based theatre company co-founded by Paul Brown in 1978. One of the major areas they have developed is 'verbatim headphone theatre'. Like Alecky Blythe in the UK, Rosalyn Oades has become particularly associated with her documentary work using headphones. Her work will be explored further in the chapter on *The Girlfriend Experience*, as the ancestry of her approach has remarkable similarities to Blythe, and can be directly traced back to Anna Deavere Smith. In 2003, Oades was commissioned by Urban Theatre Projects to create a full-length headphone production. The resulting play, *Fast Cars and Tractor Engines*, featured eight intertwined stories of survival, from war to domestic violence and abuse. It was the first of a trilogy of headphone plays; further instalments came in 2008 with *Stories of Love and Hate*, and the final part of her trilogy, *I'm Your Man*, was performed at the 2012 Sydney Festival.

Productions created using headphones are also a feature of new documentary theatre-making in New Zealand. Stuart Young and Hilary Halba have developed a series of plays in this way at the University of Otago. Their work includes *Be/Longing: A Verbatim Play* (2012), which was constructed from interviews with the many different groups of immigrants who live in the country, and *Hush*, a play about family violence (2009). Recognising both Alecky Blythe and Anna Deavere Smith as influences, their work will also be analysed in Chapter 4, focusing in particular on the subtle differences between the ways in which the headphones are used.

Sydney-based theatre company Version 1.0 have also developed documentary forms, staging intensely political works on issues of national and local importance. For example, in 2012 they staged *The Table of Knowledge*, exploring corruption allegations within the local council and New South Wales State Government. In this production, like the actors in *Aftershocks* and in Stafford-Clark's work, the cast were involved in the creation as well as the performance of the material. They blended real-life stories of sexual violence with multimedia projection and techno music in their acclaimed production *This Kind of Ruckus* (2010). Kate Champion, artistic director of theatre company Force Majeure, has also developed the relationship between movement and the words of real people. In her production of *Never Did Me Any Harm* (2012), Champion worked with seven actors and dancers to physically explore the testimony of people who had experienced domestic violence. Similarly, *Not in a Million Years* (2011) was a dance piece which took extraordinary stories found on YouTube and in the printed press as its starting point. There are clear similarities between Champion's work and the recent production of *To Be Straight With You* (2011) by British physical theatre company DV8, which saw testimony about attitudes towards homosexuality explored through dance and movement.

Finally, Melbourne Workers Theatre (MWT) has a commitment to documentary theatre at the centre of its artistic vision. One of their four 'Parameters for Making Work' states that 'Most of the performance text (in the broadest sense of the term) directly quotes real people.' The company state that, 'MWT makes work that articulates flaws in the mainstream perception of Australian culture and identity, contesting how Australians think about themselves as a nation and as a people' (MWT website). Overtly political and left-wing in stance, celebrated productions have included *Who's Afraid of the Working Class?* (1998), and *Yet to Ascertain the Nature of the Crime* (2010). The latter play focused on attacks on Indian students in Melbourne, and featured 25 interviews conducted by the cast and creative team.

My case-study productions also have close links to American documentary theatre. One of the most high-profile and influential American documentary theatre-makers is Anna Deavere Smith. Smith is internationally recognised and her work has had a great influence on Alecky Blythe and British documentary theatre more widely. Her documentary work has become synonymous with her virtuoso one-woman shows. Smith both researches and performs in these pieces, often portraying multiple individuals of different class, race, age and gender. Concerned with issues of identity and community, since the late 1970s she has worked on a series of plays under the ambitious title *On the Road: A Search for American Character*. Smith has performed over 20 plays as part of her series. Notable productions have included *Building Bridges, Not Walls* (1985), and, most famously, two plays dealing with race-related riots: *Fires in the Mirror* (1992, directed by fellow documentary theatre-maker Emily Mann), which was based on interviews conducted following the Crown Heights Riot in Brooklyn in 1991, and *Twilight: Los Angeles, 1992* (1993), which focused on the Los Angeles Riots. Central to her work has been her focus on idiomatic language:

> My goal has been to find American character in the ways that people speak...at that time I was not as interested in performance or in social commentary as I was in experimenting with language and its relation to character. (Smith 1993: xxiii)

To this end, Smith records her interviews and rehearses by listening to the testimony on headphones and repeating it. Once she has been able to reproduce the exact idiosyncrasies of an individual's speech patterns, she takes off the headphones, and performs without them. We shall see just how influential Anna Deavere Smith has been on the work of Alecky Blythe and Roslyn Oades in Chapter 4.

Smith is one of two giants of American documentary theatre, and of political theatre generally. The other is Moises Kaufman. With his Tectonic Theater Project, Kaufman edited and directed *Gross Indecency: The Three Trials of Oscar Wilde* (1997), which, like the series of tribunal plays at the Tricycle that I explore in Chapter 3, was based on the real court transcripts. Other notable successes include *I Am My Own Wife* (2004), based on hundreds of hours of interviews with Charlotte Von Mahlsdorf, a famous transvestite who survived both the Nazis and the Communists dressed as a woman; and arguably the most celebrated American documentary production to date, *The Laramie Project* (2000), and the follow-up production *Laramie Ten Years On* (2010). *The Laramie Project* used actors in a similar way to Stafford-Clark, in that they were involved in the process of collating the interview material. A team of actor-researchers travelled to Laramie, Wyoming, following the homophobic murder of Matthew Shepherd. The play featured interviews with various members of the community, including Matthew's killers, and explored the range of views towards homosexuality in the town. The research team revisited Laramie in 2010 to explore how attitudes had changed in the intervening decade. In a development of Stafford-Clark's employment of actor-researchers, the interviewers appeared as themselves as well as multi-rolling as the interviewees in the play. These plays were self-reflective, in that they were focused not only on the events portrayed, but also on inscribing the questions and problems of conducting this research into the narrative itself.

Jessica Blank and Erik Jensen have also become known for their documentary work. Their celebrated play *The Exonerated* (2002) was based on interviews with six individuals who, though later found to be innocent, spent time on death row. The work, originally performed in Los Angeles, then in New York, received a West End transfer in 2006, opening at the Riverside Studios. As well as the interviews, the play used written sources such as court records and letters, and, as in *My Name is Rachel Corrie*, the actors were involved in the editing of the material.

My interviews

My research into the four case-study productions includes interviews with 27 actors, four directors and four writers. The interviews were mostly conducted over the telephone, but eight were conducted in person. The interviews tended to last around an hour, and I conducted follow-up interviews when more detail was required.

I take an actor-centred view throughout the book, offering a counter-narrative to the dominance of directors' and writers' experiences in documentary theatre, and championing the actors' work. My research for *Playing for Real* made me aware of the amount of private work that happens outside the rehearsal room. This has always been the case; actors do a lot of work in their own time as well as collaboratively in rehearsal. This private work is partly a reaction to the sensitivities of the rehearsal room. In *Playing for Real*, it became evident that to negotiate these sensitivities some actors conducted private work unbeknownst to the director. For example, Henry Goodman stated:

> Every actor has to negotiate the politics of rehearsal, the egos ... What I've learned over the years is how to operate in the political environment of the rehearsal room, and how to assess the confidence of directors and writers. What you have to understand is that some people become frightened when actors do what they think of as a writer's or a director's job. (Cantrell and Luckhurst 2010: 73–4)

Actors, therefore, do not necessarily share their processes with the director or writer, or indeed other actors. For example, Timothy West states that 'Actors don't talk to each other very much about their own ways of working. I think many are quite private about it...how you work on your own is your own business' (Cantrell and Luckhurst 2010: 158). Thus, in this book I focus in particular on the actors' narratives of their work, rather than analysing the rehearsal process as laid out by the director. Indeed, the discrepancy between the directors' narratives of the rehearsal methods and the actors' narratives of their processes will be a focus of this work.

There are other issues associated with interviewing actors which need to be addressed here. If, as Timothy West suggests, actors are 'quite private', it follows that not all actors may want to articulate their creative processes, and some may harbour suspicion towards any project that aims to explore what they do. I was fortunate that none of the actors I interviewed appeared to view my project negatively; indeed, without exception they were enthusiastic about my pursuit, and many had also noted the curious lack of interest in their acting processes. The interviews were very detailed and were concerned with eliciting information that could not be gained in any other way. However, the intense challenge of articulating a creative process was repeatedly evident in my interviews. The actors were often analysing an experience which may have remained a partial mystery to them. Despite these challenges, this book will explore the fascinating range of processes and the highly personal ingenuity with which these actors confronted what were often new challenges. Actors have been denied the kind of access to the dissemination of their experiences generally enjoyed by writers and directors. My work clearly demonstrates that their spoken testimony is no less illuminating than written publications, and ignoring this vital resource has led to a significant gap in our knowledge.

Talking to Terrorists. From left: Lloyd Hutchinson, Alexander Hanson, Christopher Ettridge, Jonathan Cullen and Chipo Chung (photo by Geraint Lewis)

1

Talking to Terrorists

INTRODUCTION

Talking to Terrorists, written by Robin Soans and directed by Max Stafford-Clark, was produced by Stafford-Clark's company, Out of Joint, in 2005. The play was compiled by Soans from a series of interviews conducted by the writer, director and actors. The unusual involvement of the actors in the creation of the material as well as its performance led to them developing particular preparatory and rehearsal strategies. In this chapter I will focus on the actors' experiences of Stafford-Clark's working methods, particularly the foregrounding of actor-subject meetings (in which the actors met and interviewed the person they played) and the way in which the material for the play was shared with the writer and director. The little testimony that exists on this subject has generally been formulated by Stafford-Clark, who has made certain claims about how these techniques function for actors. These claims are subjected to scrutiny in this study. This chapter is based on new interview material with actors providing, for the first time, a detailed analysis of the innovative techniques the actors developed within these working processes.

Max Stafford-Clark's documentary productions

Max Stafford-Clark is a distinguished director of new plays. During his tenures as director of the Traverse Theatre, Edinburgh (1966–70, artistic director from 1968), Joint Stock Theatre Company (1974–79),

15

the Royal Court Theatre (1979–93), and more recently with his own
company, Out of Joint (since 1993), he has commissioned and premiered some of the most exciting new writers. Most relevant to this
study is Stafford-Clark's long-standing advocacy of political theatre,
and of documentary forms in particular. Indeed, he chose a documentary play as the inaugural production of Joint Stock, staging an
adaptation of Heathcote Williams' novel *The Speakers* (1966), which,
as co-director William Gaskill remembers, 'was largely [constructed
from] actual conversations and speeches recorded by Heathcote at the
time he knew the speakers in Hyde Park' (1988: 135). This was closely
followed in 1976 by *Yesterday's News*, for which the cast interviewed
those involved with what became known as the 'Colonel Callan affair'.
Stafford-Clark stated:

> I think it was David Rintoul, one of the actors, who had read about this
> incident, in which Colonel Callan...had shot some of his own troops in
> Angola, they were mercenaries which had been recruited...and we fol-
> lowed the story. (2004)

The play was thus performed almost contemporaneously with the
story it staged. Alongside these documentary productions have been
plays that whilst not wholly fact-based, have involved substantial
research periods, such as David Hare's *Fanshen* (1974), which was
based on the Chinese Revolution, and Caryl Churchill's *Cloud Nine*
(1979), which took the actors' own sexual orientations and experiences as the starting point.

With Out of Joint, Stafford-Clark's documentary plays have
grown in number. In 2000, he directed *A State Affair*, his first collaboration with Robin Soans. The production was a contemporary
response to Andrea Dunbar's play, *Rita, Sue and Bob Too* (1982),
and was based on the cast's and writer's interviews on the Bradford
and Leeds housing estates in which Dunbar grew up, and which in
2000 were still areas of severe deprivation. In 2003, he directed the
premiere of David Hare's play, *The Permanent Way*, which investigated the privatisation of the railways and the personal tragedies of
those involved in rail disasters since. His most recent documentary
play, *Mixed Up North* (2008), was, after *Talking to Terrorists*, his
third collaboration with Robin Soans, and was based loosely on the
cast's and creative team's interviews with staff and young people
in a youth drama group in Burnley, formed following the riots in
2001.

Contested ground: the received narrative of Stafford-Clark's working methods

The processes of research and rehearsal in *Talking to Terrorists* follow a path that Stafford-Clark has developed throughout his career. A key feature of his work has been creating plays by means of research phases involving the actors and the writer. In a recent interview with Hammond and Steward he stated, 'I've always used research...Extensive research was always part of Joint Stock's repertoire' (2009: 50). Michael Billington has noted that this emphasis strongly associated Joint Stock's work with fact-based plays. He stated that the group 'stimulated companies to seek their source material in fact: something that was to have enormously beneficial results for British theatre over the next quarter of a century' (2007b: 268). Actors, the writer and the director together research a theme and collate material for the writer to use as the basis of the play. This is followed by a writing period, during which the play is drafted, then the play is cast and rehearsed. John Ginman explains:

> Stafford-Clark identifies two types of new plays produced by Out of Joint: the workshop plays, where actors have contributed to the research and development of the project from a relatively unformed idea that may be initiated by Stafford-Clark himself; and those where the company rehearses and stages a writer's script from a developed or complete draft. (2003: 18)

The so-called 'workshop plays' are by no means new to Stafford-Clark in his projects with Out of Joint, but, as we have seen, date back to his work with Joint Stock in the 1970s.

In his own publications, in the recent wave of interviews, and as a result of his distinguished status in the theatre community, published accounts of Stafford-Clark's practice have almost exclusively been articulated by the director himself. Whilst illuminating, this material has meant that actors have traditionally been de-privileged in the creative narrative, their testimony sporadic and often anecdotal. This is a problem which this case-study seeks to address.

Stafford-Clark has argued that the roles of actor/writer/director are broken down during the research phases for his productions, with everyone contributing. As he states in one interview:

> all of you act as a research team during the workshop process. Your role becomes more of a conventional director during the rehearsal process.

> The roles are much looser in the workshop...and become much tighter in the rehearsal period. (Wu 2000: 58)

He has also maintained that involving the cast in the play's research period nourishes the actor in a way that is impossible in a three- or four-week rehearsal period:

> The role of the actor is often a passive one: you are summoned to do a job, you get it or you don't get it...So that to say, 'Look, this is a level playing-field, we're all in this together, and we don't quite know where it's going, and we'd like you to go off and talk to these stockbrokers', is perhaps unexpected and stimulating. (Wu 2000: 60)

It should be remembered that it was Stafford-Clark who hired or rejected the actors, and that the actors did not choose the director, writer or area to research. His suggestion that actors are often 'passive' is provocative, and many actors would entirely disagree. Yet he is adamant that the experience is empowering for an actor:

> an actor's job is first of all to observe, and by saying, 'Your observation is very important and could indeed be crucial in the formation of the play', you give the actor an importance and a role that they don't normally have. (Wu 2000: 60)

Although he may be underselling the actors' other work in order to emphasise the inclusive nature of his own processes, these comments seriously under-acknowledge the actors' role. Stafford-Clark's narrative is that actors are given a sense of ownership of the material and are hierarchically elevated by his particular working processes. This is a claim I will explore in the case of *Talking to Terrorists*.

Talking to Terrorists

Talking to Terrorists opened at the Theatre Royal, Bury St Edmunds on 21 April 2005, and toured nationally for nine weeks, before playing at the Royal Court Theatre Downstairs for five weeks. The play is a compilation of interwoven interviews from a wide range of people associated with so-called terrorist acts. Individuals depicted include those directly responsible for attacks; victims of terrorism; experts in mediation and peace-work, such as politicians and diplomats; and a psychologist who explores possible reasons for these acts.

The individuals interviewed for the play were all contacted through Scilla Elworthy, who was instrumental in the play's genesis.

Elworthy is a three-time Nobel Peace Prize nominee who is internationally renowned for her work in promoting and facilitating dialogue between nations in conflict. She is the founder of the Oxford Research Group think-tank (ORG), which negotiates between the policy-makers, politicians and the military in areas of conflict, aiming 'to promote a more sustainable approach to security for the UK and the world' (Oxford Research Group website).[1] Elworthy's involvement in *Talking to Terrorists* came about through a meeting with Stafford-Clark:

> Max read about my work in the paper and got in touch...Max asked me what I was doing, and I said 'well, in a nutshell, I'm talking to terrorists'. He said that that sounded like a title of a play...After a long discussion I told him about the various protagonists whom he could talk to, from cabinet ministers to the actual people on the ground, who are affected by terrorism as well as the people who could be classified as terrorists.

The whole project was driven by Elworthy's access to key contacts and the trusting relationships she had built with these individuals through her work. Her confidence that Stafford-Clark would respect their testimony was also paramount: 'If I hadn't trusted him, I would never have opened up my address book to him.' Based on this mutual understanding, Elworthy and Stafford-Clark arranged a series of interviews which provided the material for the play.

The multifarious nature of Elworthy's work was evident in the final production of *Talking to Terrorists*, which included 29 interviewees from a diverse range of conflicts. The first category of those who appear are the 'terrorists' of the play's title, although understandably they are all ex-terrorists, or rather, individuals who were once associated with groups which used terror as a political tool. The play features five such interviews, covering conflicts in Northern Ireland, the Middle East and Africa, with ex-members of the Irish Republican Army (IRA) and the Ulster Volunteer Force (UVF), an ex-member of the Kurdish Workers Party (PKK) and an ex-head of the Al Aqsa Martyrs Brigade, Bethlehem (AAB), and an ex-member of the National Resistance Army, Uganda (NRA). All interviewees remain anonymous in the play-text, either by use of the abbreviations above, or by changing their names.

The second category of individuals comprises those who have been direct victims of terrorism. Again, the identities of the individuals in the printed text have been concealed. However, unlike those interviewed about their membership of terrorist groups, some of these individuals are recognisable and their identity is already in the public domain. The victims of terrorist acts are: an 'Archbishop's Envoy': the celebrated humanitarian Terry Waite, who was held hostage in Lebanon for over four years (1987–91) whilst working for the then Archbishop of Canterbury, Robert Runcie; an 'ex-Secretary of State' and his wife: Norman and Margaret Tebbit, who were injured in the Brighton hotel bombing during the 1984 Conservative Party Conference; and 'Caroline', a landowner and Conservative Party activist who was also caught in the Brighton bombing.

The third category comprises neither terrorists nor direct victims, but individuals who are concerned with these struggles, such as mediators, aid workers, foreign diplomats, army personnel and politicians. This category includes an ex-Ambassador, Craig Murray, formerly Ambassador to Uzbekistan, and his partner Nadira Alieva, called Nodira in the play; an ex-government minister, Mo Mowlam, who was Secretary of State for Northern Ireland from 1997 to 1999; Phoebe, a relief worker for Save the Children; a British Army Colonel; and Rima, a freelance journalist.

Research phase one: April 2004

The material for the play was generated from interviews which took place in two research phases, and during rehearsals. The first research phase ran for two weeks, from 19 to 30 April 2004. Stafford-Clark and Elworthy were joined by the original commissioned writer of *Talking to Terrorists*, April de Angelis, and a team of 12 actors. Together they conducted research for the play. Seven of the actors were recruited from the cast and creative team of Stafford-Clark's production of Hare's *The Permanent Way*, which by April was midway through its run at the National Theatre. Only three of the initial research team, Chris Ryman, Lloyd Hutchinson and Chipo Chung, appeared in the final production of *Talking to Terrorists*.[2]

In this two-week period the first round of interviews took place, including those with ex-Ambassador Craig Murray and the ex-member of the IRA talking to the group at the Out of Joint rehearsal room. Also as part of the first research phase, Chris Ryman, Stafford-Clark and de Angelis flew out to Ireland to interview the ex-head of the AAB in Dublin and conduct further interviews with the ex-IRA member. Scilla Elworthy and Chris Ryman travelled to Luton to visit a mosque and talk to the imam, whilst Chipo Chung and Ian

Redford interviewed the British Army Colonel at his Wiltshire base. However, despite the number of interviews completed, the writing did not progress. De Angelis left the project towards the end of 2004, and was replaced by Robin Soans. Soans is an actor and playwright who has become known for his documentary plays. In addition to *A State Affair*, *Talking to Terrorists* and *Mixed Up North* for Out of Joint, his documentary work has included *Across the Divide* (1997), *The Arab-Israeli Cookbook* (2004), and *Life After Scandal* (2007). He took over from April de Angelis at the beginning of the second research period in November 2004.

Research phase two: November–December 2004

The second research phase began on the 22 November 2004, and interviews continued through December. It was the main research phase for the production, and involved Soans and the actors (the same team as for the first research phase) re-interviewing the individuals to whom de Angelis had already spoken, and talking to new individuals.

In the first research phase, interviewees had often talked to the group at the rehearsal rooms. By contrast, in the second phase, many of the team travelled to meet their subjects. For example, Soans and Stafford-Clark visited Mo and John Mowlam, and Norman and Margaret Tebbit, in their own homes. Soans also visited Terry Waite and 'Caroline' at their respective homes during this period. Soans and Lloyd Hutchinson together re-visited the ex-member of the IRA in a Belfast hotel, and with Chris Ryman talked (as Ryman had previously done with de Angelis) to the ex-head of the AAB in Dublin. Soans and Stafford-Clark also flew out to Denmark to interview the ex-member of the Ugandan National Resistance Army. Interviewees who talked to the cast in the Out of Joint rehearsal rooms in Finsbury Park included Phoebe from Save the Children and ex-Ambassador Craig Murray and his partner Nadira.

It is important to note that although the actors were present at some of the meetings, this does not mean that they were solely responsible for creating the material for the play. Soans told me that between the second research phase and the completion of the script, he had met every single individual apart from the British Army Colonel: 'I didn't interview [the Colonel]. That was on the first Monday and I couldn't go ... David Hare stood in for me that day, and wrote comprehensive notes on him.' This meant that although actors were present at the interviews, and often portrayed the individuals they met, Soans was not reliant on the actors for material. Thus, although the actors were involved with the process, Soans still functioned as a writer, assisted by the actors.

Similarly, the actors did not act as independent researchers since the questions they asked were planned and pre-determined by Stafford-Clark and Soans. Prior to their meeting, the actors were given precise instructions; as Lloyd Hutchinson stated, 'everybody's briefed before we go away'. Chipo Chung was clear that she was 'asking very particular questions', and that the actors did not work to their own open brief.

Very few of the interviews were recorded, which makes Stafford-Clark's methods unusual in documentary theatre. As he stated, 'The actors did not tend to record but rather took notes', whilst Soans confirmed that

> I only use a notepad and pencil. If someone comes to us, I think it is acceptable for there to be a microphone on the table, but if I go to talk to someone like Mo Mowlam in her house, I'm not going to start messing around with finding a plug... and also, it takes people ages to relax if you're pointing a microphone at them.

Of course this approach also allowed him a certain creative freedom. If documentary theatre is defined as 'a theatre whose practitioners, if called to account, could provide interviewed sources for its dialogue', as Mary Luckhurst argues (2008: 201), this raises interesting questions. Whilst interviewees could be identified, in the vast majority of cases there was no official interview transcript. Evidently, there is an ethical problem with the issue of transparency here, but this suited Stafford-Clark and Soans, permitting them a greater degree of imaginative freedom.

With all the material (including his own notes, actors' notes, recordings and transcripts) from both research phases at his disposal, Soans constructed the play over a ten-week writing period in early 2005, before rehearsals began on 14 March. It was during this period that the play was cast. Hutchinson noted:

> You didn't know whether you'd see it through to the production, because you might have got another job between. I mean Max kind of knows that those are the actors that he'd like to be involved in the final project, but

sometimes, depending on the nature of the way the writer has gone with the work, there might not be parts for everyone.

The actors cast after the two research phases were brought in to play particular roles. Citing the example of the casting for the British Army Colonel, Stafford-Clark explained:

> At a later stage we thought that the Colonel was going to be part of it, we don't have anyone to play him, and then we cast Alexander Hanson. So you find some of the actors first, then find the characters they are going to play, then fill in the gaps.

Stafford-Clark insisted that close physical resemblance did not inform his casting choices: 'No, no, [it was] more general than that. I wanted to cover all the bases.' Given that the actors played multiple roles, Stafford-Clark cast actors of roughly the right age, gender and ethnicity to play the interviewees, rather than foregrounding physical aptness. The actors cast after the two research phases were Jonathan Cullen, Christopher Ettridge, Alexander Hanson, Catherine Russell and June Watson, making up a cast of eight. Between them, they played all 29 characters, each playing at least three roles.

It is no coincidence that, with the exception of Alexander Hanson, all the actors in the final cast had worked with Stafford-Clark in the past. This suggests that the production demanded particular techniques and skills which Stafford-Clark must have been confident these actors could deliver. However, only Jonathan Cullen (*Falkland Sound*, 1983 and *The Permanent Way*, 2003) and Lloyd Hutchinson (*The Permanent Way*) had worked on his documentary productions before.

When the production went into rehearsal in March 2005, more meetings were arranged. For example, Alexander Hanson met the British Army Colonel at his Wiltshire military base, and Catherine Russell met Rima the journalist she played, and Phoebe from Save the Children. Similarly, Christopher Ettridge met Edward the psychiatrist during the rehearsal period, allowing both the actors who took part in the research phases and those cast later in the process to meet the individuals they played. Thus, almost all the cast (with the exception of June Watson and Jonathan Cullen) met at least one of the individuals they portrayed before the production opened.

The feedback process

The process by which the cast relayed their interview experiences to Soans was 'hotseating'. This is a technique that Stafford-Clark has used extensively to gather material for new plays: 'In this kind of work I normally use hotseating. They are able then to improvise from their notes.' The actors, using the notes they took during the interview, recreated the interviewee's responses, whilst Stafford-Clark, Soans and the other cast members repeated the original questions the actor had asked the interviewee. In the hotseating exercise, Stafford-Clark asked the actors to render 'as accurate a recreation as possible', indicating that he hoped for a detailed and precise portrayal of the interviewee. As the hotseating process is an under-explored rehearsal technique and was a major factor in the cast's experiences of the play, its function and effect on the actors' approaches will be considered in detail.

We can appreciate that whilst the actors were involved to some extent with the research for the production, Stafford-Clark's claim of 'a level playing-field', which implies that the cast acted as a team of independently functioning researchers, each with the same level of investment and responsibility, is inaccurate. In fact, Soans had edited a working draft of the script and had selected the majority of the material by the time the cast met their subjects in the rehearsal period. However, the script did change as a result of the actors' meetings with interviewees. Catherine Russell estimated that: 'About 70% of the script stayed as it was at the beginning of rehearsals, and 30% was added or changed depending upon what we had discovered and the conversations we'd had.' Soans has said that in the rehearsal process he would be 'constantly adapting... adding and subtracting', which suggests that the actors' contributions had a considerable effect on his writing. A critical question is how far they found that these particular working methods challenged their approaches, and how they adapted their work as a result of Stafford-Clark's processes.

ACTING PROCESSES

I interviewed the cast of *Talking to Terrorists* between 15 February and 9 July 2008. I found that the actors used vocabulary indebted to Stanislavski, having been taught in what Derek Paget has called 'the Stanislavski-based, stage-focused approach of British actor training'

(2007: 169).[3] However, the cast of *Talking to Terrorists* were not thoroughgoing Stanislavskians. I will interrogate the extent to which Stanislavski's theories might provide a useful terminology to illuminate the actors' processes in *Talking to Terrorists*, and explore the points at which other vocabularies may be more useful in describing their work.

My interviews revealed that the cast's major preoccupation was a process- rather than performance-based issue. The actors who took part in the bipartite process of meeting their subjects and the subsequent hotseating session recognised how formative the experience had been in their character construction and spoke about how it had affected their work thereafter. Since the hotseating exercise repeatedly emerged as a pivot-point in these actors' processes, the analysis in this case-study will centre on a detailed exploration of the actors' pre-hotseating processes; their experiences of the hotseating exercise itself; and the challenges they faced following it.

Pre-hotseating processes

In my interviews it became clear that whilst the actors were aware of the need to observe first-hand external features such as voice and appearance, these were of secondary importance to trying to absorb as much as they could about the individual's mind-set, history and attitude to the subject matter within the bounds of the pre-arranged questions they had at their disposal. One of the central acting skills they employed was the capacity for close observation. Chris Ryman's experience provides a particular formulation of this important aspect of acting.

'Empathetic observation'

Chris Ryman explained that as the writer and director took the lead in questioning in his interview with the ex-head of the Al Aqsa Martyrs Brigade, he was at liberty to observe the individual. As the meeting was conducted in the first research phase, and formed the basis of the testimony in the play, he was also able to note the emotional narrative of the man's story:

> Max and the writer were asking questions. The writer would write down various bits and pieces and I would be picking up the character aspects...because I had met him, and knowing the kind of person he was,

it was easy for me to know which emotions to act...for example when I talked about his kids I would have a real empathy.

Here Ryman links his rendering of emotions in performance to the fact that he experienced an empathetic response when he witnessed the man recount the same story. However, we must question how much credibility can be given to the assertion that he knew 'the kind of person he was'. This was a formal interview during which the individual recounted his story in front of a group of strangers with the express purpose of making a play from his words, which clearly constituted a performance from the interviewee. Nevertheless, while the claim to 'knowing' him has to be questioned, it is clear that Ryman needed to believe he had an emotional connection with the individual.

The way in which Ryman described employing the empathy he experienced through his observation can be understood through a particular (though often overlooked) formulation of emotion memory by Stanislavski. In his early to mid-career writings, emotion memory was one of Stanislavski's preferred techniques to summon an emotion in performance. The term is almost exclusively understood as it is described in the chapter 'Emotion Memory' in *An Actor's Work*: 'Just as your visual memory resurrects long forgotten things, a landscape or the image of a person, before your inner eye, so feelings you once experienced are resurrected in your Emotion Memory' (2008a: 199). However, this was not Ryman's emphasis. Later in my interview he stated: 'I wouldn't have to imagine the emotions, because I was there and saw him. It was about observation – my memory of what he was doing.' It appears that Ryman did not utilise his own personal experiences and associated emotions in the way Stanislavski describes, as he experienced an empathetic response to the man's story.

It is informative to view Ryman's work in relation to the writings of the actor Bella Merlin. Merlin appeared in Stafford-Clark's production of David Hare's play, *The Permanent Way*, and has written about her experiences. Merlin trained as an actor at the State Institute of Cinematography, Moscow, and has published widely on Stanislavski's work (see Merlin 2001, 2003, 2007b). She has explored how she used and adapted her Stanislavskian approach when playing a real person. Merlin also avoided this particular formulation of emotion memory in *The Permanent Way*:

I am not a great advocate of 'emotion memory'. Whilst I acknowledge it is a profound and important tool in Stanislavski's toolkit, I am aware that it is far too easy for actors to misinterpret its use...and overlay the play-wright's script onto their own personal histories. (2007c: 46)

In contrast to playing a fictional character, when the script is based on the words of real people, the possibility of 'overlaying' was evidently too great a risk for Merlin, who was anxious to distance this work from her own psychology or emotions. However, Ryman did use a form of emotion memory as he utilised the memory of the empathetic connection he experienced in his observation of the man's story. This is a technique which can be found elsewhere in Stanislavski's work. Although generally overlooked in favour of his chapter in *An Actor's Work*, Stanislavski also explored emotion memory in *Creating a Role*. Here, for the first time, he suggested that emotion memory can be 'acquired through study and preserved in [the actor's] intellectual memory' (1961a: 9). Thus, Stanislavski argued that actors can utilise the emotional responses they have experienced in study or research rather than via personally experienced emotion. In other words, they can draw on their emotional responses to other people's stories. Although Stanislavski does not predicate this acquisition on first-hand observation of the subject, it is clear that this lesser-acknowledged formulation is closer to the way in which Ryman worked. Ryman stated: 'It is a blessing to have a template to work from, a grounding.' He was able to ground his performance of emotion in the behaviour he had observed. However, it is also evident that he shared Merlin's concern with regard to 'overlaying' her own experiences. At no point did Ryman recall using his own personal experiences; instead he foregrounded his powers of active and empathetic observation.

Given and found circumstances: adapting a technique

A specific Stanislavskian technique that proved particularly helpful in the actors' meetings with their subjects was establishing the given circumstances of the role. However, because of the way in which the actors adapted their approaches in response to Stafford-Clark's working methods, we can add a new category – found circumstances. Comparing the experiences of Jonathan Cullen (who didn't meet the people he played and so was not hotseated) and Catherine Russell (who met both her subjects and so was) will demonstrate the impact of these meetings and also suggest some of the associated difficulties of representation inherent in this process.

Both actors were cast once the play had been written (at least in draft form), and so both could analyse the script to establish certain circumstances of their subjects' lives. Cullen commented that this was an important feature of his work: 'For every part I sit down and I note what I say about myself, what others say about me and what I say about other people ... then I list what I know about the character – the circumstances ... that can be revelatory.'

As Cullen had not met either of the individuals he played (the ex-Ambassador Craig Murray and the ex-member of the UVF), he chose to employ this recognisable technique: 'I decided very early on, if I was going to do this [play] I had to accept I hadn't met [them] and you have to do it on the basis of what is there on the page.' By contrast, although Russell's subjects Rima and Phoebe had already been interviewed, she was able to meet them one-to-one during rehearsals. The point in the process at which these meetings took place is vital here. Soans had already drafted the script of the play, and therefore he was not reliant on Russell for content. Thus, she enjoyed a greater freedom as to the questions she asked, and could formulate questions which would be helpful to her preparation. Russell consciously used these meetings to find out more of the circumstances of both their lives, 'Because I spoke to them for so long, I didn't just speak to them about their work, I spoke to them about their marriages, children – their lives.' Russell's and Cullen's comments indicate their different access to, and thus engagement with, their subjects' circumstances.

Establishing the 'given circumstances' is a Stanislavskian technique which has been widely accepted and adopted by a range of theorists and actor-trainers, including Brecht.[4] In *An Actor's Work*, Stanislavski provides an almost exhaustive list of what can constitute the given circumstances of a role:

> They mean the plot, the facts, the incidents, the period, the time and place of action, the way of life, how we as actors and directors understand the play, the contributions we ourselves make, the mise-en-scène, the sets and costumes, the props, the stage dressing, the sound effects etc., etc., everything which is given for the actors as they rehearse. (2008a: 52–3)

Given the limited access to her subject, in her interview Russell only approached some of the areas that Stanislavski identified:

> I didn't just speak to them about their work, I spoke to them about their marriages, children, their lives and childhood, upbringing – all the things

in Chekhov you would create for yourself, all of those things I found out
for real.

In her comparison between Anton Chekhov's imaginary characters and the exigencies of portraying a real person, Russell identifies a major difference: Stanislavski was primarily interested in
imagination, whereas documentary actively rejects this in favour of
fact-based sources. A meeting between strangers for the purposes
of a theatrical presentation evidently compromised the scope of
the given circumstances that she could acquire. The research that
Stanislavski lists could take weeks, and would have been impossible
to encompass in the interview, given both time constraints and the
fact that the interviewee would be unlikely to share a great deal of
personal information. We can see from Russell's comment that she
found out the facts (which suggest a Freudian emphasis) that were
useful to her. These were associated with Russell's own agenda as an
interviewer and it is clear that this information was critical in creating a character for her:

> You do get a character from the interview, as long as you don't just go for
> what is in the play, as long as you make sure your interview goes outside
> of that, otherwise you are in the normal situation of having to make it up,
> which is a waste – if the person is there in front of you, you can find out
> the real backstory.

While we must problematise the notion of a 'real backstory', and
acknowledge the highly constructed nature of their meeting, it is
clear that Russell had far greater access to her subjects' lives than
did Cullen. She was able to find circumstances *not* given in the play,
and also start to explore the circumstances that *were* given. Despite
the play's predication on interview material, Russell clearly turned to
sources beyond the script to aid her work. However, we can identify
a marked departure from Stanislavski in the way that Russell utilised
this information.

Given circumstances and the 'If ... I'

Stanislavski saw the given circumstances as being inseparably combined with the actor's imagination through their symbiotic bond with
the 'if':

> One is a hypothesis ('if'), the other is a corollary to it (the Given
> Circumstances). 'If' always launches the creative act and the Given

Circumstances develop it further. One can't exist without the other, or acquire the strength they need. But their functions are somewhat different. 'If' is a spur to the dormant imagination, and the Given Circumstances provide the substance for it. (2008a: 53)

'If', therefore, works within the structure created by the given circumstances and transports the dry circumstances into the actors' imaginative plane. This requires the actors to locate themselves within these circumstances, so as to start to imagine how the circumstances might affect them. Benedetti cites Stanislavski's illustration: '*if* everything around me on stage were true, this is what *I* would do, this is how *I* would respond to this or that event' (Benedetti 1982: 35, my emphasis). Stanislavski's deployment of the given circumstances with 'if' consequently calls upon the actor's own personality to provoke inner feeling. According to Stanislavski, this personalises the given circumstances through the actor's 'own impressions, genuine feeling and life experiences' (2010: 119). We could call this feature of the 'if' the 'if...I'. The twinning of the given circumstances with the 'if...I' is thus Stanislavski's acknowledgement that more is needed than the given circumstances themselves.

As documentary theatre above all privileges the text and the sources it is derived from, this feature was problematic for Russell. Her comments suggest a much less conscious application of the facts she discovered: 'I'm just looking at my rehearsal notebook here and my notes go on for pages. It all sinks in at some level, even if you don't consciously use it.' She used a similar osmotic analogy when she said: 'it probably did seep through...certainly her sense of absolute commitment, I hope that came through'. Like Ryman, Russell's departure from Stanislavski lies in her rejection of employing her own experiences in the role: the 'if...I'. One reason for this focus can be found in Shomit Mitter's comment that 'Stanislavski's "magic if" obliterates the claims of actuality in order to allow the actor a more compelling release into the imagined truths of character' (1992: 49). In light of Mitter's comment, the way in which Russell foregrounded observation over imagination appears largely attributable to the fact that the 'claims of actuality' were central to the production. Stanislavski formulated his techniques in relation to playing fictional roles; here, by contrast, the 'compelling release' which might result from using 'imagined truths' may not have been deemed appropriate when portraying a real person in the play.

A more helpful vocabulary through which to understand Russell's use of the given circumstances can be found in Stella Adler's development of the technique. Adler met Stanislavski in 1934, when he was working on the Method of Physical Action, a development of his thinking that will be explored in later case-studies. It was as a result of this meeting that Adler broke away from Lee Strasberg's emphasis on the personal psychology of the actor, and investigated other ways in which actors could employ their imagination. Although again based on fictional roles, Adler questioned the use of 'if' to personalise the given circumstances for the actor (the 'if ... I'). Instead, Adler stressed the importance of noting the differences in circumstances between the actor and subject, rather than the similarities.

> The playwright gives you the play, the idea, the style, the conflict, the character, etc. The background life of the character will be made up of the social, cultural, political, historical, and geographical situation in which the author places him ... Through the proper use of craft, the actor will be able to see the differences ... between himself and the character. Through his craft he will be able to translate these difficulties and use them to arrive at the character. (Adler et al. 1964: 149)

Adler's emphasis on the character's given circumstances and background life resonate strongly with Russell's technique, particularly in the departure from using the actors' own experiences. As Adler states, 'You will never have your own name and personality or be in your own house ... every word, every action, must originate in the actor's imagination' (1988: 17). However, despite the similarities with her process, Russell was much less specific with regard to her use of imagination. Although it would be glib to suggest that an actor could perform without any imagination, Russell's comments suggest a gradual enrichment of her portrayal through these circumstances rather than a developed imaginative application of them.

Russell and Cullen thus employed quite different strategies, relative to their access to the individuals they later played. As a result of her access to the interviewees, Russell was able to learn a lot more about them than Cullen, and could take this information into her hotseating sessions. Although, in comparison to Cullen's experiences, learning more about the women may have benefited Russell's understanding of the roles she played, it severely hampered her later in the process, as we shall see.

Experiments with self-analysis

When I spoke to Alexander Hanson about his experiences of meet-ing the Army Colonel, it became clear that he had developed dif-ferent strategies in his portrayal. Hanson visited the Colonel at his Wiltshire base during the rehearsal process, at which point the script was in draft form. His preconceptions about the Colonel, based on Stafford-Clark's description of meeting him, were reversed by his own experience:

> Max filled me in a bit ... and told me what he was like, so I had this image in my mind and then I met him and he was quite different – he wasn't intimi-dating at all ... he was incredibly friendly actually. We went for a walk and went for dinner and chatted.

The meeting was extremely valuable as it allowed Hanson to form his own opinion. In addition, Hanson's description of the purpose of his meeting marks a quite different emphasis from the other actors: 'It was great for me to watch him and see what he was like as a per-son, because obviously you are aiming to find the essence of him in yourself.' Hanson thus actively sought out similarities between the Colonel and himself.

One mode of interrogation into these four divergent pre-hotseating approaches is to view them according to Stanislavski's writings on 'Analysis'. Hanson's description follows this process to a greater extent than Russell's, and yet, arguably, does not follow it to the logical con-clusion Stanislavski sets out. Stanislavski identifies a five-stage system of script and role analysis, but it is the first three stages that are par-ticularly relevant here:

1. Studying the writer's work.
2. Searching for the inner and other kinds of material for creative purposes to be found within the play and the role. (2010: 103)

Ryman, Russell and Cullen all followed the first two stages, albeit on divergent paths from Stanislavski. In their search for 'material for cre-ative purposes', Ryman summoned his empathy from the interview, Russell used her knowledge of the circumstances to guide her, and Cullen listed both the circumstances and what was said about his sub-ject. However, in his approach, Hanson experimented with the next stage:

3. Searching for the same material in ourselves as actors (self-analysis) ... (2010: 103)

Of all the cast, Hanson was the only actor to report that he actively used 'self-analysis' to prepare himself for hotseating. Stanislavski subsequently expanded on this technique, stating: 'the actor's imagination has the ability to get close to someone else's life, transform it into his own, discover exciting qualities and traits they have in common' (2010: 114). In contrast to the link between Russell's process and Adler's teaching, Hanson was drawn to the Colonel and sought shared features. However, Stanislavski's third stage of analysis goes further than merely finding similarities in the actor:

3. [cont.] The material under discussion consists of living, personal memories drawn from our five senses, contained in an actor's affective memory...these memories must always be similar to the feelings in the play and the role. (2010: 103)

Hanson, therefore, sought out similarities between himself and the Colonel, but he did not recall consciously employing his own 'personal memories' to assist him. This is a critical distinction. By identifying these similarities, Hanson was able to base his portrayal on the elements of the Colonel's personality that he found reflected his own. However, like Ryman and Russell before him, Hanson made no reference to using specific experiences of his own to do this. Although he based his portrayal on his own personality to a greater extent than did Russell or Ryman, this was predicated on the shared features he observed in the meeting with the Colonel, rather than actively translating these through his own emotion memory.

Hotseating

The hotseating sessions took place as soon as possible after the actor-subject meetings, often the following day. They were held in the Out of Joint rehearsal room in front of the cast and creative team. In contrast to their pre-hotseating processes, which were private, here the actors' early work was shared and therefore subject to scrutiny from all involved. It was the first point at which the actors performed as the person they had met. Thus, their processes started by, rather than culminated in, performing as the individual. This section will identify the innovative array of processes that the actors developed in response to this unusual challenge.

In the hotseat, the cast and creative team asked the pre-set interview questions that the actors themselves had asked when they met the individual. The actor then replied as the interviewee. As few

of the interviews were recorded, the sessions were based on rec-
ollected improvisation and the actors' notes. Stafford-Clark states
that 'it makes you dependent on the actors' imagination'. However,
it should be remembered that as Soans was present at all but one
of the interviews, the actors' hotseating sessions provided add-
itional viewpoints rather than being the primary method to gather
material.

Despite the improvisatory nature of the sessions, Stafford-Clark
advised the actors to give 'as accurate a recreation as possible', suggesting that the actors were required to stay as close to their recollections
of the interview as they could. Like many documentary practitioners, Stafford-Clark places a heavy insistence on the authenticity of
the process. As the sessions were based on the actors' notes, memory
and improvised interpretation of what they had heard and observed,
arguing that the portrayals are 'accurate' is potentially misleading. As
Lloyd Hutchinson observed:

> Basically what happens is you'd come back to rehearsal room with notes
> [or] with the audio tape, you probably might have listened to the interview
> on the way back, or gone over your notes, but what happens is the rest of
> the group sits at one end of the room, or one end of the table, you sit at the
> other and they basically ask you questions... You try and keep to the truth
> of what the person had said to you in the interview. If you don't know the
> answer to a question that's being given to you, you can act your way out
> of that, or tell them you don't know... that's basically how it worked, it's
> always out of improvisation.

Similarly, Christopher Ettridge laid out the journey of the hotseating
process: 'It is a very gentle shift; Max starts by asking you what he [the
interviewee] said, and then saying "just do that as him". You get asked
questions and you answer as the character.' Chipo Chung described
the process as a mixture of reportage and re-enactment:

> When we reported back, we'd still be reading from our notes, but
> re-enacting at the same time. That's something that Max would often
> do. He'd get us to re-enact simultaneously so that we would both be
> playing them and at the same time able to give different aspects of the
> character.

A word of caution regarding the term 're-enactment' may be necessary for clarity. The formulation of 're-enactment' in this case-study
should be understood as referring to the creative enterprise of

reproducing and reconstructing the words of the interviewee; although Stafford-Clark aimed for 'as accurate a recreation as possible', he also commented that 'the script would be filtered through their memory in a rather curious way'.

Responding in the third-person: 'simultaneous re-enactment'

Chung's term 'simultaneous re-enactment' is useful to describe this first stage of hotseating, as it indicates the dual awareness of the actor in the process. As Chung suggests, in the 'simultaneous re-enactment' stage, the actors were aware of their role both as a reporter, narrating and describing the interviewee, and as a performer, actually responding in character as them. Chung's and Ettridge's comments suggest that the early stages of the hotseating sessions included recognisable Brechtian strategies.

Brecht's description of a 'double role', wherein the actor 'does not disappear in the role he is playing', shares certain features with the hotseating process (Willett 1964: 194). Citing the example of Charles Laughton playing Galileo, Brecht states:

> The actor appears onstage in a double role ... the showman Laughton does not disappear in the Galileo whom he is showing ... Laughton is actually there, standing on stage and showing us what he imagines Galileo to have been. (Double and Wilson 2006: 55)

As in Brecht's description, by responding in the third person, Chung was able to share her own subjective view of the interviewee. The 'double role' is also explored by Brecht in his essay 'The Street Scene', which he used to illustrate the dramatic functions of his epic style. In it, Brecht analysed the way in which an individual, standing on a street corner, could describe a recent traffic accident to a group of onlookers (Willett 1964: 121–9). The way in which the demonstrator functions as the guide, describing and recounting what happened, whilst also quoting those involved, shares basic features with the re-enactment stage in the actors' hotseating:

> The event has taken place; what you are seeing now is a repeat ... the street-corner demonstration admits it is a demonstration (and does not pretend to be the actual event) ... There is no question that the street-corner demonstrator has been through an event, but he is not out to make his demonstration serve as an 'experience' for the audience ... He is not interested in creating pure emotions. (Willett 1964: 122)

Brecht goes on to state that 'It is most important that one of the main features of ordinary theatre be excluded from our street scene: the engendering of illusion' (Willett 1964: 122). In the 'simultaneous re-enactment' stage, there was a lack of illusion, and rather an emphasis on describing and recreating the content of the interview.

The technique of transferring speech into the third person is also a Brechtian rehearsal exercise, and was indeed one of the exercises Brecht conducted with his actors to create a 'double role'. In his essay 'A Short Description of a New Technique of Acting which Produces an Alienation Effect', Brecht investigated techniques by which the actor could interrupt the audience's identification with his/her character, and thus 'make the spectator adopt an attitude of enquiry and criticism' (Willett 1964: 136). In Brecht's view, avoiding a complete transformation was critical to achieve this:

> He reproduces their remarks as authentically as he can; he puts forward their way of behaving to the best of his abilities and knowledge of men; but he never tries to persuade himself (and thereby others) that this amounts to a complete transformation... Given this lack of total transformation there are three aids which may help to alienate the actions and remarks of the characters being portrayed:
>
> 1. Transposition into the third person
> 2. Transposition into the past
> 3. Speaking the stage directions out loud
>
> (Willett 1964: 137–8)

Brecht's comments have a very strong resonance with this first stage of hotseating. 'Simultaneous re-enactment' represents a move away from an emotional or psychological rendering of character, and rather allows the actor to comment on the character, thereby promoting a critical engagement with the unfolding narrative in the spectator (here the other actors and the creative team).

First person recollection: experiments with inhabitation

The process of 'simultaneous re-enactment' was only the first stage in the hotseating process. As Ettridge states, after answering in the third person, he was instructed to 'do that as him' and respond in the first person. Chris Ryman echoes Ettridge: '[After meeting them] we'd then come back and we would just say what happened, what we saw, what we heard, and then we'd go into the scene, we would re-enact and improvise the kind of things we heard.' Ettridge recalled that in the second stage of hotseating 'you drift in a quite seamless way into becoming that character... It is a very gentle shift that Max does.' Hutchinson described that 'you take on the character', whilst Catherine Russell recalled that 'you'd become the character in the room.' In articulating the move from third to first person, these actors appear to suggest they are entirely transformed into the individual. When I questioned the actors further about the specific nature of this transformation, the complexity of the experience became clear. Alexander Hanson recalled: 'the cast sat round the table, and I was there as the Colonel, and basically they asked me questions about army policy, so you are really on the rack. You are taken out of your comfort zone'.

As the actors did not read from their script, they were both physically and mentally engaged in improvising responses to the questions, whilst staying as close to what they could remember of the interviewee's testimony as possible and trying to capture, unrehearsed, the way in which it was given. This represents a departure from Brecht's view that:

> the actor must remain a demonstrator; he must present the person demonstrated as a stranger, he must not suppress the '*he* did that, *he* said that' element in his performance. He must not go so far as to be wholly transformed into the person demonstrated. (Willett 1964: 125)

Hanson found that answering as the Colonel felt 'false'. He said, 'I did a very bold version of him... It feels false if you try to do it.' Similarly, Lloyd Hutchinson commented that:

> I would say to begin with I was sort of impersonating in the hotseat, I didn't completely inhabit him. Then after a while, later in the process, that just goes out the window when you're faced with things on the page, intentions that the writer had.

Perhaps as a result of the timing of the session, so soon after the meetings, these actors were aware of the limitations of their inhabitation and remained particularly conscious of the duality in their performance. This may well have also been a product of the preceding 'simultaneous re-enactment' stage, which meant that when they replied as the individual, they did not lose the narratorial quality the previous stage had established. Whilst this second stage may have departed from Brecht's writings, the actors' awareness of duality finds resonance in Stanislavski's writings, most fully explored in *An Actor's Work*.

Hotseating and Stanislavski

Although Stanislavski does not use the term 'hotseating', in *An Actor's Work* he places the young actor 'Kostya' in a similar situation. Kostya takes part in an improvisation in which he plays an acerbic critic. After the improvisation, he stays in character when questioned by the director, Tortsov. He notes: 'I'm happy because I know what being someone else requires, what *transformation and physical characterisation are*' (Stanislavski 2008a: 526). However, when Stanislavski explains the nature of this 'immersion', he notes a duality not dissimilar to that which Cullen and Hutchinson noted was created through the two-stage hotseating exercise:

> while I was living the Critic I still didn't lose contact with myself, Kostya. I drew this conclusion because all the time I was acting I took enormous pleasure in observing my own physical transformation...The Critic came out of me. I, as it were, split down the middle. One half was the actor, the other watched like an audience. Strange. This sense of being split in two wasn't a hindrance, it fired and encouraged the creative process. (2008a: 527)

Stanislavski expounds a duality in which part of the actor's awareness is focused on observing the character created. This represents a significant overlap with Brecht's theories, and yet in academic discourse on Stanislavski's work his comments on duality are often overlooked, arguably in an attempt to polarise the work of the two theorists.

When playing a real person only hours after meeting them, it is little surprise that the actors in *Talking to Terrorists* were preoccupied with adhering to the specifics of the original interview. This may well have been more keenly felt in Stafford-Clark's and Soans' working processes (as Hanson said, he was 'on the rack') because they were not only portraying a real person, but also a person the writer and (often) the director had met. The added pressure of the writer's and director's familiarity with the subject appears to have increased the actors' dual awareness, since they had to monitor, censor and control their portrayals.

Post-hotseating processes

Alexander Hanson: from a 'false' portrayal to a 'half-way house' and Chekhov's 'imaginary body'

As we have seen, Hanson sought to establish the similarities between himself and the Colonel in his meeting. By contrast, Stafford-Clark's demand for an 'accurate recreation' meant that Hanson moved away from his own mannerisms to replicate the Colonel's responses: 'The next day I went in the hotseat, I did a very bold version of him. Particularly his way of speaking. It feels false if you try to do it, but eventually you begin to own the actions.' It is informative to consider what Hanson meant by 'a bold version' of 'his way of speaking'. Hanson implies that he exaggerated his portrayal; an enlargement which meant his performance felt 'false'. However, his comment that 'eventually you begin to own the actions' suggests that his journey post-hotseat was predicated on using the shared features he established in the meeting to psychologically justify and thereby 'own' his portrayal.

Hanson stated that a critical stage in this journey was establishing a 'half-way house' between himself and the Colonel. This was based on a combination of his observations in the meeting and his awareness of what was theatrically viable:

> You bring what you have as an individual...and you create that half-way house. You want to maintain the integrity of the person you are playing, but you also know what works – what interests an audience – what keeps attention, which is your craft.

In contrast to the other actors' descriptions of their preparation for the hotseat, here Hanson more readily acknowledges his own creative agency and interpretive interventions in constructing the role. The creation of this 'half-way house' between Hanson and the Colonel allowed him to develop his portrayal beyond the performance he gave in the hotseat. He stated: 'You're not really copying the individual, you try and be him, but ultimately of course you find a half-way house between yourself and that person.'

Hanson's description of the 'half-way house' has many similarities with Michael Chekhov's description of the 'imaginary body'. His 'bold version' in the hotseat necessarily emphasised the differences between, for example, his voice and the Colonel's. Chekhov suggests that a character is defined by the ways in which it is distinct from the actor: 'That which constitutes their *difference* makes them *characters*' (2002: 78). Using a similar vocabulary to Stella Adler, Chekhov writes that the actor should therefore ask 'What is the *difference* – however subtle or slight this difference may be – between myself and the character as it is described by the playwright?' (2002: 78). Chekhov states that the character should be created through these differences, and calls this creation an 'imaginary body': 'You are going to imagine that in the same space you occupy with your own, real body there exists another body – the imaginary body of your character, which you have just created in your mind' (2002: 78). This imaginary body 'influences your psychology... your *whole being, psychologically and physically*, will be changed' (2002: 79). Chekhov warns against '"performing" your imaginary body prematurely' (2002: 80):

> Do not exaggerate outwardly by stressing, pushing and over-doing those subtle inspirations which come to you from your 'new body'. And only when you begin to feel absolutely free, true and natural in using it should you start rehearsing your character with its lines and business. (2002: 80)

This relates very closely to Hanson's experience in the hotseat; his 'bold version' may have felt 'false' because his session took place so early in his preparation for the play. He was, to use Chekhov's words, 'outwardly... stressing, pushing and over-doing' his portrayal, because of Stafford-Clark's request for an accurate representation of the Colonel so soon after the meeting. However, Hanson's remark that he began to 'own the actions' has a strong resonance with Chekhov's statement that 'you begin to feel absolutely free, true and natural'. Though acting is clearly highly constructed, and Chekhov's terms are not particularly helpful, we can understand these comments as referring to the actor's physical and emotional confidence in the role. Seen through Chekhov's description, therefore, we can identify Hanson's performance in the hotseat as an exercise which both fulfilled Stafford-Clark's wish for accuracy and at the same time set the parameters within which his 'half-way house' or 'imaginary body' could be located.

Chekhov's tripartite construct and emotion memory

Chekhov's advice with regard to the rendering of emotion within the 'imaginary body' provides a further frame through which to understand Hanson's process. Like Hanson's description that he did not consciously use his own emotional memory in his preparation, Chekhov states that 'the imaginary body stands, as it were, *between* your real body and your psychology' (2002: 79).

Chekhov's theory of the actor–imaginary body–character is mirrored in his tripartite construct of the 'self' (a term which he uses interchangeably with the '*I*'). This is composed of three different levels of consciousness, which he terms the 'everyday *I*', the 'higher *I*' and the 'character's *I*'. On the most basic level is the 'everyday *I*', which is the actor's own 'emotions, voice and mobile body'. The features of the 'everyday *I*' provide the material with which the 'higher *I*' can work. Chekhov explains that the 'higher *I*' is the 'expanded self', a feeling the actor experiences in the moment of creation. Thus, when an actor is performing, 'you are two selves'. It is the relationship between these two selves that allows inspiration to occur, by 'putting you into a *creative* state' (2002: 87). Chekhov identifies the 'everyday *I*' as a solid base on which to build; it is the 'common-sense regulator', which 'controls the canvas upon which the creative individuality [the higher *I*] draws its designs' (2002: 88). This higher self is quite detached from the actor's everyday personality, as it is present only when on stage in the moment of creation. The third consciousness is the 'character's *I*', which is created by the 'everyday *I*' and the 'higher *I*'. This third entity 'becomes the focal point of the higher self's creative impulses'. To apply this directly to Hanson's comments, he was able to bring 'what you have as an individual' (the 'everyday *I*'), but also 'your craft' (the creative 'higher *I*'), which together Hanson used to create 'a half-way house' between himself and the Colonel.

The crucial departure from Stanislavski (and one which aligns Hanson's process more closely with Chekhov) is in the way in which the actor's own experiences are deployed in the 'character's *I*'. As examined earlier, Stanislavski used 'if' to draw on the actor's own experiences in relation to the circumstances of a role. Although Chekhov acknowledges that the material for character creation stems from the actor's own experiences, he states that the emotions engendered by the 'higher *I*' are 'as "unreal" as the "soul" of the character itself' (2002: 90). As they are so strongly linked to the moment of inspiration, they are not part of the actor's 'everyday *I*', but rather a product of imagination and creative individuality. Although Stanislavski suggested a dual awareness of the actor and role, and that the actor is never completely lost in the character, he never deconstructed the psychological side of character creation to this extent. Indeed, unlike

Stanislavski, Chekhov warns the actor against using experiences directly sourced from his or her 'everyday *I*'; if they do:

> they would become forever yours, indelibly impressed upon you after the
> performance is over... You would not be able to draw the line of demarca-
> tion between the illusory life of your character and that of your own. In no
> time you would be driven mad. If creative feelings were not 'unreal' you
> would not be able to enjoy playing villains or other undesirable characters.
> (2002: 90)

Chekhov develops, like Stanislavski, an understanding of rendering emotion on stage which acknowledges the use of the actor's own
feelings. However, through his elaboration of the 'higher *I*', Chekhov
foregrounds imagination, rather than the provocation of personal
experiences, which means that specific analogous events are not
called upon. As Mel Gordon argues in his introduction to Chekhov's
Lessons for the Professional Actor:

> Where Stanislavski's emotion memory exercises played upon the actor's
> sensory recall of an actual event, which then had to be used as a substitute
> in a similar occurrence in a script, Chekhov schooled his students in find-
> ing imaginary, external stimuli to fire their imaginations. (1985: 18)

Hanson thus combined his pre-hotseating approach of establishing
the similarities between himself and the Colonel with his hotseating session in which he moved his portrayal away from himself and
started to embody another 'imaginary body' which lay between the
two. In contrast to his pre-hotseating approach, the way in which
Hanson described his rehearsal process shows a conscious accept-
ance of his own creative endeavours. This is perhaps best summarised by his comment that 'the person I was portraying sort of wasn't
him, but it was his words'. Hanson did not attempt to recreate what he
had observed minutely, but still based the character he created on the
individual he met.

A major determinant in Hanson's process was his relaxed sense of
accountability to the real life Colonel. Indeed, when I asked how he
felt about the Colonel's presence at a performance of the play, Hanson
answered: 'I was rather proud of what I was doing... that didn't faze
me.' There are several possible reasons for Hanson's relaxed approach
to playing the Colonel. The Colonel talked to the group (and later
to Hanson personally) in his capacity as a senior member of the
British Army. His testimony in the play thus focuses on official policy. Although the Colonel may describe harrowing events he (or his

soldiers) witnessed, he does so with reference to army policy rather than reliving deeply personal memories. This is in contrast to other characters in the play who recount their own terrorist acts, or the way in which they have been acutely affected by such acts.

A further determinant was the Colonel's personality. Hanson did not need to radically alter what he saw to make his representation theatrically viable. Hanson said, 'The Colonel was very open, confident and charismatic.' Thus, although his recreation in the hotseat felt 'false', there was an inherent theatricality to the Colonel that meant that Hanson's task of translating his behaviour for the stage was relatively straightforward. Equally critical to his unconstrained experience was the fact that Stafford-Clark was also satisfied by his portrayal in the hotseat. By contrast, the issue of theatrical viability was central to both Lloyd Hutchinson's and Catherine Russell's approaches.

Adaptation and theatrical viability

Hutchinson met the ex-IRA member that he played in Belfast with Robin Soans during the second research phase. The individual had previously spoken to the cast in the first research phase at the Out of Joint rehearsal room, where his interview was recorded, so there was already a draft version. Throughout his process, Hutchinson was aware of the importance of theatrical viability. As the interviewee was well versed in recounting his story, in the interview Hutchinson and Soans searched for new, dramatically interesting information to enrich the testimony that April de Angelis had already collated. Hutchinson recalled:

> [He's] been involved in reconciliation work, so he'd told his story many, many times both on television, radio and the printed media. What we wanted was something from him that wasn't basically him giving us a load of sound bites. Something from a more human angle. Something that would be ultimately more theatrical, I suppose, something that would work in a theatre.

Hutchinson's concern with theatricality was realised with regard to the content; the ex-IRA member's story of planting the Brighton bomb is utterly chilling, particularly as Soans inter-cuts the bomber's story with testimony from the victims of the attack, constructing a powerful montaged polemic. However, Hutchinson found that recreating the *manner* in which this information was given was more problematic.

In addition to his description of his 'impersonation', Hutchinson described that in the hotseating sessions 'you take on the character, and they ask you questions and basically you try and give an impression of the person that you met'. The way in which he foregrounded externality as a means to achieve this in the hotseat became clear when he said: 'You maybe start by using certain physical things and vocal things that they have, but then you kind of forget about them.' However, the care Hutchinson took in replicating these external features resulted in difficulties because of the theatrical viability of his subject. To illustrate these challenges, Hutchinson contrasted his experiences of playing the ex-IRA member with his portrayal of the Archbishop's Envoy, Terry Waite:

> The problem with [the ex-IRA member] is that he is an unbelievably soft spoken man, so I had to find a way that you could convey his naturally subdued behaviour in a theatre; whereas Terry Waite has quite big and expansive gestures, so that's pretty easy to do.

It is evident from Hutchinson's comments that whilst an accurate recreation was helpful in his portrayal of Terry Waite, it was not theatrically viable for the ex-IRA member. Due to Terry Waite's larger than life physique and personality, Hutchinson felt he did not consciously have to adapt his observations for his portrayal: 'I mean why do you feel you need to create something when you've already got the living, breathing model of them sitting there in front of you? If you're playing a real person there are indications of how the role should be played.' Whilst this is evidently true of his portrayal of Waite, Hutchinson certainly had to 'create something' to adapt his portrayal of the 'unbelievably soft spoken' ex-IRA member to make it theatrically viable (or at the very least, theatrically audible).

Here, we can acknowledge that the term 'adaptation' is understood to refer to the differences, consciously imposed by the director and/ or actors, between the person interviewed and the actor's portrayal of them. Stafford-Clark states that: 'Adaptation has to take place as you are performing in public. You are performing in front of four hundred people, where in the interview, it was to one person.' There can be no performance without some degree of adaptation, and yet Stafford-Clark's direction for the actors to be 'accurate' in the hotseat was clearly an effort to limit adaptation as far as possible. The journey for the actors was thus to develop a theatrically viable character from the precise recreation they gave in the hotseat, a journey that clearly varied depending on the interviewee.

Whilst observation is unanimously hailed as one of the most important tools for an actor, the way in which the actor can utilise observed
behaviour has been explored in various ways. For example, Sanford
Meisner instructs a young actor that: 'When you put the real situation
on the stage, you need to keep its reality so that it's believable both to
you and to the audience, but you have to raise it to a level above real
life. Otherwise it doesn't communicate' (Meisner and Longwell 1987:
146). Brecht was similarly mindful of avoiding exact recreation:

> Observation is a major part of acting. The actor observes his fellow-men
> with all his nerves and muscles in an act of imitation which is at the same
> time a process of the mind. For pure imitation would only bring out what
> had been observed; and this is not enough, because the original said what
> it has to say with too subdued a voice. (Willett 1964: 196)

For Brecht, therefore, it is the 'process of the mind' which is the actor's
key creative aid to avoid reliance on 'pure imitation'.

However, Hutchinson's comments most closely relate to
Stanislavski's writings on 'theatrical truth' or 'theatrical fact'. The
concept is one of the cornerstones of Stanislavski's system. In *An
Actor's Work* he states:

> in the real world, genuine truth and belief create themselves... But when
> there is no reality onstage and you have acting... truth and belief first
> arise in the imagination, as an artistic fiction, which is then translated
> onto the stage... [You] create theatrical truth and belief onstage. So, in
> life there is truth, what is, what exists, what people really know. Onstage
> we call truth that which does not exist in reality but which could happen.
> (2008a: 153)

Elsewhere in *An Actor's Work*, Stanislavski states that to perform
'actual truth' is impossible for an actor:

> Genuine 'facts', the normal world, do not exist on stage. The normal world
> is not art... The actor's task is to use his creative skills to transform the
> story of the play into *theatrical fact*. Our imagination has an enormous role
> to play here. (2008a: 60)

Hanson and Hutchinson described how they developed their role
beyond 'impersonation' and the 'false' feeling they experienced in the
hotseat. As we have seen, for Hanson this was predicated on creating
a 'half-way house'. For Hutchinson, the notion of choice and selection
was critical. This issue came to the fore when he considered how to
adapt the quietness of his subject: 'You choose the elements that will

work. So I didn't copy [ex-IRA's] quiet voice, but I did use his stillness. It is about selecting what is going to work.'

Hutchinson's comments are consistent with Stanislavski's statement
that the actor must choose 'what is essential' in his/her portrayal,
which is evidently an entirely subjective intervention by the actor. In
his short note 'On Being Truthful in Acting', Stanislavski asked:

> What does it really mean to be truthful on the stage?...Does it mean that
> you conduct yourself as you do in ordinary life? Not at all. Truthfulness in
> those terms would be sheer triviality. There is the same difference between
> artistic and inartistic truth as exists between a painting and a photo-
> graph: the latter reproduces everything, the former only what is essential.
> (1968: 20)

Hutchinson, therefore, created a theatrical truth by finding an alternative approach to portraying a feature that was not theatrically viable,
which clearly involved his observational skills. His comments echo
those of Bella Merlin, who states:

> The process that the actors were asked to engage in with Stafford-Clark
> and Hare was, I would argue, the distilling of 'actual fact' into 'scenic truth'.
> This distillation...was not the *diminishment* of truth, rather the condensa-
> tion of 'truth' into a palatable and manageable artistic form. (2007c: 42)

Continuing an emerging trend of experience among the cast,
Hutchinson's approach was more associated with observational memory, here adapted to create a 'theatrical truth', than it was with his
own experiential recall. Stanislavski stated that

> Not all the truths we know in life are good for the theatre. Truth in the
> theatre must be genuine, not glamorized. It must be purged of unneces-
> sary, mundane details. It must be true in a realistic sense but made poetic
> by creative ideas. (2008a: 192)

Stanislavski's comment has a strong resonance with Hutchinson's
process, although 'creative observation' may be closer to his working
method. Like Stafford-Clark's statement that 'I make no claim to the
absolute authenticity of it, but it is true to the spirit of it.' Hutchinson
was able to maintain the qualities that he felt were indispensable
(here the ex-IRA member's stillness) by consciously adapting his performance to create a 'theatrical truth'. Hutchinson actively intervened
with character creation, and thus his post-hotseating processes moved
away from the impersonation he gave in the hotseat. He identified,
and was able to fix, the problem of theatrical viability in his portrayal

of the ex-IRA member. However, Stafford-Clark's notion of staying 'true to the spirit of it' is significantly problematised by Catherine Russell's experiences.

Catherine Russell: adaptation/reinvention

Catherine Russell played Rima, the journalist, and Phoebe, the relief worker for Save the Children. As we have seen, she used her meetings with them to establish the circumstances of their lives and careers which were outside the testimony Soans had already drafted. However, Russell's experience of hotseating fundamentally challenged her approach.

Russell found her hotseating session as 'Rima' was very helpful due to the inherent theatricality of her subject: 'she is an extremely theatrical character and her personality transfers very well to the stage as she is very entertaining'. But her portrayal of Phoebe was a very different experience. She recalled that in the hotseat:

> Max was saying, 'well that is not very entertaining'. Poor woman! So actually that really set me back a few weeks meeting her, as I had her very firmly in my mind but that is not what the director and the writer wanted, it didn't fit in. So I had to create somebody who wasn't her.

This represents a complete contrast to the experiences of the other actors and provokes serious questions about Stafford-Clark's working methods. Although Hutchinson had to adapt certain elements to make his portrayal theatrically viable, the core of his observational work remained intact. When translating something to create a 'theatrical truth', Stanislavski only proposed finding the 'poetical equivalent', rather than entirely re-inventing the character. The care Russell had taken to find out more of Phoebe's circumstances in her pre-hotseating work was of very little use to her, as she felt she had to dismiss it and 'create somebody that wasn't her'. The changes demanded by Stafford-Clark severely hampered her approach:

> It made it really, really difficult, it's the same with most things, once you've learnt or got your head around something, it is very difficult then to change. I found it an incredibly difficult rehearsal process from that point of view.

Russell thus had to completely re-imagine a character; one unrelated to the 'not very entertaining' (yet more accurate) portrayal she gave in the hotseat. The contrast between her pre-hotseat preparation and what was imposed on her by Stafford-Clark was enough to make her ask: 'was it useful meeting her? Not really... what I wanted to do was to play her.' This evidently was not the agenda shared by the director. Stafford-Clark's comment that he'd 'always go for theatricality' meant that he privileged a workable dramaturgy over a precise rendering of the interviewee; thus a high level of adaptation (indeed complete re-invention) was admissible in order that the portrayals were interesting, which evidently presented a very problematic conundrum for Russell.

To return to the comparison between Catherine Russell's and Jonathan Cullen's experiences, as Cullen didn't meet anyone he played before the production opened, he was wholly reliant on Stafford-Clark and Soans for guidance. Despite the fact that this vested power in the director and writer, it also meant that he was spared the problems that Russell experienced. Cullen himself noted that the actors who took part in the research phases 'were coming from a very different place as they had done the interviews themselves and knew the people they were talking about'. However, he did not see himself as being at a disadvantage:

> I think there are two big dangers... one is that you get too attached to the person you have interviewed, and you don't want to betray them, so you want all of their words in, and the other one is that you know too much about them, and you forget to represent that, to make it dramatic for the audience, who don't know that person. But I was spared these problems, I was in the same situation as the audience, I was coming to it fresh.

Here Cullen alludes to some of the problems which were evidently informing Stafford-Clark's advice to Russell. For Cullen, bypassing the hotseating session avoided this very delicate negotiation, which, in the example of Russell, was detrimental to her preparation. In addition, when viewed in comparison to Cullen's experiences, Russell's comments are highly significant in relation to Stafford-Clark's claims regarding his research processes. Her process was far more problematic than Cullen's, who didn't meet his subjects at all. The experience was evidently frustrating, and reinforced the status of the director to the detriment of her own work. Indeed, although Russell did not feel her hotseating session as Phoebe helped her, there were aspects of it which assisted both Soans and particularly Stafford-Clark. With regard to content, it should be remembered that Phoebe talked to the research team at the Out of Joint rehearsal room during the second research phase, before Russell had been cast in the play. This is in contrast to *The Permanent Way*, in which the actors had a much larger role to play in the generation of material. For example, David Hare relied on Bella Merlin for the content of the script as well as the way in which the testimony was given. Derek Paget has suggested that the hotseating exercise in *The Permanent Way* 'was also a kind of audition' in that the actors were pitching their interviewees to the director and writer (2007: 171). When Russell became involved, Soans and Stafford-Clark had already decided that Phoebe would appear in the play, and furthermore, that Russell would play her. Russell, therefore, was not 'pitching' Phoebe, who had been included, but rather her performance of Phoebe. Thus, Russell's hotseating process assisted Stafford-Clark as he was able, at the earliest possible opportunity, to change Russell's portrayal to fit his own notions of theatrical viability.

Russell's experience prompts wider questions about Stafford-Clark's and Soans' manipulation of the stories of a real person. Summarising her feelings, Russell stated: 'There is the question of accuracy for an actor. Like with Phoebe from Save the Children, an accurate portrayal of her would not have been theatrical. So when you are presenting the truth, you are not really presenting the truth.' Russell's experiences can be juxtaposed with Stafford-Clark's comment that 'observation and accuracy, which are part of any actor's training, are very much what you look for' (Hammond and Steward 2009: 65). As we have seen, Russell's innovative strategies in both these areas were dismissed by the director. Her comments also cast severe doubt over Stafford-Clark's argument that 'I make no claim to the absolute authenticity of it, but it is true to the spirit of it.' Evidently, we can add the highly problematic caveat: *when the interviewee is interesting enough*. It appears that, in the depiction of Phoebe, Stafford-Clark's foregrounding of theatricality over accuracy eclipsed his claims to be 'true to the spirit' of the interview.

However, in his defence, it was Stafford-Clark and not the actors who had a perspective on the whole play. The capacity of the writer and director to have an overview is an important consideration which is echoed in the experiences of Bella Merlin in *The Permanent Way*. During the previews for the play, the real-life 'Second Bereaved Mother', who Merlin portrayed, attended a performance with her husband. After the show, she told Merlin that she felt her portrayal 'had been rather "hard"' (Merlin 2007a: 132). Merlin wrote: 'My quandary as an actor was whether or not I was right to "forsake" the real person to some degree in order that the theatricality of the subject matter and the play's overall visceral quality was maintained' (2007a: 132).

In order to create a powerful polemic, David Hare organised the play so as to juxtapose events, stories and characters in a montage of scenes and speeches. Merlin's portrayal and Hare's narrative thus may have depicted the character as 'hard'. Merlin commented that Hare 'had no wish to show her temperate side; he had other characters to demonstrate temperance at other places in the play' (2007a: 132). We thus have to acknowledge that these individuals carry a function in the play. In the montage of speeches in *Talking to Terrorists*, Stafford-Clark was able to see the narrative function of the characters in the play as a whole. This was a luxury which, in their multiple roles and counter-pointed monologues, the actors themselves were denied.

CONCLUSION

It is evident from the actors' testimony that their involvement in the production's research phases, particularly their meetings with the individuals they later played, had a significant effect on their work. Although in all cases the meetings stimulated their creative processes, for some, problems arose in the disparity between the actors' relationship to their subject and the director's personal plans for their portrayals.

Firstly, it is worth noting that despite the actors' research, the working methods in *Talking to Terrorists* did not necessarily give the cast a higher status in the production as Stafford-Clark has claimed. The fact that Robin Soans met all but one of the subjects himself, and Stafford-Clark the great majority, meant that the actors did not have sole ownership of the material. Their input was controlled by Stafford-Clark, who did not always share the actors' preoccupations about their roles. Indeed, as we have seen in the case of Catherine Russell, the creative impulse which resulted from the actor-subject meetings could very easily be stifled by Stafford-Clark as a result of his own notion of theatrical viability. As has been evidenced by the comparison between Russell and Cullen, those involved in the research periods were not necessarily placed in a more advantageous position than those who conducted no research at all. In fact, given the power vested in the director, Russell was at a distinct disadvantage having conducted her own research. This is not to suggest, however, that the actors were passive in the work; far from it. The unusual working processes presented the actors with challenges which prompted them to develop innovative strategies in their preparation for the play.

We have found that these strategies tended to focus on the psychology of the individuals that the actors were tasked with portraying. This is not surprising given that the actors met their subjects, and thus were able to humanise the script they had been given. It was arguably this concern with psychology that led to their testimonies being infused with a Stanislavskian terminology. Stanislavski's teaching has provided a useful framework through which to analyse these actors' processes. We have repeatedly seen that the starting-point for the actors was very much along Stanislavskian lines. Examples have included the way in which Ryman used his observational skills to explore an individual's psychology; how Russell placed an emphasis on exploring the circumstances of their lives; the way in which Hutchinson worked to develop a theatrical truth in his portrayal of the ex-IRA member; and Hanson's experiments with self-analysis. These are examples of what has emerged as a common theme in this case-study: that actors find innovative ways to adapt recognised techniques when playing a real person. The way in which both Russell and Ryman, through their meetings, were able to develop these techniques beyond the framework which Stanislavski lays out suggests the impressive pragmatic capacity of the actors.

Through the actors' testimonies we can begin to identify specific ways in which, in the service of playing a real person, their processes developed beyond Stanislavski's teaching. The primary departure from a Stanislavskian rendering of character occurs on the question of the role of the actor's own emotion memory and experiential recall in character creation. All the actors here distanced their work from their own emotions and experiences, or what I have called the 'if … I'. In a documentary play such as *Talking to Terrorists*, which is based on complex notions of a privileged proximity to the words of a real person, it has become clear that the actors downplayed the use of their own personality in character creation. It is arguable that this was because they felt it would leave them open to accusations of being unfaithful to what they had observed. This is despite the fact that Stafford-Clark's working methods are centred on improvisation and memory rather than on recorded sources.

Where the actors found that their work started to depart from Stanislavski's teaching, the writings of particular post-Stanislavskian practitioners have proved helpful in illuminating the precise way in which they approached character-building. The applicability of these writings is no coincidence. Both Stella Adler and Michael Chekhov reformulated Stanislavski's teaching as a result of their experience of working with his techniques as actors. Crucially, their adaptation of his work focused on moving away from using the actor's own experiences as the root of summoning emotion on stage, and thus is more relevant here. Adler's emphasis on imagination rather than experience and Chekhov's identification of the 'higher I' provide useful frames for furthering our understanding of these actors' processes. However, though they may move the emphasis away from the actor's own experiences, they still place importance on imagination. This is a critical term which underpins all these writings; yet in the service of playing a real person in documentary theatre, and in these actors' experiences in particular, we find that this term is complicated.

What role does imagination play in the service of playing a real person whom the actor has met, and whose words become the text of the play? In this chapter we have seen that to negotiate this problem the actors developed alternative strategies to employing their imagination. For example, the exigencies of playing a real person using Stafford-Clark's particular working methods meant that Hanson's focus was not, as Chekhov would have it, on imagination, but rather on the creative manipulation and utilisation of what he had observed in his meeting with the Colonel. This creative manipulation, whilst acknowledging the artistic skills needed to construct a viable performance, places emphasis not on imagination, but on the actor's sense of serving the individual. It privileges observation and the actor's own creative dramaturgy. In short, it is based on the ways in which actors can harness and utilise their observational skills. We have seen that different strategies were employed to achieve this. Hutchinson's creation of a scenic truth was achieved by taking elements that he had observed, and adapting others for the stage. Similarly, the creative ways in which Ryman and Russell employed observation and establishing the given and found circumstances further distances their processes from relying on imagination. Ryman's empathetic reaction to the man's story, and Russell's discovery of facts outside the text of the play, enabled them to work on the psychological aspects without consciously moving beyond their observation of the individual. However, we must also sound a note of caution here. By downplaying the use of elements of character creation beyond what they observed, the actors were able to focus on how they served the individual they played. We must ask questions of this, and not confuse it with passivity. It is my contention that the actors' belief that they could emotionally remove themselves from their portrayals, and act as conduits for what they had witnessed rather than creatively adapting it, might be necessary when articulating processes within the ethical minefield of performing such sensitive material. I believe this is a critical factor in the lack of research into this field. By foregrounding the individual rather than their own processes, actors can easily obscure their own creativity. This case-study has explored the subtle ways in which the actors foregrounded the individual they played, whilst remaining active in their work. The detailed articulation of their processes strongly suggests that the prevailing narratives about actors' work voiced by non-actors need a more sceptical treatment.

My Name is Rachel Corrie. Megan Dodds (photo by Geraint Lewis)

2

My Name is Rachel Corrie

INTRODUCTION

My Name is Rachel Corrie, edited from the writings of the eponymous activist by actor Alan Rickman and the *Guardian* journalist Katharine Viner, was produced by the Royal Court Theatre in 2005. The production was directed by Alan Rickman with Tiffany Watt-Smith as associate director, and Elyse Dodgson acting as producer for the Royal Court. American actor Megan Dodds played Rachel Corrie in this one-woman play. Rachel Corrie was a young American woman who died in 2003 at the age of 23 protecting Palestinian homes from an Israeli bulldozer, 50 days after arriving in the city of Rafah to work with the International Solidarity Movement (ISM) on the Gaza strip. The play, after running successfully in London, hit the headlines on both sides of the Atlantic when the planned run at the New York Theatre Workshop was abruptly cancelled by the Workshop's artistic director, James Nicola, in what Alan Rickman called an act of 'censorship' (Borger 2006). This decision significantly raised the stakes of the play, elevating it into a politically contentious event, and protests, as we shall see, included demonstrations outside and inside the theatre.

Performing in such a controversial production resulted in a unique experience for Megan Dodds. This chapter features new interview material with Dodds, Rickman, Viner and Watt-Smith, but focuses particularly on Dodds' analysis of her experience of portraying Corrie. Unusually in documentary theatre, and unique in this book, the actor portrayed a real person who had died.[1] The emotional and performance challenges of this will be explored in detail. In addition, Dodds was performing in a one-woman show. Again, this separates the challenges of performance from the other experiences analysed here. This chapter will focus not only on Dodds' own acting processes, but also on the difficult context in which she had to perform, and the measures taken to protect her safety.

The genesis of *My Name is Rachel Corrie*

Rachel Corrie was killed on 16 March 2003. The story of her death made the front pages in Europe and America. For example, the day after Corrie's death, the *New York Times* led with an article entitled, 'Israeli Army Bulldozer Kills American Protesting in Gaza', by Greg Myre (2003). On the same day, in Britain the *Telegraph* ran an article reporting Corrie's death (Philips 2003). The story of the circumstances of her death was reinvented by both pro-Israeli and pro-Palestinian groups to suit their own particular agendas. For example, on a news website run by Arutz Sheva, the Israeli media network, Bruce Ticker wrote an Op-Ed article which began: 'Maybe, just maybe, Rachel Corrie knowingly aided and abetted cold-blooded murderers' (2004). After linking the International Solidarity Movement to the tunnels used to transport weapons, Ticker insisted that any 'reasonable person must conclude that the ISM members knew they were aiding and abetting terrorists' (2004). Others, however, called Corrie a saint and martyr. Arguing that the heavily armed and organised Israeli forces were attacking defenceless civilians, a news anchor on the All Voices website wrote that Corrie was a 'messenger of humanity', in a piece entitled 'Remembering Rachel Corrie – the martyr of peace in Gaza' (All Voices 2010). Christopher Wallenberg, writing in the *Boston Globe*, was correct when he observed: 'Corrie herself has been praised as a heroic martyr and denounced as a misguided, ill-informed naïf' (2008).

Mahmoud El Lozy has noted that 'It is highly unlikely that the Western consumer of corporate media would have ever heard of the Palestinian town of Rafah in Gaza had it not been for the life and death of Rachel Corrie' (2008: 102). El Lozy's comment provokes searching questions about the nature of Western press coverage of the Israel-Palestine conflict, in which the deaths of Palestinians go largely unreported, and it was not until an American citizen was killed that the city hit the headlines. Sandra Jordan, writing in the *Observer* a week after Corrie's death, echoes this sentiment:

> There are those who dismiss Western activists as just well-intentioned 'political tourists', naïve and ineffectual do-gooders. On the night of

Corrie's death, nine Palestinians were killed in the Gaza Strip, among them a four-year-old girl and a man aged 90. A total of 220 people have died in Rafah since the beginning of the intifada. Palestinians know the death of one American receives more attention than the killing of hundreds of Muslims. 'It is a fact', agrees Richard Purcell, who shared a messy, run-down flat with Rachel Corrie in Rafah. 'That's the way things are in this world. I wish it wasn't.' (2003)

Within days of the death of their daughter, Cindy and Craig Corrie publicly shared a series of Rachel's emails about her experiences in Gaza on the internet, sparking a heated online discussion, and catching print, television and radio press attention. The *Guardian* published many of these emails over two days on the 18 and 19 March 2003. Katharine Viner, then the features editor at the newspaper, remembered that:

> A couple of days after Rachel was killed, a different team from mine in the *Guardian* published some of her emails. One of the team had spotted them up on the internet and they were fantastic. Among them was the email that ends the play as well as many more.

Viner's comment that they were 'fantastic' relates to the quality of Corrie's writing, and her ability to capture both the atmosphere of Rafah and her own response to the work she was doing. Corrie's emails printed in the *Guardian* also caught the eye of Alan Rickman, who told me:

> There would have been no production, or notion of one, without my initial response to the emails published in the *Guardian* shortly after Rachel's death. These were words and images bursting off the page, wanting to be spoken.

It is clear that Rickman immediately saw the theatrical and political potency of these emails. He discussed the possibility of making a play from Corrie's words with Ian Rickson, the artistic director of the Royal Court. In the Autumn of 2003, Elyse Dodgson, the Royal Court Theatre's associate director and head of the International Department, contacted the Corries:

> We found out that the Corries were stopping off in England on the way back from the Middle East and I set up a meeting, but I couldn't be there. I asked Kath Viner to go because she'd been in Palestine with me. Nothing happened for a year. There was a lot of correspondence with the Corries but it was too painful for them. But a year later Sarah [Rachel's sister]

found everything that Rachel had written since she was ten and sent it in.
(Little and McLaughlin 2007: 426)

Thus, in November 2004, a year after the project had first been
mooted, Sarah Corrie sent the Royal Court Theatre a 184-page
document which included journals, diaries, emails and letters that
constituted Rachel's life-writing. As Megan Dodds remembered:
'There was such a huge amount of material...Pretty much everything she'd ever written. Craig and Cindy sent us so much material.' With this material available, the editing process could begin.
Corrie's family was in contact with the Royal Court throughout the
preparation of the production. This is important to note, as there
have been spurious arguments about the legitimacy of using the
words of Rachel Corrie to make a play. For example, El Lozy has
suggested that:

> One would assume that journals and diaries belong to a person's private
> realm. What is essentially a private text, or at least parts of it, has been
> thrust into the public realm. In its vulgar manifestations, an exercise of
> this kind provides the readers/spectator with the cheap thrill of the voyeur.
> (2008: 111)

Similarly, reviewing the premiere for *Time Out London*, Brian Logan
stated that 'There's a discomfort of eavesdropping on journals that
were never meant for public consumption' (2005). This can be seen
as part of the confusion surrounding the production. In 2008, Rachel
Corrie's family published *Let Me Stand Alone*, a collection of her
writings (which includes some of the writing that appears in the play).
In it, her family makes it absolutely clear that she was writing, at least
in part, for a public audience:

> This book is a milestone for Rachel and our family. It started, in a sense,
> with Rachel's email correspondence from Rafah to her mother. She hoped
> her writing from there would be published, at least in her local newspaper,
> may be as a human interest story. (Corrie 2008: xviii)

El Lozy's and Logan's points, in this light, are without foundation. In
addition, it was Rachel's parents who decided to publish the emails,
and it was their decision whether or not to allow the Royal Court to
make a play from Rachel's writings. However, El Lozy's statement is
useful as it demonstrates the naïve and unfounded questions of legitimacy which have plagued the play.

Working under the auspices of the International Department at the
Royal Court, Katharine Viner co-edited the play with Alan Rickman.

Viner was aware that her experiences as a journalist brought a particular set of skills to the project:

> I got involved because I'm on the board of the Royal Court and I've been on lots of trips with Elyse Dodgson to the Middle East – the Middle East is quite an interest of mine. They were looking for someone with an interest in both the Middle East and theatre. Elyse felt, I think, that Alan had had this great idea and had a great knowledge of the theatrical side of things and how it would work on stage, but they wanted someone who understood the region and the context. Also, from my journalistic background, I understood narrative and story... It was a difficult process; we were coming from such different places, with different traditions. However, at the end we both felt that the balance of me fighting for the story and Alan for the theatrical was what it needed.

It is important to note that whilst Viner may have known the region, this was still from a British perspective. It is evident that there were tensions between the editors, which, as Viner suggests, was to be expected from two individuals coming from such different traditions. This issue was noted by Tiffany Watt-Smith who was appointed associate director before the workshop period:

> Kath was brought on board as a co-writer which perhaps was a rather complicated situation and I don't think one that Alan was anticipating. There were frictions – of course Kath is not a playwright either, so it was a slightly awkward situation. She has, however, a lot of political knowledge about the area.

Soon after they began work on the project, the story broke that Rickman and the Royal Court were involved in a play based on Corrie's writings. The press immediately identified this as a politically controversial endeavour. The first mention of the play in print was in December 2004 when Guy Adams, writing in the *Independent*, announced that 'Alan Rickman is about to become the latest Hollywood star to light the blue touchpaper on the powderkeg that is Arab-Israeli politics' (2004). As a journalistic prediction goes, Adams' statement proved to be disconcertingly accurate.

Viner and Rickman edited Corrie's writings into a 90-minute monologue which follows several years of Corrie's life. Corrie was the white, middle-class daughter of Craig and Cindy Corrie. Her father, an insurance executive, described his family as 'average Americans – politically liberal, economically conservative, middle class' (Banks 2005). The play opens with her early writing, aged 11, in which she describes her childhood in the leafy suburbs of Olympia, Washington.

The play quickly (within the first five minutes in performance) skips on several years and focuses on her developing political awareness of and engagement with the Israel-Palestine conflict, and her desire to move to the Gaza Strip to assist the Palestinian cause. For example, leaving an answer-phone message for her mother, she warns her about her choice of words when talking to the local press:

> If you talk about the cycle of violence, or 'an eye for an eye', you could be perpetuating the idea that the Israeli-Palestinian conflict is a balanced conflict, instead of a largely unarmed people against the fourth most powerful military in the world. (Rickman and Viner 2005: 12)

The vast percentage of stage time focuses on Corrie's first-hand experience of the Israeli-Palestinian conflict in Rafah. The later emails to her parents and her own journal entries paint an increasingly dangerous picture of her life in the city. For example, on 7 February 2003, she notes that 'Today, as I walked on top of the rubble, Egyptian soldiers called to me from the other side of the border: "Go! Go!" because a tank was coming' (Rickman and Viner 2005: 29). Corrie's last email was dated 9 March 2003, only a week before she was killed. With the exception of a short voice-over report of her death by her friend Tom Dale, this journey is told exclusively through Corrie's written testimony.

The actor in the workshop period

Rather like the involvement of some of the actors in *Talking to Terrorists*, Megan Dodds was cast as Rachel Corrie very early on in the process, and so was involved in the production from the early workshops. Dodds is an American actor who trained at the Julliard School in New York. Early in her career, she moved to London, and worked in the West End and on British television. At the time of being cast as Rachel Corrie, she was most associated for British audiences with her television role in *Spooks* (BBC, 2002–4). She was 35 when she played the 23-year-old Rachel Corrie. With regard to her casting, she had worked with Alan Rickman at the Royal Court on a workshop for Terry Johnson's play *Hitchcock Blonde*, and as she recalls:

> It was during this time [March 2003] that the *Guardian* started publishing the letters of Rachel Corrie. Alan immediately wanted to do something with these letters. At this point he wasn't sure what it was, but Ian Rickson was also passionate about the idea of creating something from them and so we had a workshop at the Royal Court.

Rickman has noted that he offered the part to Dodds without an audition, such was his confidence that she was right for the role (see Little and McLaughlin 2007: 427).

The workshop sessions were held sporadically over the course of several months as Rickman and Viner edited the script. As Dodds was engaged on other projects, these were organised around her work, and since she was not contracted at this stage, she was paid a session fee. Rickman was also involved in several film projects, which meant that he missed some of the workshops and rehearsals. Thus, Tiffany Watt-Smith was appointed associate director to be a continuous directorial presence throughout the project. The sessions, which took place in the meeting room at the Royal Court Theatre, comprised meetings between Viner and Rickman to edit the material, and workshops to share their edits with Dodds and Watt-Smith in which Dodds read the material aloud. During this period, all members of the team were involved in the discussions, and as Megan Dodds recalled, 'We all fought our own battles over what material could be included.' Similarly, Watt-Smith remembers:

> That process was pretty collaborative. We all had an input and discussed certain bits. We went through this process until we had whittled it down to a workable shape. I remember there were certain bits that Megan particularly loved – such as the lists and the opening in the bed. There were certain bits that as an actor she connected to, that she felt were a real insight into that woman's life.

This was a critical period, which included decisions about the structure of the piece and allowed Dodds to begin to become familiar with the material and identify the challenges of staging the testimony. She remembered that 'We sat round and read out the letters. At this point we were trying to find a shape for the piece ... This was still before we had decided what sort of work it would be.' As Dodds notes, the form of the piece did not take shape for some time. Viner also recalls that at the beginning of the workshop the plan had been to supplement Corrie's own writing with interview material from other people:

> At the beginning, I did lots of work researching what it is like to be an Israeli soldier in Gaza, what it is like to drive a bulldozer, what it is like to be a citizen in Gaza. We built up quite a big and complicated picture, and we didn't really know where it was going, which is really interesting for me coming from a journalistic background. But we kept on sifting the material and what kept rising to the top were Rachel's words ... this voice, striving for truth and goodness all the way through, and it became clear that all the contextual stuff, interesting though it was, was not needed.

The gradual realisation that this was a solo-performance unsurprisingly came as something of a shock to Dodds, who recalled that

> At no point did Alan ever say this is a one-woman show. If he had, I would have moved quickly in the opposite direction! But because of the long process of editing, by the time we realised that was what it was, it was too late to back out.

Evidently Dodds was deeply concerned by the notion of giving a solo-performance in this play. This element of her performance experience and preparation will be addressed in detail in the Acting Processes section.

The performance history

After four weeks of rehearsals, which due to the detailed work with only one actor often lasted only four or five hours each day, the play opened on 7 April 2005 on the smaller stage at the Royal Court, the 80-seater Theatre Upstairs. After playing to sell-out audiences over its three-week run (until 30 April), the play later transferred for three weeks (11–29 Oct 2005) to the Royal Court's larger theatre, the Theatre Downstairs (seating 395). Though tensions ran high and, as we shall see, there were demonstrations by pro-Israeli campaigners, Guy Adams' prediction that Rickman was lighting the 'blue touchpaper' by staging the play was not fully realised in the London run. However, it certainly was borne out by the series of events that took place when the play was prepared for its American transfer.

The success the production enjoyed in London was eclipsed by the events surrounding the proposed New York transfer. James Nicola, the artistic director of New York Theatre Workshop (NYTW), planned to bring the play to New York. The NYTW is an off-Broadway theatre with a remit to

> Include international artists – including playwrights, directors and designers – and to focus upon issues of non-traditional casting and the inclusion of diverse voices, representing all of the constituencies in NYTW's theatrical community. (New York Theatre Workshop website)

The NYTW is a nonprofit theatre, which means that it relies heavily on funding from benefactors. Shawn-Marie Garrett, who in April 2006 chaired a high-profile panel discussion on the play in New York entitled 'Who's Afraid of Rachel Corrie?', reported that 'Nicola told the Royal Court he was interested in producing the play, and on

January 19 [2006], the Workshop's board of trustees unanimously supported Nicola and the staff's decision' (Carlson et al. 2007: 56).

My Name is Rachel Corrie was scheduled to open on 22 March 2006, and to run until 14 May. In London, flights had been booked, set loaded into containers and the production prepared for the transfer. However, on 17 February, Nicola decided to postpone the play indefinitely. Less than a fortnight later, the story broke on both sides of the Atlantic and journalist Julian Borger, writing in the *Guardian*, quoted Nicola's explanation of his decision:

> In our pre-production planning and our talking around and listening in our communities in New York, what we heard was that after Ariel Sharon's illness and the election of Hamas, we had a very edgy situation ... We found that our plan to present a work of art would be seen as us taking a stand in a political conflict, that we didn't want to take. (Borger 2006)

On the same day, an article by Jesse McKinley appeared in the *New York Times*, which included more detailed information about Nicola's decision:

> James C. Nicola ... said he had decided to postpone the show after polling local Jewish religious and community leaders as to their feelings about the work. 'The uniform answer we got was that the fantasy that we could present the work of this writer simply as a work of art without appearing to take a position was just that, a fantasy,' he said. In particular, the recent electoral upset by Hamas, the militant Palestinian group, and the sickness of Ariel Sharon, the Israeli prime minister, had made 'this community very defensive and very edgy,' Mr. Nicola said, 'and that seemed reasonable to me.' ... But Mr. Nicola said he was less worried about those who saw the show than those who simply heard about it. 'I don't think we were worried about the audience,' he said. 'I think we were more worried that those who had never encountered her writing, never encountered the piece, would be using this as an opportunity to position their arguments.' (2006)

Nicola's decision appears to have been a direct response to pressure from the funders of the theatre to stop the play from being performed at the venue. His reticence over 'taking a stand' or 'position' is an oddly spurious argument for an artistic director of a theatre committed to 'representing all of the constituencies in NYTW's theatrical community'. As part of the 'Who's Afraid of Rachel Corrie?' panel discussion on the play, American academic Marvin Carlson echoed this point:

> the decision to pull back from the sort of play that defined its enterprise created a significant sense of betrayal. This betrayal was felt all the more

keenly because the NYTW was one of the very few prominent theatres in New York where audiences expected to find drama with serious political and social concerns. (Carlson et al. 2007: 59)

Despite being presented as a postponement, the decision was a cancellation in all but name, as *My Name is Rachel Corrie* was never performed at the New York Theatre Workshop. Soon after the decision was made public, Rickman was interviewed in the *Guardian* and stated that Nicola's decision was an act of 'censorship' (Borger 2006), while Dodds commented that 'I feel a little bit ashamed in a way that happened. It's your country, you know, and that kind of thing can happen. But it also gives fuel to the fire, it makes sense of why this play should get made' (2006a).

In an effort to regain trust and respect, the NYTW ran a series of discussions on the topic of censorship. This was received cynically by commentators. Janelle Reinelt, for example, noted that:

> The theatre tried to recover some of its prior stature by holding a series of forums on artistic representation, including one on censorship issues, and invited a highly respected group of artists and activists to speak on those questions (including Anna Deavere Smith, Emily Mann and Jessica Blank). Was this a genuine effort to repair its relationship with the theatre community and to compensate for the original decision, or was it just an effort to exert damage control through a gesture rather than a substantive engagement which could heal the situation? Informal discussions with people who were there indicated that views ran in both directions. (2007: 12)

More damning was playwright Christopher Shinn, who, writing in the *Index on Censorship*, recalled that

> many weeks after the cancellation, in an overt effort at damage control, the theatre ran a series of panel discussions about political art and censorship to which the community was invited. Unfortunately, these discussions were organised by a PR firm, did not include voices that have been highly critical of the Workshop's decision to cancel the play, and limited audience involvement by making all audience members write questions and comments on note cards that were collected and given to moderators, allowing them to filter the responses before presenting them to the panel and public. No open debate or spontaneous questioning was allowed. (2008: 89)

Shinn concluded that 'A politically progressive East Village off-Broadway theatre was behaving like a huge corporation', engaging in exactly the kind of practices which a politically engaged theatre company spends its time attacking.

Nicola's action, and Rickman's branding of it as censorship, provoked debate in the British and American theatre industries, press
and academia about the freedom of speech on the stage. As Houchin
noted, 'It was at this point that polemics, accusations, and outrage
exploded with a force rarely seen in New York theatre' (2008: 17).
In an open letter to the *New York Times*, high-profile British writers
including Stephen Fry, Harold Pinter and Gillian Slovo wrote:

> We are Jewish writers who supported the Royal Court production of *My
> Name Is Rachel Corrie*. We are dismayed by the decision of the New York
> Theatre Workshop to cancel or postpone the play's production ... In London
> it played to sell-out houses. Critics praised it. Audiences found it intensely
> moving. So what is it about Rachel Corrie's writings, her thoughts, her
> feelings, her confusions, her idealism, her courage, her search for mean-
> ing in life – what is it that New York audiences must be protected from?
> (Fry et al. 2006)

The letter goes on to state that 'The various reasons given by the workshop ... make no sense in the context of this play and the crucial issues
it raises about Israeli military activity in the occupied territories' (Fry
et al. 2006). British actor Vanessa Redgrave went even further, calling the cancellation 'The Second Death of Rachel Corrie' in her open
letter to James Nicola (2006).

As a result of the storm around the cancellation, in scholarly
work on the play and in critical responses to post-cancellation performances, the focus shifted away from the death of Rachel Corrie.
Rather, the event of the production – its actual appearance in a theatre, as opposed to its content – became the political signifier. At the
aforementioned panel discussion on the play, Shawn-Marie Garrett
commented that *My Name is Rachel Corrie* has

> introduced theatre people in New York and London to Rachel Corrie in
> the forms of, first, Rachel Corrie the Docudrama, the Royal Court Event,
> the Award-Winning Performance, the West End Transfer. They were fol-
> lowed in the United States by Rachel Corrie the Scandal, the Censored,
> the Cause Célèbre, the Voice That Must Be Heard. (Carlson et al. 2007:
> 55–6)

This list provokes several questions about attitudes towards the death
of Corrie and further demonstrates that the controversy moved the
focus away from the actual content of the play. This central issue is evident in Christopher Shinn's assertion that '*My Name is Rachel Corrie*
is not a formally radical play. Rachel Corrie herself was radical. It's an

effective play and it should be done, but to hold it forth as the epitome of radical, political drama is a mistake' (Carlson et al. 2007: 64). Shinn here seems to be reacting (and contributing) to the hype surrounding the production, rather than the production itself. None of the people involved with *My Name is Rachel Corrie* asserted that it was a radical play; indeed, as we shall see, they have argued the opposite. It is clear that through the hype surrounding the cancellation, both the act of staging the play and the death of Rachel Corrie were adapted and given new significance and meaning. Just as James Nicola was concerned not about offending his audience members, but rather 'those who had never encountered her writing, never encountered the piece', we can see that the controversy moved the focus away from the actual story of Rachel Corrie and rather became a vehicle for strong and hysterical views. El Lozy notes that

> It is not the play itself as a final product, as much as the road that has been travelled towards its coming into existence, that is the source of much of the angry responses that have been expressed. The history of the play's text transcends the text itself. (2008: 110)

Megan Dodds certainly experienced this. These views had a direct effect on her, and made her performance an even more challenging experience. As a result of the inflammatory rhetoric which surrounded the controversy, Dodds experienced a profound loss of status as an actor:

> The artistry was lost in the controversy. For example, when the reviewers came, they came to write about whether it should be put on, and its politics. They reviewed it as politics, not as a theatrical production, as a one-woman show. So in fact, my role as an actor was lost as they seemed less interested in the acting than the political controversy of the event.

One of the central questions for this chapter is how the actor coped when her work was so overlooked, and when much of the debate surrounding the controversy was voiced by people who had not seen the play.

The centre of the storm: the challenge for Megan Dodds

The production, denied its staging in New York, opened in London's West End. It ran from 28 March–21 May 2006 at the Playhouse Theatre (800 seats), before short runs at the Galway Festival Theatre and the Edinburgh Festival. The play eventually received its American transfer in late 2006. The Minetta Lane Theatre in New York, a 406 seat off-Broadway theatre, gave the play its American premiere on 15 October. The theatre is a receiving house, meaning that it has no resident company and does not produce its own work, nor does it have an artistic director or board. Rather, it is a commercial theatre, and the transfer was produced by Dena Hammerstein and Pam Pariseau for James Hammerstein Productions. After extending due to popular demand, the play closed on 17 December, after 80 performances.

The reaction to the cancellation and furore around the transfer of the play differs between those commenting on it, and those artistically involved in it. In terms of the status and profile of the production, the cancellation and hype outlined above certainly made *My Name is Rachel Corrie* a politically contentious work. However, we can acknowledge that much of the political significance came about though the storm over its initial censorship, not through what actually happened on stage.

How, then, do we expect the actor to respond to such a problem? Megan Dodds went into the production with her own political agenda. She stated that: 'there has never been a time where Americans have needed more to hear stories about people going out into the world and finding out the impact of their own foreign policy on other parts of the world' (2006b). Though she did not go into detail, it is evident that Dodds viewed the play as a form of protest against the United States' foreign policy of financially supporting Israel, and the impact of this policy on the Palestinians. But she was also aware that the play consisted of the words of a real woman:

> The play is a beautiful insight into the view of the world through the eyes of a young woman. But people came and saw it and either couldn't work out what the fuss was about and felt it should have gone further, so neither response were what you want as an actor.

Dodds' responses are symptomatic of working on a political piece of theatre. The production, as Dodds herself clearly understood, would divide opinion, and the voices for and against it were likely to be loud. However, it is evident from her comments that she did not expect the level of reaction the play received, and that the cancellation significantly upped the stakes in expectations about the production.

To illustrate Dodds' point, it is informative to consider the differences between the play's reception before the cancellation, and the reviews following it. When the play opened at the Royal Court, the reviews were almost unanimously (if not unreservedly) positive.

Brian Logan called the play 'desperately poignant' (2005), whilst
Michael Billington stated that 'Theatre can't change the world, but
what it can do, when it is as good as this, is to send us out enriched by
other people's passionate concern' (2005). Charles Spencer called it a
'thought-provoking and deeply moving piece of theatre' and praised
Dodds' performance in particular, commenting that

> Alan Rickman and Katharine Viner, who have edited Corrie's writings,
> offer a fully rounded picture of this passionate, idealistic and at times
> infuriating young woman, vividly brought to life by an astonishing solo
> performance by Megan Dodds. (2005)

However, the reception in America following the controversy was
rather different. A case in point was the review of the run at the
Minetta Lane Theatre that appeared in the *New York Times*, and
which Megan Dodds referenced during my interview. The start of the
review reads:

> Few plays have travelled to New York with as much excess baggage as
> *My Name Is Rachel Corrie* which opened last night at the Minetta Lane
> Theatre. This small, intense one-woman drama, first staged last year at
> the Royal Court Theatre in London, makes its delayed American debut
> freighted with months of angry public argument, condemnation, celebra-
> tion and prejudgment: all the heavy threads that make up the mantle of a
> cause célèbre. So how does it stand on its own, this quiet, 90-minute work
> that has been preceded by so much noise? Towards the end of the perform-
> ance I attended, I heard one man choking back sobs and another snoring.
> I could sympathize with both responses. (Brantley 2006)

Of this review, Dodds stated

> Some people found it boring. One of the *NYT* reviewers said that he didn't
> know whether to cry or fall asleep. I mean thanks!... We were so happy
> that it was being performed, but I think it didn't have the power it did in
> London, it felt a bit of a let-down. No one seemed to take it on face-value –
> as a show about Rachel.

Although she notes that this increased the profile of the production, Katharine Viner also identifies that the controversy was to the
detriment of the play:

> I think it was bad for the play, as it made it a kind of cause célèbre, so
> people didn't look at it as a play... They took it as a political, controver-
> sial event, not a 90-minute monologue about a girl's experience that was
> true. It couldn't arrive and be itself... It meant that people came with
> preconceptions.

This, as we shall explore, put Dodds in a very complicated position, and gave rise to particular concerns and preoccupations in her process.

ACTING PROCESSES

Although the absence of focus on the actor in documentary theatre has become clear, the lack of attention on Dodds' performance of Rachel Corrie is particularly pronounced. Yet at the centre of this controversial play was an actor, speaking the written words of a young woman, alone on stage for 90 minutes. A crucial element of Dodds' experience and an important factor in her working conditions was the steps taken by the Royal Court to protect her from protests against the play. Exploring how the theatre sought to mitigate the risk to the actor alone on stage further moves her experiences away from anything else we will find in this study, and demonstrates how unusual and challenging the work of the actor can be in politically sensitive documentary projects.

Protecting the actor

From the outset of the project, the creative team behind the play clearly understood that the performance would leave Megan Dodds exposed on the stage. We have seen in the previous case-study that the actors in *Talking to Terrorists* found the performance of the play immensely challenging. As Catherine Russell stated 'I've been working since I was 21, and that was without doubt the most scared I have ever been on stage.' However, the nerves that Russell felt were entirely attributable to her portrayal. As I have suggested, the working processes in *Talking to Terrorists* were uniquely challenging and prompted an innovative pragmatism in the actors' processes. It is important, though, to acknowledge that the stress the actors felt was limited to their craft; particularly to the unusual scrutiny with which their performances were viewed. By contrast, Dodds' involvement exposed her not just in artistic terms, but also personally, to threat of interruption and protest from the audience.

When the production opened at the Royal Court, peaceful protests took place outside the theatre. The focus of these protests was on the Israeli deaths suffered in the Israel-Palestine conflict, which the campaigners argued were not represented in the play. Protesters handed the audience leaflets which read:

> Rachel Corrie should be alive today. So should Rachel Ben Adu, Rachel Thaler, Rachel Levy, Rachel Levi... Rachel's death was accidental and

tragic. It occurred as a counter-terrorism bulldozer was uncovering one of 90 underground tunnels that terrorists were using to smuggle weapons into Gaza... One Rachel dies by accident. Many Rachels were killed by suicide bombers. Each of these deaths is tragic. (Stand With Us 2003)

The leaflet further demonstrates the ways in which the facts around Corrie's death have been a subject of heated debate and disagreement. The protesters' facts are unproven – there is no evidence to support their contention that the bulldozer was uncovering terrorist tunnels. Katharine Viner remembered that before one of the early performances, she spoke to the protesters with Craig Corrie:

> We had some people protesting outside and I went to talk to them and so did Craig Corrie. He was brilliant. An Israeli group did a demonstration 'What about all the other Rachels?' Obviously being a common Jewish name, lots of people called Rachel have died in intifada and conflict, and they made a leaflet which asked about the other Rachels. And Craig went out there and said that it was absolutely terrible that these young women are dying – he told them that 'I've lost a daughter and I don't want any other father to go through what I have.'

However, critically for Dodds and the production team, these protests also extended into the theatre itself. One experience in particular has clearly stayed with Dodds:

> I was repeatedly heckled in one of the West End performances. There was a woman sitting a couple of rows back who kept shouting out throughout the performance. Things like 'What about the Israeli children?' That made me terrified. There were lots of people protesting outside the theatre against the play, and goodness knows who might have bought a ticket. I was aware of it throughout the performance, but I couldn't quite make out who it was without stopping. But you see these things were why I did it. I was clear how important it was for these words to be heard.

The level of anger in the audience, and the potential threat to Dodds on stage, were not side-issues, but actually formed part of her preparation for the role. Dodds told me that 'I rehearsed a line that I would say if I had to stop, but I never had to use it thankfully.' Katharine Viner spoke about this decision in more detail. She said:

> We were concerned about protests, and we had a series of contingency plans for what to do if someone started protesting during the play. Someone did protest, but Megan just carried on... You see we needed this because she was exposed. No one else could come on... She had to deal with it herself. The plan was to say to the audience 'I'm going to stop speaking now because of this woman, and I will come back on when she has been removed.'

Having to invent a line to stop the play quickly and allow the actor to get off stage safely is not a situation the other plays discussed here ever had to address. It is clear that Dodds' experiences position this work even further from what we might expect of an actor's performance. What was particularly pronounced in my interviews with both Dodds and Viner was the matter-of-fact way in which they talked about the decision to prepare this exit line. It appeared to be a completely normal and logical part of the rehearsal process. However, if we take a step back, we can appreciate that this is a shockingly unusual performance necessity. No other production in this book was so contentious that the actors felt personally threatened, and none came close to initiating this kind of intense emotional response from the audience. The threat to Dodds was exacerbated by the fact that she was alone on stage, without scene breaks or blackouts to structure the piece and allow her respite or, indeed, a convenient moment at which to exit.

As Viner suggests, the rehearsal of an exit line was only one of several systems that the Royal Court Theatre put in place to protect the actor. Tiffany Watt-Smith outlined the different procedures. As is the norm, in the performance itself, it was the responsibility of the stage-manager, Charlotte Padgham, to ensure the actor's safety. Due to the controversial nature of *My Name is Rachel Corrie*, Padgham had a slightly different brief, as Watt-Smith explains:

> One of the things we agreed on was that if there was a protest from the auditorium that Megan was not aware of, the stage-manager would walk on stage and walk her off – although there were no actual interruptions, the process was rehearsed.

These measures also extended to the booking process for the show, as Watt-Smith explained:

> Among the various strategies implemented to protect Megan and the show from protestors was a box office policy of not accepting block bookings. There was a fear that a protest group might decide to buy out the whole stalls for example, and then not show up, or conversely, show up and interrupt the performance.

The theatre also took steps to ensure Dodds' safety after the performance:

> Elyse discussed with the front of house management about making it safe, and although we didn't in the end, we discussed having additional security on the doors. We had a range of support mechanisms in place.

We wouldn't let her walk to her car from the stage door. She got cabs so that no one would follow her car. It sounds over-blown, but these were genuine concerns.

Summing up the rationale behind the need to protect Dodds, Watt-Smith explained that:

It was discussed from the beginning. The idea was that if we could be very clear and explicit about it, it would put Megan's mind at rest, as she could be assured that people were looking out for her safety. This is the critical thing – she would be the person who would be targeted rather than Alan or me or Elyse. She was the face in the newspapers and in the reviews. She was very vulnerable.

To this end, a member of the creative team would be present at every performance. The norm in most professional productions is that once the play has opened, though the director will often attend performances intermittently throughout the run and give notes, the actors and backstage team take ownership of the show. However, in *My Name is Rachel Corrie*, it was critical that Dodds did not become isolated by the run of performances. As Watt-Smith states: 'No one wanted Megan to feel "left with it" as it were, particularly because the material was so upsetting.'

A particularly unsavoury and threatening aspect of the hype surrounding the production was extreme posts on websites focusing on Dodds herself. Watt-Smith recalls that:

Alan told her not to read the hype around the play...It was not about her. For example, Vanessa Redgrave's letter was more about Vanessa Redgrave than what Megan was doing. It was not for her to worry about. The main thing we told her was not to Google herself. That was Alan's prime advice. There was one evening when she did and she came in the next morning ashen-faced and devastated. There were a lot of extreme views on websites.

The production team thus built a support structure around Dodds that ensured she did not feel isolated by the experience. This was based on a combination of emotional support as well as the implementation of procedures to safeguard her. We have seen that it included almost every area of the institution, from the backstage team, to the box office and the front of house staff. It is clear that this was an atypical working environment, and one which unsurprisingly led to particular changes in her working methods.

'Just inside someone's head': Dodds' departure from intentions and objectives

Given the unusual material with which she was working, and the level of concern for her own safety, it was no surprise that at the beginning of my interview, Dodds noted that 'I don't think that I have ever worked in this way. It really is not the same.' This, in light of what we now know, is something of an understatement.

Dodds has identified particular ways in which the challenge of playing Corrie prompted her to move away from what she describes as her 'usual' approach to a role:

> It was very different approaching playing Rachel...Usually when I am approaching a character, I break that character down to its intentions and objectives and what that character's function is in order to serve the play. I build the character from what it needs to do. But in this case, when all the writing was Rachel's own, the process of excavating personality or character was completely different. (2005)

Dodds' articulation of the centrality of 'intentions and objectives' in her usual approach to character-building demonstrates a strong Stanislavskian influence. This is unsurprising given her training at the prestigious Julliard School in New York, which provides actors with a rich array of techniques, including Stanislavski's approaches to script analysis. We must thus ask what it was about *My Name is Rachel Corrie* which necessitated the move away from her customary approach. Why was she unable to break the play down into intentions and objectives in the way she would normally do with an invented part?

Stanislavski saw objectives (usefully retranslated into the more user-friendly term 'Tasks' in Jean Benedetti's recent re-translation of Stanislavski's work) as the creative heart of an actor's performance. He explains that:

> Life, people, circumstance and we ourselves endlessly set up a whole series of obstacles one after the other and we fight our way through them, as through bushes. Each of these obstacles creates a Task and the action to overcome it...Learn not to play the result onstage but to fulfil the Task genuinely, productively, and aptly through action all the time you are performing. You must love the Tasks you have, find dynamic actions for them. (2008a: 143–4)

According to Stanislavski, these tasks 'must invariably be defined by a verb...Say to yourself: "I want to do..."' (2008a: 148–9). However, the particular use of testimony in *My Name is Rachel Corrie* denied

Dodds the crucial ingredients needed to employ this, her usual approach to script analysis. To refer to Dodds' comments above, she was also unable to 'build the character from what it needs to do', because there is a fundamental stillness to the writing. This highlights a crucial factor. Uniquely among the plays in this study, *My Name is Rachel Corrie* is based on written, rather than spoken, evidence. Unlike the texts with which Stanislavski was working, Corrie's writings were never designed to be spoken. We can thus ask what constitutes an active task or objective when the script is taken from reflective writings and reportage in a diary, journal and emails. It is evident that Dodds found that the differences in the type of script on which she was working necessitated an adaptation of her usual techniques.

We must note, however, that Dodds' rejection of intentions and objectives does not suggest a lack of interest in internal processes, but rather the dismissal of a particular mode of script analysis. It was obvious in my interview that Dodds was keenly interested in working on the psychological determinants underpinning Corrie's words. Dodds stated that she 'tried to work out her thought process – the logic of what she was saying and how she was thinking'. This strategic departure from intentions and objectives can be understood as one manifestation of a move away from an 'active' or 'future-focused' rendering of the character. By this I mean replacing the questions that Stanislavski suggests are central to establishing objectives or tasks – such as 'what does she want to do?' or 'what does she want to achieve?' – with more circumspect questions such as 'why does she feel this?' or 'why did she write that?' Dodds states that:

> The last scene translated really well as it was very theatrical. The first half of the play was much more of a challenge. You are just inside someone's head. So as an actor you need to give it something else. You have to figure it out – what is she trying to say? What are you demonstrating? It was working out which bit of her we are hearing. All the scenes are different facets of her humanity. It is about her values and her beliefs. That was the most difficult.

Dodds' identification that she was 'just inside someone's head' neatly captures the specific challenge of this testimony. However, although the piece was inherently still, because the play is a 90-minute engagement with one individual, it does allow the audience (and thus the actor) to see different sides to Corrie's personality. These differences were critical to Dodds, and through these she was able to begin to find a shape to the piece. Sarah Hemming's review suggests that Dodds was successful in her aim of capturing these different aspects. In the *Financial Times*, Hemming wrote that Dodds portrayed Corrie as 'compassionate, funny and wise, but also naive, bombastic and even infuriating' (2006). To return to Dodds' identification of her usual process of using objectives to shape a performance, we can identify that in her analysis of 'working out which bit of her we are hearing', Dodds was able to start to develop the Stanislavskian technique of finding different units, or 'bits' within the piece. These bits, according to Stanislavski, help the actor to navigate her way through the play. He writes:

> Bits…that are laid out during the length of the play, serve us as a fairway which shows us the right course to follow, and leads us through the dangerous shoals, reefs and complex threads of the play, where we easily get lost. (2008a: 141)

Even in a play such as *My Name is Rachel Corrie*, which does not immediately lend itself to clearly defined 'bits', Dodds was able to identify these by the different elements of Corrie's personality she was portraying. She noted that this process stemmed from the early workshop period with Viner and Rickman: 'It was very difficult to find a shape for the play, as there is very little action, but rather we tried to create a linear narrative shape. So we would have different piles according to the sort of tone that Rachel was using.' With regard to developing her work on these bits, and establishing the different elements of her personality, Dodds had the added resource of the 184-page document the theatre received from the Corries: 'I was in a very privileged position in that I could read much more widely about Rachel than was included in the play, and that really was incredibly helpful.' This document functioned in a similar way to the interviews that Catherine Russell conducted in *Talking to Terrorists*. It helped Dodds probe more deeply into Corrie's writings that formed part of the play, and assisted her understanding about the background to these beliefs.

Emotion in *My Name is Rachel Corrie*: audience and actor's circumstances

Ironically, given the reaction of the critics and the furore which surrounded the play in America, Dodds' performance has a lightness of touch and humour. The emotional aspects of Corrie that she identified were, emphatically, not what might have been expected from the storm the play generated. Rachel Corrie did not know her fate in

Rafah, and Dodds portrayed her as a young woman with an energy
and verve for a cause that inspired and motivated her. As Watt-Smith
states: 'Megan found a lot of humour in it. Alan was also very keen
that she did not play the tragedy from the beginning, and so quite a lot
of rehearsal was finding the fun and the lightness in what she wrote.'
Dodds was keenly aware that some of Corrie's enthusiasm could be
viewed cynically by the audience, and that it was important that she
did not judge Corrie through her portrayal:

> I was very aware that she's a 23-year-old girl saying that she is going to save
> the world, and that everyone might be rolling their eyes. I felt it was critic-
> ally important that I did not judge her. Not to look back and acknowledge
> the naivety of her words through my performance.

Of course 'not judging' a character is a rather abstract notion. However,
Dodds was able to identify tangible ways in which she approached this
issue, one of which involved focusing on Corrie's point of view:

> There was a lot of work on her point of view – on how she felt about differ-
> ent situations. This is where the documents her sister sent were so useful.
> Normally you don't have the luxury of finding out a character's feelings in
> such detail.

Avoiding judging the character was also a central concern of
Watt-Smith in her work with Rickman and Dodds in rehearsal,
and the associate director provided details as to how the directors
approached this area:

> We wanted her to avoid standing outside the character and commenting
> on it; she had to be within it...that was the challenge of working with
> this particular material. We wanted to avoid her putting it in quotation
> marks and illustrating it, we didn't want her to demonstrate it. She had
> to trust that the words are interesting enough. As it was not written for
> performance, there was the worry that it needed dramatising, and that
> some of it, alongside the interesting sections, might be rather banal. So
> she might lose her nerve and want to demonstrate it, which is the usual
> actor's response.

Here we have a dual concern from the associate director – both an
emphasis on inhabitation and also on avoiding over-dramatising the
individual. These two areas were also guiding principles for Dodds.
She stated that:

> This piece is a tribute to Rachel as much as anything, and needs to stay
> completely truthful to the real person. You can't impose any ideas about

what would make her more attractive or dramatically interesting. You just have to tell the truth. (2005)

Dodds' concern with understanding the background to Corrie's comments, and how she felt about certain aspects of her time in Rafah, were ways in which she could begin to psychologically inhabit the role.

In the previous chapter we heard that Max Stafford-Clark would 'always go for theatricality'; by contrast, Alan Rickman was keenly aware of the need to avoid over-dramatising and letting Dodds' performance become too big, as Dodds explained:

> Alan could be very hard on me. He would notice if I was becoming lazy or the section was becoming too general. He would be very careful to avoid me being 'showy'. He hit that on the head straight away. That was one of his key words. I couldn't allow it to become 'showy'.

One of Dodds' discoveries, which she used to avoid being 'showy' or 'dramatising' and 'demonstrating', was the realisation that 'the audience would feel emotional, but I didn't need to emote to make this happen. They would view it very powerfully.' This is an important distinction for the actor. Dodds has clearly made the key identification that, in this play, the audience's emotional response stems from their knowledge that Rachel died. Thus, the audience's awareness of the circumstances, rather than the actor's conscious foreshadowing of the tragedy, gave the play its power. Here, unlike the other plays in this study, the audience were in the position of knowing the outcome of the individual's actions. The other plays tend to focus on individuals looking back and describing events to the audience. In this way, the individuals depicted become the authority as they provide the audience with new information. In *My Name is Rachel Corrie*, by contrast, the audience knew an outcome of which Corrie herself was unaware. I would argue that this is one of the reasons why the hype that surrounded the play tended to ignore the actor. The tragedy of Rachel Corrie's death sits outside the performance itself. After Dodds has left the stage, the audience hear the news report of her death and see archive footage of the ten-year-old Corrie talking about world peace at a school event. In the play itself, the actor is not directly involved in any reference to Corrie's death.

Physical action

We have seen that Dodds could not break the play down into objectives (or 'tasks') in the way that Stanislavski lays out, but that she was able to adapt this mode of script analysis and identify a shape to the play, and thus her own journey through it, by the use of 'bits' which were marked by the different elements of Corrie's personality in different scenes. It is perhaps of little surprise, given the nature of the source material, that the problem of finding active psychological objectives in Corrie's written testimony was mirrored in the lack of physical objectives in the piece. This was a challenge that was another product of the type of testimony used to construct the play, and the resultant use of direct address. Though the same could be argued for the monologues in *Talking to Terrorists*, the critical difference in *My Name is Rachel Corrie* is the fact that Dodds was alone on stage, and had to hold the audience's attention for 90 minutes, whereas Stafford-Clark's cast only had to contend with a few minutes of stage time before the narrative focus switched to a different speaker. However, developing simple physical objectives became of real importance for Dodds, and was one of the ways in which she filled the void left by the lack of psychological objectives. She remembered that:

> Once we got it into rehearsal, it was mainly walking it in the rehearsal room and starting to find the actions she might be doing and how we might employ the different areas of the stage. That gave me a clearer logic to work by.

In performance, the blocking was structured around small changes of placement on the stage. There was only one complete change of location, which was the move from Olympia to Rafah. This was simply indicated by Dodds pushing the bed and the flat which formed her American bedroom wall to one side to reveal the bullet-ridden, bombed-out room behind. She then inhabited this space for the remainder of the play. Within this there were a series of small changes of position which were evidently useful for Dodds to create a structure to the piece. For example, she sat at the front of the stage, on a chair behind a small computer desk to read the emails aloud, and at one point climbed up onto the wall at the back. This series of physical actions also supported Dodds by giving the play a shape for her:

> I kept referring to it as a journey in the rehearsal room and Kath would roll her eyes, but that was the best way in which I could describe it. As her writings span a considerable length of time, she develops, she goes on a journey – both physical and emotional – and charting that development was one of my ways into the role.

However, rather than functioning as a mechanical series of physical actions, the relationship between Dodds and these different areas of the set became of real psychological importance for her:

> The wall was really helpful. Having somewhere to hide and to sit. Props were also very helpful to me. In a one-woman play, finding sign-posts for yourself from one moment to the next is very important. Most helpful was the notebook. I really latched on to that. I would make notes in it in performance, and it became a useful anchor for me – actors are always looking for something to hold or something to do. In one performance the notebook slipped out of its folder behind the wall and at first I was terrified, I thought I can't do the play without it, but it was funny because through the performance I found that in fact I did not rely on it in the way in which I thought I did. Afterwards when I looked at it, I didn't write in it as much as I thought, but I had clearly made a psychological association between it and what I was saying.

This close relationship between physical action and inner processes was an important concern for Stanislavski. In his chapter 'Bits and Tasks' in *An Actor's Work*, Stanislavski writes that:

> These are physical actions. Yet how much psychology there is in them ... Use the ambiguity of the borderline between physical and psychological Tasks ... Carrying out a physical Task truthfully helps you create the right psychological state. (2008a: 147)

Stanislavski thus recognised the close interdependency between the physical and the psychological. He most fully explored this in 'The Method of Physical Action' which will be analysed in Chapter 4. Though Dodds came to realise that she did not in fact rely on the physical action of writing in the notebook in the way she had expected, it is clear that her rehearsed set of actions provided her with not only physical tasks to achieve and the 'sign-posts' that she mentions, but also contributed to her internal, psychological processes. It thus appears that the combination of physical actions and dividing the play into bits according to different elements of Corrie's personality took the place of objectives in Dodds' approach to character-building.

Her reliance on the set and props also demonstrates the extent to which Dodds felt exposed by the experience, which is in part attributable to her unusual relationship with the audience. Several of the other actors' interviewed in this book also note that documentary theatre often denies them the kind of interaction with other actors on stage that they would normally expect. This issue was particularly prevalent in the experiences of the *Talking to Terrorists* cast. Due to the absence of the interviewer, the play featured long sections of direct address, with some actors talking to the audience almost exclusively. This was described variously by the cast as 'scary' (Ettridge), 'restrictive' (Chung) and 'torture' (Russell). It was clearly a significant issue for Dodds too. She stated that 'my biggest challenge was getting over my own fear about standing up in front of that many people with no one else there' (2005). We have also heard that had she known in advance that it was to be a one-woman play, she would have 'moved quickly in the opposite direction'. Elaborating on this in my interview, she stated: 'The great thing about most other plays, and all the other plays I have worked on, is that you have another actor to work with. I love working with other actors – it is what we do. You completely lose that interaction.'

In *My Name is Rachel Corrie*, Dodds found that the sole communication was between her and the audience:

> The audience take the place of the other actor. It is them that you are in communication with... That is how it developed. The audience changed it. Because it was so much direct address they changed it – their reaction. But there was a threat from them here.

Herein lies a specific challenge for Dodds. The main problem becomes evident when we consider her exclusive use of direct address in the context of the theatre's concern to protect her. Not only did Dodds talk directly to the audience throughout, she had the constant threat of interruption from them. Thus, her only point of communication was with the very people who might present a threat to her. As Watt-Smith states, she had to talk to them 'with the possibility of interruption ever-present'. This, unsurprisingly, was very exposing for the actor. It is therefore of little surprise that such rudimentary elements of performance, here a wall and a notepad, took on such significance for the actor.

One of the ways in which Dodds negotiated the challenge of direct address was to 'cast' the audience. She told me that 'they became the people that Rachel was talking to... I could see their eyes, and imagine that they were who she was writing for.' The concept of 'casting the audience' is a technique described by James Nicola (incidentally, not the same James Nicola who runs the NYTW). According to Nicola, rather than merely talking to the audience, an actor can establish a role for them: 'In direct address, no contrivance is required on your part to talk to the audience, for that is indeed to whom your character is talking... [but] you can go further and actually cast them in a role' (2002: 13). This was one way in which Dodds was able to make an imaginative leap which provided a context and focus for her performance. Thus, despite the type of documentary testimony in *My Name is Rachel Corrie* initially denying her those aspects she was accustomed to utilising – objectives and the presence of other actors – Dodds was able to replace them with a quite different set of strategies.

Posthumous performance: playing the dead

In my interview with Dodds, it became clear that playing a person who had died also brought specific challenges for her, making her involvement in *My Name is Rachel Corrie* a very different endeavour from the other productions explored in this book. It placed her in an unusual position, as the headline of a review during the run at the Minetta Lane Theatre made clear: 'Rachel Corrie Brought Back to Life' (Lappiny 2005). Dodds was as close as the audience could get to Corrie, and thus it was her performance that, to use Carol Martin's phrase, was responsible for the 'restoration of behaviour' (2006: 10). Where Martin uses 'behaviour', Franklin and Lyons use 'personal effects' – those things that the individual owned and left behind. They write: 'We are interested in "personal effects" because sometimes it is only testimony that is left behind. "Personal effects" refers to the belongings of the dead, and testimony constitutes a narrative remainder' (2004: viii). From beyond the grave, as Franklin and Lyons state, Corrie's words are all that exist. They are the personal effects in the play, and thus the speaker, in this case Megan Dodds, became an important signifier of presence.

Playing a dead woman made Dodds' performance a powerful act of surrogacy. As Martin states: 'The absent, unavailable, dead, and disappeared make an appearance by means of surrogation' (2006: 10). Unlike, for example, Lloyd Hutchinson as the ex-IRA bomber, there was no real person living to tell this story. Several commentators have identified that this surrogacy was a strong contributor to the political power of the play, particularly following the cancellation. For example, John Houchin notes:

> The literal political message of the play is obviously threatening. It is, however, the fact that we experience a dramatic representation of the living Rachel Corrie after having internalized images of her dead body that transforms political disagreement into a potentially violent confrontation. (2008: 18)

Houchin usefully identifies the significance of the bodily presence in the production. It is also worth noting his assertion that the play is 'threatening' and that it raises the potential of a 'violent confrontation'. Both these phrases suggest the vulnerability of Dodds in performance. El Lozy develops this identification of the material body's importance in his analysis of the play:

> when Rachel comes back to life on the stage at any given performance of *My Name is Rachel Corrie*, through the actor's performance, it is similar to the appearance of the ghost of Hamlet's father coming back from the dead to reveal to us the true story of a crime that has been covered up as a natural death. (2008: 113)

Notwithstanding El Lozy's grandiose rhetoric, it is clear that the notion of reincarnation or resurrection through the actor's performance sets this play apart from documentary productions which focus on living people. As El Lozy states, the embodied presence of Corrie to 'set the record straight' was a politically contentious act. In this light, we can more fully appreciate why the Royal Court took the procedures to safeguard Megan Dodds so seriously. Through the corporeal presence of Dodds as Corrie, Rickman and Viner were able to give a voice to the voiceless, or rather a bodily presence to the absent.

Dodds was keenly aware of the likelihood of audience members identifying her as a surrogate for the real person she played. It was evident in my interview that she found this to be very problematic, particularly in the talk-backs and discussions organised in conjunction with the performances. She said: 'I didn't take part in them as much as Alan and the Corries. I'm an actor. I'm not Rachel, I'm not her, and when I did take part in discussions, people seemed to want me to answer for her, which of course I can't do.' It is clear from Dodds' comments that some members of the audience wanted her to stand in for the dead woman she portrayed, and that naturally this was something she resisted. The complex relationship between actor-role and actor-audience is further illustrated in Dodds' comment that: 'It is nothing to do with me, it's Rachel, it's her story, the way she communicates her ideas to the world. That is it. That's why people come, they want to sit in a room with her' (2006b). Here Dodds simultaneously denies her own agency and capacity to act as a surrogate, and promotes it by suggesting that it is not about her, but that through her the audience can gain a privileged access to Rachel. This contradiction is at the centre of questions of acting in documentary theatre. It is notable that in the comment above Dodds misrepresents her role by suggesting that she is passive. In this chapter we have seen the ways in which she creatively developed new working processes in the play. She has also been clear about her political agenda in the play. This articulation of passivity is arguably a product of the ethical implications of playing someone who has died.

We must add another level of meaning with regards to an embodied presence here. After the cancellation in New York, it was not only the presence of the actor as the dead Corrie that was powerful, but also the statement this made in the face of the censorship. In the post-cancellation performances, in London, Edinburgh and New York, attendance at the theatres to witness the staging of the play became a powerful show of support against the suppression of free speech in the arts. It is thus doubly bemusing that although her presence on stage was so significant, Dodds experienced such a loss of status. It appears that as the play came so loaded with expectation, it was her presence, rather than what she was actually doing in performance, that became significant.

Surrogacy and Rachel's parents

Dodds' portrayal of Corrie resulted in a strong sense of responsibility, as Dodds has noted: 'I feel a big responsibility towards the work, to communicate it in a way that I think it deserves to be communicated. I put a lot of pressure on myself to do that' (2006b). Part of this stemmed from the involvement of Rachel's parents in the production. Dodds has stated that she had 'to consider all the people in [Rachel's] life who are still alive' (2005). Elaborating on her concern about Rachel's parents, Dodds told me that 'I had to convince myself that I could do it and that I wouldn't be a disappointment. I just didn't want to disappoint Rachel's parents really.' Unlike the other actors I've included in this study, Dodds was in contact not with the individual she played, but with her parents. However, it is clear that she did not talk to them during the rehearsal process, and that being entirely concerned with their reaction would have made her task impossible: 'I think with playing any real person that if you worry too much about what people who knew them might think of your portrayal, and if you are like them, you would not be able to start.' Thus, although she was keenly aware of her responsibility to the parents, she worked independently to create the role herself, rather than being in contact with them throughout her process. She stated that:

> They had been in touch with Kath and Alan during the process more than me. I didn't meet them until a couple of days before. It was odd I suppose, because at that point in the process I was completely concentrating on the play and the challenge of performing it...I was in a different headspace. I felt really responsible when I met them. It reminded me that this was a real person – their daughter...They were very supportive however. They loved it. They had this great kind of enthusiasm, it was lovely to meet them.

Corrie's parents saw the play several times at the Royal Court. Indeed, they have continued to follow productions since – Cindy Corrie noted that a production in Oregon in 2008 was 'around the fourteenth they had seen' (Haedrick 2011: 17). There were examples in the previous chapter of an individual watching themselves portrayed on stage; for example, the ex-British Ambassador came to watch *Talking to Terrorists* many times. Here, however, we have a rather different negotiation. It is evident in the Corries' writings about the experience of watching Dodds portray their daughter that they also experienced moments in her performance as powerful acts of surrogacy. In an article in the *Guardian*, they stated that:

> It is disconcerting, but also comforting, to watch an actor who looks much like Rachel...the resemblance is almost too much. But Megan lives Rachel's words in ways that are sometimes familiar but also sometimes surprising, so that we learn from her what Rachel may have been thinking. At several points in the play, Megan enacts receiving emails from us – real emails that we actually sent to Rachel. We had never before imagined our daughter's reactions to receiving our messages until we saw them on stage. (Corrie 2005)

This is a fascinating statement, which again suggests why Dodds felt responsible when she met them. Katharine Viner also spoke in detail about this moment:

> The first time they came to see it, we sat them very close to the door and we said, just leave, we'll come with you if you can't bear it, but they loved it. They came to every single performance for about nine days, and then they found it very difficult to leave. There is a scene which I really love when we show Rachel reading an email from her dad, and getting upset about his concern for her. Craig said that when he saw it he had never before imagined her responding to his emails, so the play had opened up a whole area of his imagination that he had never thought of. Isn't that beautiful? Maybe the way that Megan responded isn't the way that

Rachel responded, but that is a private place for them to go and think about it.

With regard to this moment, Dodds stated that in the intimate surroundings of the play's premiere at the Royal Court Theatre Upstairs, she could see Corrie's parents:

> I remember the first performance they came to. It was in the Royal Court Theatre Upstairs. I think that that theatre suited the play best. I could see Craig's face, he had this look of shock and recollection, and at the end they were both in floods of tears. I think we had given them something.

The relationship between the performer and the family of the woman she played in performance clearly affected Dodds. However, her resistance to being viewed as a surrogate for Rachel Corrie manifested itself in other ways in Dodds' process.

We have seen that Rachel's parents felt that the 'resemblance is almost too much'. Similarly, John Houchin wrote that the play 'placed an eerily accurate representation of the deceased activist on stage' (2008: 17). However, part of Dodds' wish to avoid becoming a surrogate was her lack of interest in recreating Rachel Corrie's appearance, voice or physicality. In my interview Dodds stated: 'I didn't really worry about looking like her. They spent a very long time working out what I should wear – but I only have one costume. They told me to tie my hair back. It really wasn't a concern.' We should note that although Dodds was over ten years older than Corrie when she played her, she shares the same blond hair and slim build. Despite her lack of interest in looking like Rachel Corrie, such was the power of the surrogacy in the play that some commentators, like Houchin, experienced a much closer resemblance. Though video material was available, Dodds chose not to watch it, as Watt-Smith remembers:

> There was a video that I don't think Megan wanted to see in which Rachel is interviewed…There is this awkwardness when playing a real person about seeing her and feeling that you don't quite measure up. There were a few books around, but it wasn't approached as a research project in the way that lots of verbatim pieces are.

It is thus clear that Dodds' identification of the need 'to consider all the people in her life who are still alive' did not mean developing a way to work on Corrie's external features, or that she should be in contact with these people. Rather, as we have seen, it meant that she was very much focused on finding a clear route through the play and on identifying the different aspects of Corrie's personality in her portrayal.

CONCLUSION

This chapter has focused on how Megan Dodds developed nuanced and subtle strategies within both a very challenging form of documentary theatre and extremely difficult working conditions. Dodds' description of her experiences has thrown the differences between the hype surrounding the play and the actor's own work into sharp relief. The way in which the play was received was evidently very challenging for Dodds, as the furore not only ignored her work, but also led to a set of assumptions and prejudices which were in no way based on what she was doing on stage. Dodds' frustrations about the critical reception are thus completely understandable. Whilst overlooking her performance, writers in print and viral media built up an unmanageable and unjustified set of expectations surrounding the play, and then proceeded to express dissatisfaction when it did not live up to the feverish hype they had themselves constructed for it. In short, we have seen how a play and a performance can be re-signified and overshadowed by events. To this end, the cancellation in New York gave the play its political kudos and cultural legacy, but disadvantaged the production, and particularly the solo performer within it.

The extent to which this was a profoundly challenging performance environment has become clear through my focus on the context of Dodds' work. Dodds had to contend with the threat of interruption on stage, with demonstrations outside the theatre, as well as with deeply offensive material about her and her portrayal on the internet. In this chapter I have dedicated substantial room to analysing these challenges. Not only are they unusual for an actor, and include the sort of organisational procedures which are rarely considered in research into acting, but also we have seen that they underscored her processes throughout. However, not only did Dodds have to contend with these personal challenges, she also carried the responsibility of portraying Rachel Corrie in front of Corrie's own parents, in a production in which they had been heavily involved. What has become clear in my analysis of her portrayal are the subtle ways in which she strove to preserve integrity in her work against this almost intolerable backdrop.

It is thus in this context that I have analysed how Dodds worked on a very difficult task in itself – the process of adapting written word into spoken performance. Dodds was very clear that the written testimony of *My Name is Rachel Corrie* rendered her usual reliance on intentions and objectives obsolete. She found that developing ways to create momentum and shape through the play based on what the character wanted to do was impossible for her. However, as we have seen, when faced with new challenges which denied the actor her usual approach, Dodds adapted and reinvented her working process to navigate those challenges, and was able to replace objectives with an alternative set of processes. She placed a greater reliance upon the various elements of Corrie's personality that she was portraying in different scenes, informed by her use of the extensive collection of Corrie's writing which the Royal Court had received. This evidently gave a shape to the play for Dodds. However, she was still challenged by the lack of momentum left by the absence of objectives. This was filled by her emphasis on physical actions and her belief in the psychological attachment she developed with these actions and her use of props. These, rather than psychological objectives, gave her simple tasks to complete through the play. This pragmatic capacity demonstrates the ability of actors to respond sensitively to the particular exigencies and contexts of character creation.

We have also seen the use of terms by the directors which could have been taken as questioning the actor's craft in this play. However, Dodds made it clear that Rickman's advice to avoid being 'showy' was one of the directing team's strategies in response to the type of testimony they were using. Dodds' articulation of the importance of playing the piece from Corrie's point of view also flew in the face of the expectations for the production. By ensuring that she did this – in part thanks to the extra material sent by the family – Dodds performed the piece not as an elegy to a dead pro-Palestinian protester, but as what she has called a 'testament to Rachel' – as a focused and optimistic portrayal which captured Corrie's passion and youth.

Called to Account. From left: Thomas Wheatley, Diane Fletcher, Charlotte Lucas and David Michaels (photo by Geraint Lewis)

3

Called to Account

INTRODUCTION

Called to Account: The Indictment of Anthony Charles Lynton Blair for the Crime of Aggression Against Iraq – A Hearing opened at the Tricycle Theatre in Kilburn, North London, on 19 April 2007, where it ran for seven weeks. It was edited by Richard Norton-Taylor and directed by the then artistic director of the Tricycle Theatre, Nicolas Kent. *Called to Account* focused on the British government's decision to go to war in Iraq in 2003, and whether, due to the charge that he breached the UN General Assembly Resolution 3314 (1974), there is a case for charging Tony Blair as a war criminal. The play was constructed from testimony from a range of high-profile witnesses who were cross-examined by eminent lawyers about their knowledge of the circumstances and the decision-making process in the lead-up to the war. The cross-examinations were subsequently edited by Norton-Taylor and 11 of the interviews were included in the play.

Although considered to be one of a series of 'tribunal plays' (documentary plays edited from court cases) at the Tricycle Theatre, *Called to Account* was qualitatively different from both Kent's and Norton-Taylor's previous productions. Here, the interviews were not edited from a legal trial, but arranged specifically for the purposes of a theatrical production. This difference resulted in innovations in Kent and Norton-Taylor's working methods: because the interviews were arranged for the play, the testimony was not subject to the rules of a law court, and thus the witnesses and lawyers could be filmed. Each actor was thus given a DVD of their subject's interview. In comparison to the previous tribunal plays and the other plays analysed here, in *Called to Account* the actors had unprecedented access to the specifics of the original interview. This resulted in a quite different set of challenges from those encountered in *Talking to Terrorists* and *My Name is Rachel Corrie*, and prompted a particularly focused concern with restraint and precision among the cast.

Tribunal theatre

The term 'tribunal play' refers to a documentary production in which the primary document is an official legal case. Kent is correct when he states that 'I wasn't doing anything spectacularly new...but it seems like I reinvented the wheel' (2005b). Although often credited otherwise, as Kent recognises, he and Norton-Taylor did not create the form as much as reinvigorate and revitalise it for the contemporary stage. The influential exponents of the form were working in Germany in the 1960s and had a direct link to Erwin Piscator's experiments in the 1930s. Piscator's production of *Trotz Alledem* (*In Spite of Everything*) in 1925 was arguably the first documentary play, and thus Piscator is considered the founder of documentary theatre. The leading documentary dramatists who worked with Piscator were Rolf Hochhuth, Heinar Kipphardt and Peter Weiss. The latter two writers staged tribunal versions of contemporary legal cases. Heinar Kipphardt's play, *In the Matter of J. Robert Oppenheimer*, was first performed in 1964 in Berlin and Munich, directed by Piscator. It was particularly successful, becoming, according to *Time Magazine*, 'the talk of Europe' (1964). The play is a condensed version of the investigation into Oppenheimer, an American nuclear physicist, and focuses on his appearance in front of the House of Un-American Activities Committee in 1953. Peter Weiss' 1965 play, *Die Ermittlung* (*The Investigation*), was like *In the Matter of J. Robert Oppenheimer* an internationally significant theatrical event. *The Investigation* was an edited dramatisation of the Frankfurt War Crimes Trials (1963–65), which tried 22 Nazis involved in the death camp at Auschwitz. It was performed simultaneously in 16 cities across East and West Germany shortly after the conclusion of the trials on 19 October 1965. Piscator directed the West Berlin production, and the play received a rehearsed reading at the RSC, directed by Peter Brook, which Kustow notes 'pioneered, in this country at least, the stage as courtroom...Nick Kent at the Tricycle Theatre...continues this moral and civic stance today' (2000b: 134). Megson similarly identified the formative influence of *The Investigation* on the Tricycle tribunal plays: 'Weiss'

The Investigation... clearly establishes a template for the Tricycle's approach' (2009: 196).

Nicolas Kent was the artistic director of the theatre from 1984 to 2012. Like Weiss and Kipphardt before him, through the tribunal plays Kent created a national debating house and situated the Tricycle at the forefront of contemporary political theatre. As Charles Spencer declared in the *Daily Telegraph*, 'There is no theatre in Britain that has told us more in recent years about the way we live now than the Tricycle in Kilburn' (2004). The theatre won the Olivier Award for 'Outstanding Achievement in an Affiliate Theatre' in 2006 for *Bloody Sunday*, and it was for its political work that the Tricycle won the Evening Standard Theatre Awards' Special Award in the same year.

Kent and Norton-Taylor: the partnership and the plays

Richard Norton-Taylor is the Security Affairs Editor for the *Guardian*. He has worked for the newspaper since 1975, and in that time has published a number of books, often highly critical of the structure of government. Norton-Taylor's partnership with Nicolas Kent has included, to date, seven tribunal plays, dating back to 1994, all of which Norton-Taylor has edited and Kent has directed. It is noteworthy that Kent approached an investigative journalist rather than a playwright to edit the transcripts. Norton-Taylor is a political expert with a long history of investigating institutions, policy-makers and the British justice system. As well as lending what Kent has called 'serious credibility' to the plays, this decision suggests the type of skills required to maintain a full grasp of the legal and political complexities whilst sculpting a logical and coherent narrative out of the vast proceedings of an inquiry (Hammond and Steward 2009: 164).

Kent and Norton-Taylor's first collaboration was entitled *Half the Picture: The Scott Arms to Iraq Inquiry* (1994). It was the only tribunal play to include fictional monologues, written by the famous political playwright John McGrath. The production was immediately acknowledged to be of national importance, and became the first play to be performed in the Houses of Parliament, staged in the Grand Committee Room in front of an audience of parliamentarians. It was subsequently televised on BBC2 and broadcast on the BBC World Service. This was followed two years later by *Nuremberg: The 1946 War Crimes Trial* (1996), timed to commemorate the fiftieth anniversary of what Norton-Taylor notes was 'the world's first war crimes trial', and which followed the rich heritage established by Weiss and Schneider of Nazi trials in tribunal theatre (Hammond and Steward 2009: 108). The play was performed at the Tricycle and again broadcast on the radio by the BBC World Service. *Nuremberg* was presented alongside short documentary pieces from contemporary tribunals, including Kent's solo project, *Srebrenica* (1996), which drew attention to the similarities between the trial of the high-ranking Nazis and the war crimes in the former Yugoslavia. Their most celebrated venture to date, *The Colour of Justice: The Stephen Lawrence Inquiry*, was staged in 1999. The play, which condensed the Macpherson Inquiry that investigated the police's handling of the racist murder of Stephen Lawrence, a black teenager, by a white gang, was performed at the Tricycle and the Theatre Royal Stratford East. The production was the first West End transfer for Kent and Norton-Taylor, performed at the Victoria Palace. A television production of the play was also broadcast on BBC2. *The Colour of Justice* is now on the curriculum of many schools, colleges and universities and is also used for teaching purposes at some police training institutions (see Norton-Taylor 2007c). In 2003, Kent and Norton-Taylor investigated the scapegoating and subsequent suicide of Dr David Kelly over the question of weapons of mass destruction and the decision to invade Iraq, in *Justifying War: Scenes from the Hutton Inquiry*. Again the production was televised, on BBC4. In 2004, Kent continued the rich tradition of documentary at the Tricycle, directing Victoria Brittain and Gillian Slovo's *Guantanamo: 'Honour Bound to Defend Freedom'*, which, after its run at the theatre, transferred to the West End and then to New York. Kent and Norton-Taylor's fifth collaboration was *Bloody Sunday: Scenes from the Saville Inquiry*. Following the run at the Tricycle in 2005, the production toured Ireland, visiting Belfast and Dublin, and was also performed in front of 65 members of the victims' families in Derry. Kent's final tribunal play as Artistic Director of the theatre was *Tactical Questioning: Scenes from the Baha Mousa Inquiry* (2011), which examined the death of Mousa, an Iraqi detainee, after being beaten by British army soldiers whilst being held in custody in Basra.

Perhaps the critical motivating factor behind the plays is that filming was prohibited in the inquiries. Although 'public' inquiries, the number of seats available was very limited. As actor William Hoyland, who has appeared in six of the tribunal plays, explained:

> Cameras were not allowed in the previous inquiries. In fact that is one of
> the reasons that Nick was so keen to do plays like the Stephen Lawrence

Inquiry – they are not televised. In many ways, that was the raison d'être for the whole tribunal shows.

In other words, the public has had to rely on journalistic reporting of the inquiries, which Kent found inadequate for the proper investigation of these complex cases. He commented that 'Because of the television age we're in and even newspapers, we're getting sound bites. We get very short coverage of stories…They don't get to the bottom of issues' (2005b). Similarly, Norton-Taylor notes that the inquiries have been 'written about in short newspaper articles, or mentioned all too briefly in television and radio news bulletins' (Hammond and Steward 2009: 122). The tribunal plays have thus enabled a broader public consumption of neglected material.

Both Kent and Norton-Taylor are convinced that theatre is the most potent form through which to get this information out to the public. Kent has stated that: 'In theatre you've got a captive audience…The doors are closed and people stay in there and they wrestle with something for an hour and a half' (2005b). The shared experience of the audience also emphasises the campaigning element of Kent's theatre. The social act of attending these plays can be seen as an act of solidarity with the issues raised.

The timing of the tribunal plays is also critical to their power and their potential to make political interventions. Many of the plays staged the inquiry before the findings of it were published. For example, *The Colour of Justice* was first performed in January 1999, a month before the findings of the Macpherson Inquiry were made public. Similarly, *Bloody Sunday*, which staged excerpts of the Saville Inquiry, opened in April 2005, following the final hearings which were held in November 2004. The Inquiry's final report was eventually published in June 2010. Like Weiss' *The Investigation*, the tribunal plays provide what Kritzer calls an 'immediate form of political engagement' (2008: 223) by the fact they are performed contemporaneously with the events they depict.

Called to Account

When viewed in relation to the past tribunal plays, it is clear that a profound relocation of the form took place in the staging of *Called to Account*, as it was not edited from a real inquiry, but rather constructed from a series of interviews set up by Kent, Norton-Taylor and a lawyer, Philippe Sands QC, for the purposes of a stage production.

Sands, using lawyers from his own chambers, conducted the interviews according to the UN Definition of Aggression. From the outset the interviews were designed to be edited into a piece of documentary theatre and thus did not constitute a legal hearing. The reviews of the production illustrate the differences between *Called to Account* and previous tribunal plays. Kate Bassett, writing in the *Independent* asked, 'This is some kind of fantasy, isn't it?' (2007). Similarly, Lloyd Evans in the *Spectator* branded it 'wish-fulfilment drama' (2007). On the whole, the critical responses were less favourable towards the production because of the fact that it was not a real inquiry.

The cross-examinations were, however, carried out in the way in which a hearing would function if lawyers were briefed to establish whether there was evidence to indict Tony Blair. Similarly, the title and marketing of the play draw on the veracity of the previous tribunal plays. In both the programme for *Called to Account* and the printed text, it is listed alongside previous legal inquiries staged, most noticeably in a double-page spread in the programme entitled 'From Iraq to Iraq: The Tricycle Tribunal Plays', which draws parallels between *Called to Account* and *Half the Picture*, and on the Tricycle Theatre website, which describes *Called to Account* as 'the most recent play in the Tribunal series' (2007). By drawing on the rich heritage of the previous plays, the marketing implies that *Called to Account* is also an edited version of a legal inquiry, thereby giving this pseudo-hearing a similar gravitas.

The political topicality of *Called to Account*

The 'Don't Attack Iraq' protest march on 15 February 2003 was London's largest ever peacetime demonstration. It was a public expression of the concern about both the motivations to go to war and the legitimacy of doing so. The Iraq war was in the headlines continually following the invasion which started on 20 March 2003. Although Saddam Hussein was executed in December 2006, when *Called to Account* opened the situation in Iraq was bleak, the country seemingly spiralling towards civil war.

The play was performed in Tony Blair's tenth year as Prime Minister. It was public knowledge long before it opened that he would not stand for another term. In September 2006, at the Labour Party Conference in Manchester, he announced it would be his last as leader. By April 2007, when the play opened, predictions as to the precise timing of his departure had become a media obsession. Blair formally stood down as leader on 30 June 2007, shortly after *Called to Account* closed. Kent has noted how important it was to perform the play whilst Blair was still Prime Minister: 'We had to do it before Blair left Parliament. I was never going to do it after he left' (Hammond and Steward 2009: 144). The play was thus an incisive critique of a standing Prime Minister at a time of considerable public dissatisfaction with the government's foreign policy.

Through the cross-examinations, the play interrogates Blair's style of leadership, and explores to what extent his approach meant that the governmental system could be exploited. It alleges that the Attorney General, Lord Goldsmith, the most senior lawyer and legal advisor to the government, was subjected to pressure from the Prime Minister, and questions the relationship between the two with regard to the legitimacy of the war. The crux of the play is the strikingly different advice the Attorney General gave Blair between 7 and 17 March 2003. During this ten-day period, Lord Goldsmith declared the war illegal and then made an about turn, legally sanctioning the war without hard evidence as to what had changed and who had authorised it. *Called to Account* asks why this was the case, and explores how the decision came about.

The creative team

The team which Kent recruited for the project is revealing with regard to the political motivation in staging the play. Importantly, he was able to gather together a group of lawyers of the calibre that might have worked on a real inquiry. Philippe Sands is the co-founder of Matrix Chambers and Professor of Law at University College London. Matrix Chambers is internationally recognised as one of most important human rights practices. Particularly relevant to this project is Sands' book on the Iraq war, *Lawless World: Making and Breaking of Global Rules* (2006), in which he argues that without the second UN resolution, the war was illegal. The book is highly critical of both Tony Blair and the British government. It is consequently no surprise that in addition to being instrumental in the play's genesis, Sands also represented the prosecution in the cross-examinations.

Richard Norton-Taylor was a critic of the war from the outset and regularly wrote for the *Guardian* on the subject. Long before the invasion, he wrote a scathing indictment of the Anglo-American attitude towards Iraq. In the article, 'Don't trust Bush or Blair on Iraq', he wrote, 'Whatever the reasons, and there are many, for seeing the back of Saddam, don't listen to Bush or Blair when they talk of morality, democracy and good governance' (2002). With regard to his involvement in *Called to Account*, Norton-Taylor stated: 'the point, for me, is to get out even more of the evidence against Blair, and the people defending him too for that matter' (Kent and Norton-Taylor 2007). In a later article he stated his intent even more strongly:

> In *Called to Account* we have set out our own stall, asking whether – given all the evidence that has yet to be properly investigated in public, whether in the Commons or elsewhere – Tony Blair has a case to answer. That must be a legitimate role for the theatre. (Norton-Taylor, 2007a)

Norton-Taylor's question has been validated by the launch of the Chilcot Inquiry (which began on 24 November 2009) into the Iraq war. In an equally impassioned statement, Kent declared:

> I think we live in a democracy and I firmly and passionately believe in calling our politicians to account... Over the last few years the House of Commons has been totally devalued because we've had this presidential style of government, so we've not been able to call our politicians to account enough, and I feel that's a very important part of the democratic process. (Kent and Norton-Taylor, 2007)

The need for transparency and public accountability in government was one of the motivating factors in staging *Called to Account*. It is thus clear both from the choice of project and the team Kent recruited to work on it that *Called to Account* was a provocatively interventionist play which, using high-profile lawyers, attempted to challenge the legality of Blair's conduct over the Iraq invasion. As we shall see, the political topicality of the play and the stakes involved in laying out the case to indict a serving Prime Minister had a significant effect on the actors' processes.

Interviewers and witnesses

For the first time in his tribunal plays, the onus was on Kent, with Sands' help, to recruit witnesses. The pair found individuals reticent to come forward. Kent told journalist Matthew Amer, 'initially people were slightly distrustful about the whole thing' (Kent 2007). This is unsurprising, as the risk involved in publicly speaking out against the current (if out-going) Prime Minister would discourage many from volunteering.

The final production included eleven cross-examinations, conducted between 5 January and 15 February 2007. Norton-Taylor
crafted the play from 28 hours of interview material. The editing
process continued throughout rehearsals. Like Soans' work during
rehearsals, and symptomatic of working on a new play, the piece was
constantly re-edited.

In the production, Philippe Sands (played by Thomas Wheatley)
acted for the prosecution in the interviews, assisted by Alison
MacDonald (played by Morven Macbeth). Julian Knowles (played
by David Michaels), acted for the defence, assisted by Blinne Ni
Ghralaigh (played by Charlotte Lucas). Unlike previous productions, as there was no set order of witnesses, Norton-Taylor was able
to craft the cross-examinations into a logical and dramatic shape.[1]
In my interview with Thomas Wheatley, the actor described his view
of the play's structure, which is very useful in understanding how
the evidence was ordered. It opens with what Wheatley described as
the 'Iraqi point of view', with Dr Shirwan Al-Mufti (played by Raad
Rawi), an Iraqi national and academic in Astrobiology at Cardiff
University, interviewed. Then three witnesses appear in a section of
the play that Wheatley identified as 'setting up the case against': Scott
Ritter (played by David Beames), an American who from 1991 to 1998
was a Chief UN Weapons Inspector in Iraq; Michael Smith (played
by Ken Drury), a journalist who specialises in defence issues for the
Sunday Times and who was the first journalist to get sight of, and
report on, the Downing Street Memo; and Sir Murray Stuart-Smith
(played by William Hoyland), a former Security and Intelligence
Services Commissioner (1994–2000) and Lord Justice of Appeal
(1988–2000).[2] Then Wheatley described 'testing the case at home'
which begins with the first of what he identified as 'two star witnesses',
Clare Short MP (played by Diane Fletcher), an ex-cabinet minister
and Labour MP. Her testimony closes the first act before the interval. The 'case at home' continues with Michael Mates MP (played by
Roland Oliver), a Conservative MP and member of the Butler Inquiry
(set up by Blair to investigate the intelligence on Iraq's weapons of
mass destruction, which were never found). The cross-examinations
then switch to 'testing the case overseas', in which Edward Mortimer
(played by Jeremy Clyde), who was Communications Director under
Kofi Annan at the UN from 1998 to 2006, and Juan Gabriel Valdes
(played by James Woolley), Chilean Ambassador to the UN Security
Council in 2003, are interviewed. The thrust of the play next moves
back to England, with an interview with Bob Marshall-Andrews

QC MP (played by Terrence Hardiman), a Labour MP and criminal court judge. Marshall-Andrews' interview is followed by the second 'star witness', Richard Perle (played by Shane Rimmer), an eminent American politician who worked for Reagan and then for the Bush administration as Chairman of the Board at the time of the Iraq war. The final cross-examination is with Sir Michael Quinlan (played by William Hoyland, the only actor to play two roles), former Permanent Under-Secretary in the Ministry of Defence, which Wheatley described as a 'coda' to the play.

Predictably, the balance of pro- and anti-war witnesses tips heavily in favour of those against the invasion. This was noted by many of the reviewers. Charles Spencer found it 'worryingly partisan' (2007), whilst Ian Shuttleworth labelled it 'immensely one-sided' (2007). However, considering the scope of the production, one wonders why these reviewers were surprised. The play set out to make the case for indicting a Prime Minister, and thus was designed to be an incisive exposé of his alleged deceit.

Casting

As with Stafford-Clark's casting of *Talking to Terrorists*, Kent used many actors with whom he had worked previously. Indeed, *Called to Account* was the first tribunal play for only four of a cast of 14, which led Jeremy Clyde to call the experienced ensemble 'Tricyclists'.[3] This also suggests that Kent was very specific about the type of performance he wanted, and that having found actors adept at certain skills, he tried to maintain an ensemble of experienced actors.

Like the cast of *Talking to Terrorists,* none of the actors were well known to the general public. Marvin Carlson has noted that famous actors are 'entrapped by the memories of the public, so that each new appearance requires a renegotiation with those memories' (2001: 9). Here, however, although some were recognisable, none carried the weight of memories of previous roles in the way that Carlson suggests. Arguably, the cross-examinations in *Called to Account* benefited from an unknown ensemble cast, rather than a star who would be likely to draw the focus away from the issues, or call undue attention to one character.

Thomas Wheatley and David Michaels, playing Sands and Knowles, were cast at the beginning of the process, and so were able to observe first-hand the interviews later edited and recreated on stage. The casting of the witnesses, by contrast, took place at various points later in the process – partly because of the difficulties in persuading people to give evidence and in finalising the line-up. The actors playing the witnesses were all cast specifically to play a particular individual. In contrast to *Talking to Terrorists*, they were employed on a much more familiar contract: they rehearsed for three weeks followed by a production week, then started the run.

The most formative aspect of the actors' experiences arose as a direct result of the fact that in *Called to Account* the interviews were recorded, both on audio and on DVD by means of a camcorder. Ken Drury recalled that in some previous plays, such as *The Colour of Justice*, the cast were given audio recordings, but never before had the interviews been filmed. With the exception of two actors, the cast were given a DVD and audio version of the full-length interview in addition to the complete transcript and Norton-Taylor's edited cross-examination (two witnesses, Valdes and Ritter, were interviewed over the phone using a conference call machine, and thus James Woolley and David Beames only received an audio recording). As we shall see, this new material had a profound effect upon the actors' work.

ACTING PROCESSES

Foregrounding politics

I interviewed the cast of *Called to Account* between 8 May 2007 and 27 May 2009. All the interviews were conducted over the telephone, with the exception of the interview with Thomas Wheatley, whom I talked to in person at the Tricycle Theatre. We have seen that the primary focus of the cast of *Talking to Terrorists*, and of Megan Dodds in *My Name is Rachel Corrie*, was attempting to understand the psychology of the individuals they played. Catherine Russell's research into Phoebe's circumstances was not restricted to the content of the script, but included trying to learn as much about her formative psychological experiences as possible. Likewise, Chris Ryman's approach was also based on his perceived need to identify psychologically with the individual he was portraying. Indeed, it appears that Stafford-Clark encouraged actor-interviewee meetings in the play's preparation in order to foster the actors' belief in a personal bond with their subject. Similarly, critical to Dodds finding a shape for the play was identifying the different elements of Corrie's personality that she hoped to communicate. By contrast, in *Called to Account*, the engagement was with a professional, public persona; as Clare Short said of her responses in the cross-examination, 'most of it is in my book' (2008). These were not personal trauma narratives in the way in which interviewing a victim of a bombing in their own home was for Soans and Stafford-Clark; *Called to Account* presented legal and political arguments surrounding a particular conflict. This difference was most succinctly articulated by Ken Drury when he talked about his performance as Michael Smith: 'This material is not emotional for Smith – there is little emoting for any of the characters really. It is Smith's intellectual professional side. He comes from a certain point of view. So it wasn't psychological analysis.'

Although the cross-examinations were not devoid of emotion, it is true that the vast majority of questions called upon the witnesses' powers of justification, reasoning and intellect more often than they elicited an emotional response. Like Drury, Raad Rawi and Terrence Hardiman identified the play as unusual in its lack of focus on the psychology of its characters. Rawi stated:

> Plays are driven by character and emotion. Most plays. You approach a play through the emotional life of your character. In most plays that develops. You latch onto what makes people tick, what triggers an emotion. Why certain things are said. But with *Called to Account*, a lot of it is recollection. All those characters were recalling what happened.

Rawi's comments suggest that he had previously relied on a Stanislavskian approach to character, which he evidently found was redundant in this play. Terrence Hardiman also noted that the lack of emphasis on an emotional journey negated a Stanislavskian approach: 'You can't use Stanislavski or method as you are not there to emote, you are there to present an argument as honestly as you can and fairly to the script you have.'

The different emotional landscape to which these actors allude was pre-empted in performance by the way in which the testimony was framed in *Called to Account*. In the opening exchanges of the play, Julian Knowles informs the audience that they 'will hear' the evidence (Norton-Taylor 2007b: 10). By contrast, in the opening scene of *Talking to Terrorists,* Edward, the psychologist, tells the audience about the people they 'are about to meet' (Soans 2005: 36). Likewise *My Name is Rachel Corrie* opens with Corrie lying in bed stating:

> if you are concerned with the logic and sequence of things and the crescendo of suspense up to a good shocker of an ending, you best be getting

back to your video game and amassing your wealth. Leave the meaning-less details to the poets and the photographers. And they're all meaningless details, my friend. (Rickman and Viner 2005: 4)

The different tone of these introductions anticipates the audience's engagement with the individuals depicted. To 'meet' someone suggests a reciprocal relationship in which audience members experience a personal investment in the individual, as does the use of the term 'friend'. To 'hear' evidence, by contrast, suggests a more intellectual, forensic quality.

This quality of intellectual engagement was further nurtured through direct appeals to the audience to act as the jury and decide for themselves whether Blair was guilty. Sands and Knowles were invited to write opening statements, which, unlike the cross-examinations (but consistent with the scope of the 'hearing'), were works of fiction, written *as if* the hearing was official. In his speech Sands says:

> the prosecutor seeks the authorisation of the Court to investigate the facts, to ascertain whether they provide a basis for indicting Anthony Charles Lynton Blair for the crime of aggression. As the Court assesses the evidence, we invite you to focus on four facts ... (Norton-Taylor 2007b: 9)

The speech was rich with official legal terms that did not actually apply, but framed the testimony to appear official. 'The Court', for the performance's duration, was the audience, and so Sands readied them for a display of politics, not personalities. Similarly, Knowles' speech was written as a direct address to the audience: 'The prosecution ask you to consider a number of issues' (Norton-Taylor 2007b: 10). These comments, the first speeches in the play, immediately enlisted the audience and cast them as the jury, asking them to evaluate the evidence.

Perhaps the most explicit way in which the production planned to involve the audience was by holding a vote at the end of the play, in which the audience was invited to decide the fate of Tony Blair. Reminiscent of the first generation of tribunal productions, this device of politicising the audience can be seen as a literal employment of a technique endorsed by Brecht:

> once illusion is sacrificed to free discussion, and once the spectator, instead of being enabled to have an experience, is forced as it were to cast his vote; then a change has been launched which goes far beyond formal matters and begins for the first time to affect the theatre's social function. (Willett 1964: 39)

The day before the production opened, Michael Billington published an article in the *Guardian* entitled 'Theatre wants your vote', in which he wrote: '*Called to Account* – a piece of documentary theatre which puts the case for and against the prosecution of Tony Blair over the invasion of Iraq, and which gives the audience on the night the final vote' (2007c). However, the vote was dropped from the production at the last minute, in a move which Billington, despite his earlier intrigue, stated was wise, 'since it avoids any suspicion of a kangaroo court' (2007a). Instead, the performance ended with closing statements from the defence and prosecution. Again, these speeches were delivered directly to the audience. Sands asked, 'You have now heard the evidence. Are there grounds for a full investigation as to Mr Blair's involvement in the crime of aggression?' (Norton-Taylor: 2007b: 89). In what reviewer John Peter described as 'a very British ending' the defence is given the last word (2007). Here, Knowles also appealed directly to the audience: 'At the close of this hearing I submit that you should find Tony Blair does not need absolution. He has done nothing that justifies condemnation' (Norton-Taylor 2007b: 92). Although the vote did not materialise, the production provoked the audience into a political and legal engagement. This gave rise to particular challenges for the actors.

PRECISION AND RESTRAINT

The DVD and linguistic precision: the language of law and politics

One of the acting challenges which arose from the play's engagement with politics and law was comprehending and recreating the precise language employed by all involved. As the title 'A Hearing' and Knowles' invitation to the audience 'to hear' the evidence suggest, the British legal system is based on using spoken testimony in order to prove guilt beyond reasonable doubt. Frequently associated with a battle of wits and a virtuoso command of the spoken word, it is naturally an arena which lends itself to the stage. Couple the legal system with politics, as is the case in *Called to Account*, and the result is a sparring between the two professions which prize public speaking, rhetoric and verbal precision most highly. Although we no longer refer to 'hearing a play', we still 'hear evidence', such is the foregrounding of spoken testimony in law. James Woolley's comment that 'Nick knows when it is sounding how he wants it', suggests an emphasis on verbal rather than visual precision. Norton-Taylor's cynical view of the language of these professions suggests why they are ideal for depiction on stage:

> There are many effective weapons available to those determined to prevent the truth from emerging. They include dissembling, euphemism, deliberate ambiguity and plays on words. Civil servants, diplomats and government ministers are past masters at it. (Hammond and Steward 2009: 113)

Although evidently ideal fare for a stage production, the language was a challenge for the actors. Shane Rimmer recalled that:

> The first thing is that it is very much governmental political talk. It is not the kind of talk you or I would come out with ... It is a lingo that one has to get used to in order to make it sound natural. He [Richard Perle] sounded, if nothing else, completely natural.

As all the characters who appeared in the play were connected with politics or law, this challenge united the whole cast, with both the actors playing lawyers and those appearing as witnesses noting the difficulties they faced. Thomas Wheatley cited a particular question asked by Sands to illustrate the need for clarity and precision to which Rimmer alludes:

> The key to the work is that everybody understands what they are talking about, because if we do, there is a chance the audience will ... There are a couple of very odd sentences: 'Do you believe the British government behaved honourably and honestly on the issue of intelligence and related matters in the context of the series of issues in Iraq?' ... so understanding it is the key, but Nick is very good at that. He makes it clear.

This language is a direct consequence of the editing process. As we have seen, Soans' script for *Talking to Terrorists* was only loosely based on the interviews, and should be understood as an amalgam of the interviewees' words and Soans' own stylistic imprint. By contrast, the witnesses' words in *Called to Account* were not reformulated by a playwright but rather recorded. We must consequently appreciate that the documents from which these plays were constructed are qualitatively different. With regard to the precision necessitated by the witnesses' and lawyers' language, without exception the DVD was hailed by the actors as both a very important aid and a major influence on their approach to the play.

The recordings proved particularly useful for line phrasings and emphasis, which in this production, far more so than in the plays discussed in previous chapters, were critical in understanding the intricacies of the witnesses' stance and in being able to recreate their speech with precision. Like Thomas Wheatley's problems with the length and logic of some of Sands' questions, Shane Rimmer noted that:

> [The recording] was very helpful because words can only take you so far. You can get a lot of indications in the words about the person you are playing, but to see him [Richard Perle] is a couple of steps on from that...I played it firstly to get all that, and secondly, a lot of what he talked about I couldn't really understand, as you have to be in the scene there.

By 'in the scene' Rimmer refers to how helpful it was to see Perle's comments in the context of the cross-examination. Both Raad Rawi and Ken Drury found the recording revealed unexpected vocal features. Rawi stated:

> He [Shirwan Al-Mufti] was very nice, very charming. Even when he was talking about really horrific details about the Kurds in Iraq in the '70s, he was extremely calm and maintained this air of serenity about him...I could tell he had a great humility about him. You'd never get that from the text alone.

Similarly, Drury noted:

> The DVD is fascinating vocally, because this stuff is actually quite hard to learn. People speak in really strange ways – they never quite say things the way you would expect them to say them. They certainly never say things the way a writer would write them.

The DVD thus revealed unexpected tones in their witnesses' testimonies which the actors would not likely have adopted had it not been for the recording. We can thus start to identify how the actors understood the term 'precision'. Closely associated with this was 'restraint'. To investigate these terms further, and analyse precisely how they manifested themselves in the actors' work, the following sections will consider several actors' processes which we can identify as different forms of restraint.

Restraint: responsibility and 'colouring' the part

For the cast of *Called to Account*, the presence of the DVD produced a particular kind of responsibility towards their subjects which was qualitatively different from that encountered by the actors in *Talking to Terrorists* but evidences similarities to Megan Dodds' concerns. Raad Rawi stated:

> Prior to rehearsals I studied the tape... As an actor it is essential that we remain pure to what is being said and not do any kind of elaborate reading, not try to colour it in any way... You are conditioned as an actor to make things colourful... People normally talk in a flat monotone which as an actor is the opposite of what you usually do. [Here] there is no need to demonstrate to the audience, whereas in a normal play you often make things seem larger than life. So you don't have that pressure, but you have the pressure of being true to the intent of what was behind that person saying what he does.

Rawi's comments provide a direct contrast to the experiences of some of the *Talking to Terrorists* cast. The changes demanded by Stafford-Clark to Hutchinson's and, notably, Russell's portrayals can be understood, to use Rawi's terminology, as requiring them to 'colour' and 'elaborate' on what they had observed; such was the aim of creating a 'scenic' or 'theatrical truth' for Stanislavski. In a play in which the audience was told they would 'meet' the individuals, Stafford-Clark evidently wanted interesting personalities to appear. However, this kind of restraint has some overlaps with Dodds' process, and particularly Rickman's emphasis on her avoiding being 'showy'. In *Called to Account*, it was the witnesses' legal and political contributions, not their personalities, that were critical. Thus, physical and emotional restraint, rather than elaboration, was emphasised.

It is evident that in the same way in which Rawi felt that the political narrative and associated emotional restraint precluded him applying a Stanislavskian approach to character, the presence of the DVD required further departures from the way in which he had previously worked. Throughout his interview, Rawi's emphasis was on the logic of, and intent behind, Al-Mufti's testimony. Thus, his preoccupation with Al-Mufti's cognitive processes was apropos of his political stance rather than the emotional and psychological root of his comments. Rawi recalled that this emphasis underscored his preparation: 'As much as we try and look like them and behave like them, that is only in order to be closer to who they are, in order to be closer to the purity of their message, closer to what is the kernel of what they are saying.' Visual and behavioural precision was thus subsumed, and only deemed helpful in so far as it supported his work on what Al-Mufti *said*, which strongly indicates the high stakes for the actor and the political significance of the subject matter.

Rawi's own ethics of representation in avoiding 'colouring' and 'elaborating' on the words was a preoccupation echoed throughout my interviews. For example, Clyde noted: 'You just have to be true to the video version. You try not to colour it too much, other than what this man has given you.' Similarly, Hardiman stated that 'you have to work on it in such a way that you don't comment on the character'. In a slightly blunter fashion, David Michaels stated that 'your responsibility is to give the right account of what he said...your job is not to decide whether he is a twat or defend him'. Therefore, although the DVD recording provided a tangible, concrete source that *Talking to Terrorists* lacked (and so spared the cast the ethical dilemmas inherent in Stafford-Clark's and Soans' modus operandi), the need for restraint and precision resulted in a quite different set of associated demands.

Restraint: precision and legality

Shane Rimmer and David Beames shared similar ethical concerns about playing their parts. Both noted that due to the political significance of the testimony included in the play (as Wheatley noted 'there was a certain amount of scoop in it: fresh material'), this responsibility was not limited to the actors' own ethical compass. Rather, the need for verbal precision had legal as well as artistic roots. Rimmer stated:

> You have to be very careful not to misrepresent them in any way. That feels quite confining in the first part... you can get into a hell of a lot of hot water if you do, and possibly face libel if they chose to pursue it. So you do have to work within certain confines.

The actors' accountability evidently had legal consequences. Any slip of the tongue, memory failure or verbal inaccuracy could result in court action. These were very real concerns, as in the run of any play, human error inevitably occurs. David Beames recalled that: 'Nick is very strict about the precision of the language. For example, he'd pick me up if I said "isn't" instead of "is not", because for legal reasons if you are reproducing something it has to be exact, so he is very hot on that.' The legal issues raised by Beames and Rimmer thus explain why ensuring precision and restraint regarding the testimony was such a preoccupation for the cast and director in this play.

Not all the actors, however, felt these high levels of accountability. James Woolley experienced the documentary script as a safeguard: 'You do feel responsible to him, but it is not huge because you are only quoting from the words he said, and they are not taken out of context...you are not being libellous or slanderous or anything else like that.' Woolley evidently did not feel the weight of responsibility experienced by the actors above due to the fact that the witnesses' responses were staged in the context of the questions they were asked. In *Called to Account*, as the interviewers (in this instance the lawyers) were inscribed in the play, all of the responses were in context. By contrast, in *Talking to Terrorists* and *My Name is Rachel Corrie*, this context was removed – the interviewer did not appear in *Talking to Terrorists*, and thus the audience did not have access to the questions to which the interviewees responded, and the context of Corrie's writing was re-imagined in Rickman's production.

Restraint: playing from the witness's point of view

Like Megan Dodds, one strategy by which the actors exercised restraint and attempted to limit 'colouring' their portrayals was by ensuring that they saw the play from the point of view of the individual they played. To this end, they employed various research methods. Kent's dissemination of material dictated a particular view of the play that was critical to the cast's processes. The actors playing witnesses only received their own interviews in advance of rehearsals. Although they were furnished with a CD, a DVD and both edited and full transcripts of their interview, they were not sent the full script of the play. When the play went into rehearsal, these actors were only called to rehearse their own cross-examinations. This continued even in performance: the interval marked a dressing room 'changing of the guard', as the actors for the second half arrived and the actors who had already performed left. As Oliver noted: 'In the performance the dressing room was so small that we had a shift system, so Raad Rawi was on first and we shared a spot, so we would just cross over.' To explore the way in which this functioned, it is informative to contrast the experiences of the actors playing the lawyers with those playing the witnesses.

Diane Fletcher noted that 'it's quite a lonely experience really because...although we're a team...you go in on your own, apart from the actors playing the lawyers'. Similarly, Ken Drury noted that 'You can feel quite detached during it, a bit lonely.' Of all the actors, it was Jeremy Clyde who most fully explored the way in which the limited dissemination of material and the resulting isolation functioned:

> You can only see really where your piece comes in late on...you are not aware of the shape of it. We can't get an overview, unless you are on stage

all the time as one of the lawyers. Maybe it is important we don't. It means you play it from the character's point of view ... as a witness it must be from their point of view.

Rather than attempt to identify the significance of his cross-examination in the wider context of the play, Clyde could only recreate the testimony he observed on the DVD as precisely as possible. He reported that without understanding the significance of their witnesses' testimony, previous casts had often worried about whether their interview was interesting:

> There has always been a moment in every single tribunal play where the cast have all looked at each other and said 'oh I'm not sure – is it going to work? How dull is this?' But every time it has worked, and it has worked because Nick and Richard can see the whole thing. Whereas we only see our little bits – they have the overview.

None of the witnesses are through-characters (in that none reappeared); rather each witness was seen once in the synoptic accumulation of evidence. It is intriguing to speculate as to whether restricting the actors' knowledge in this way may have been a strategy Kent employed to avoid the actors 'colouring' their portrayals, and further restrain their performances. This was certainly the product of the rehearsal process; as the actors were unaware of the significance of some of their witnesses' comments, the potential for them to see recurrent chimes and motifs, and so give extra weight to these moments, was reduced. Arguably, these actors are thus alienated from the grand-narrative by Kent, who has adapted a Brechtian device for his own purposes.

The way in which the actors playing witnesses were denied an overview of the play may also explain the absence of a Stanislavskian vocabulary in the actors' articulation of their processes. 'Perspective' was critical for Stanislavski, who dedicated a chapter to the concept in *An Actor's Work*:

> Only when an actor has thought about, analysed and lived the entire role and a broad, distant, clear, colourful, alluring perspective opens out before him can his acting, so to speak, take the long view and not the short view as previously. Then he can play not individual tasks, speak not individual phrases but whole thoughts and passages. (2008a: 458)

Through this perspective, Stanislavski continues, the actor can pick out 'the richest colours ... because of its [a particular moment's] significance in relation to the whole play'. As Rawi has stated, the restraint he exercised denied him the possibility to 'colour' the role. Kent's dissemination of the script thus precluded the actors from being able to 'play whole actions, and speak whole thoughts'.

In his interview in *Verbatim: Verbatim*, Kent argues that 'the actors can be quite possessive of their character', which he attributes partly to the timing of the plays: 'you're conscious that your character might be in the news tomorrow. That gives it an edge, and it means you must never betray your character' (Hammond and Steward 2009: 157). As Kent states, in *Called to Account*, any of the witnesses could find themselves in the headlines at any time, and so shift the focus of the play.[4] Kent thus found that the actors were adamant that their witness was given a fair hearing:

> I had big tussles with Diane Fletcher, who played Clare Short, because we had to cut the play down, and she felt that if I cut some of the evidence Clare gave, it diminished Clare's intelligence ... Now that's wonderful, because people are so engaged with their characters that they feel it's necessary to defend their characters' positions. (Hammond and Steward 2009: 157)

However, from analysing Clyde's comments, we can posit an alternative explanation for the actors' sense of ownership. It is evident that the lack of access to the overarching shape of the play was a critical contributing factor. Consequently, without an appreciation of how Norton-Taylor's re-edits functioned, the actors were justified in seeking to protect their witnesses' testimony. Kent's limited dissemination of material pre-rehearsal and his separate calls for actors during the play's preparation, despite being isolating, thus maintained the actors' focus on precision with regard to the details they had observed in the interview.

The experience of Thomas Wheatley and David Michaels, playing the lawyers, was quite different. Wheatley remembered that they were in rehearsal 'all day, every day' and, due to their early casting, were able to attend some of the interviews from which the play was constructed. As suggested by Wheatley's description of the shape of the play, the fact that they were onstage almost all the time meant that they had a clear understanding of the play's narrative arc. Wheatley stated: 'in my head I do have a theatrical shape ... it's one of the ways you make it bearable for the audience – you tell a story'. Similarly, Michaels (2009) noted:

> One shape was that some were mine – they were witnesses for the defence, and others were prosecution witnesses. Obviously my purpose with our

own witnesses was to bring out the comments you wanted your witness
to say. Leading your witness as they were leading their witness. [You] are
trying to lead a witness or trap them essentially.

The lawyers, in the words of James Woolley (who also played lawyers
in *Justifying War* and *The Colour of Justice*), were 'in all the time,
calling the shots and…running the show'. Thus, through their 'perspective', they had an appreciation of the play's shape as a whole and
so were able to 'tell a story', or in Stanislavskian terminology, create
a 'throughaction' (Stanislavski 2008a: 312). Michaels and Wheatley
thus 'led' the narrative, and provided a spine through the play. For
the other actors, though, their perspective was more limited, which
led to a focus on their witness's point of view. In my interviews there
were three main research strategies employed by the actors to work
on their understanding of their witness's attitudes. These were individual research, cast discussion and actor-subject meetings.

Individual research

Several actors talked at length about their witness's background, and
were passionate about the themes of the play and proud of the knowledge they had acquired. This, they found, gave them confidence in
their performance. Shane Rimmer's comments about Richard Perle
are particularly noteworthy. Perle is an eminent Republican politician. He was an Assistant Secretary for Defence during the second
Reagan administration (1987–89) and Chairman of the Defence
Policy Board Advisory Committee under the first Bush administration (2001–03). Rimmer, a Canadian actor based in the United
States, recalled that when he started working on the play, 'I didn't
know too much about him. I knew he was a hard-liner…He is called
"The Prince of Darkness".' However, his own private research, outside of rehearsal time, provided a fuller understanding of Perle's political stance:

> He had a mind like a steel trap. He is a brilliant man. Totally misguided,
> but brilliant…Perle doesn't suffer fools. I think the CIA had its fair share
> of them…I think they were 'yes men'. Pretty good organisers I suppose.
> And they were nasty. No matter how much the government was involved
> with Guantanamo Bay, they were the ones that were running it, and extra-
> ordinary rendition questioning. Although he was a neo-conservative, I
> don't think he was an extremist. Although he served with Dick Cheney, he
> didn't like Rumsfeld, who he thought was a bit of a brute – I think he called
> him a Nazi once, but not on tape.

Rimmer's experiences are noteworthy in light of the actors' focus on avoiding 'colouring' and 'commenting' on their portrayals. Although he calls Perle 'totally misguided' and in the same interview stated that 'I didn't have much sympathy for his political policies', Rimmer's description is notably sympathetic considering he clearly has very different political allegiances himself. Rimmer deflects the criticism that might be levelled at Perle to the CIA. Whether justifying Perle's testimony in this way helped Rimmer as it enabled him to feel positive about the man he played was not a question on which Rimmer would be drawn, and thus remains a matter of conjecture. In his research, Rimmer appears to have submerged his own political inclinations and judgement in order to give what he called 'a fair representation'.

It is evident from his description of Perle's political agenda that this knowledge gave Rimmer confidence that he understood his responses, which was important considering his earlier observations regarding the need to reproduce Perle's relaxed performance under cross-examination. Rimmer was not the only actor to note the self-assurance which resulted from research. Jeremy Clyde stated that 'you do a lot of reading and research that can't be brought to the stage, but it gives you confidence'. Similarly, Roland Oliver commented: 'when you have done all the work, you don't think about playing Mates, it is me talking about what I know'. This vocabulary is notably less emotional than that of Merlin and some of the actors in *Talking to Terrorists* who suggested they had an emotional connection with the individual they played. Rimmer, Clyde and Oliver do not suggest any connection of this kind, but rather that researching their roles gave them confidence.

Cast discussion and the politicised actor

Jeremy Clyde noted that it was when 'talking backstage' that the wider political issues were discussed. He elaborated on how central these discussions were to his experiences of both *Called to Account* and *Bloody Sunday*:

> You get twelve people in a very small space, and because we were all reading the papers and everybody is up to date with the issues and has done the research, some of the most interesting debates and discussions I've ever had took place backstage at the Tricycle. Enlightening conversations. Often talked about from a position of great knowledge, from the position of your character. So if you were playing a Northern Ireland priest [as in *Bloody Sunday*] you would have really researched that area. So someone

would ask you, 'what was the position of the church at this point?' It was fascinating. We were quite well informed. It wasn't 'luvvie' at all, but rather very pertinent and interesting discussions backstage. Really arguing out the politics was another great element of the process.

The cast was energised and politicised by the play, and much of the debate was based on the research they had conducted into their witnesses' political point of view. This investment in the play's themes is in part attributable to the topicality of both plays, performed contemporaneously with the legal cases they depicted, and the political significance of their themes. This level of politicisation is reminiscent of Brecht's actors, for whom a central part of the rehearsal process was discussion and debate:

> Without knowledge one can show nothing; how could one know what would be worth knowing? Unless the actor is satisfied to be a parrot or a monkey he must master our period's knowledge of human social life. (Willett 1964: 196)

Brecht claims that without learning more about 'human social life', the actor is restricted to being a mouthpiece for the director. In fact, without these discussions and research, the actor can only 'parrot', that is replicate, the original speaker. Like Clyde, Brecht saw accumulating this knowledge as a fundamentally collaborative act: 'The actor learns as the other actors are learning and develops his character as they are developing theirs. For the smallest social unit is not the single person but two people' (Willett 1964: 197).

However, again we see a divergence from Brecht's aims in this technique. For Brecht, learning about the social and historical specificities was associated with his 'historicisation' techniques which represented a move away from viewing behaviour as natural and eternal to seeing it rather as culturally specific and thus capable of change. In *Called to Account*, by contrast, the learning was associated with the actors' confidence that came from understanding their subjects' political allegiance and attitudes. Given that the play's political argument was designed to indict the Prime Minister, this confidence was crucial.

Meetings between actors and subjects

The third approach to establishing the point of view of the character was to meet them in person. In comparison to *Talking to Terrorists*, in which meetings were strongly encouraged, and all but two actors met at least one of the individuals they played in their preparation of the play, in *Called to Account* only three of the 12 actors discussed the project with their subject before the play opened. Again, the actors playing the lawyers had a slightly different experience. Due to their early casting, Thomas Wheatley and David Michaels observed some of the cross-examinations first-hand. Michaels stated:

> I went to see the interview with Michael Quinlan, so I was there ... without telling Julian [Knowles] that I was going to play him ... I said I'll operate the camera whilst I'm here, so I made sure I had a lot of footage of Julian on it. Otherwise it was always on the interviewee, so I pointed it at him to make sure I had everything I needed.

Michaels' main aim was thus to ensure that he had the same DVD material with which to work as the actors playing the witnesses, and so he used the cross-examination to observe and record rather than use it as an opportunity to meet Knowles and discuss the play with him. Like the actors playing witnesses, later in the interview Michaels stated that 'You lean on that tool the whole time really', suggesting just how important the DVD was to him. Wheatley said that he too 'operated the camera' and so was 'having a good old squinny at Philippe Sands'. However, as will be explored later in this chapter, Wheatley's first-hand observation led to a quite different experience.

　The three actors who discussed the play with their witnesses in specifically arranged meetings during rehearsals were Roland Oliver, Jeremy Clyde and Ken Drury. Their comments were remarkable in the unanimous lack of importance they placed on these meetings. In response to my question 'when you met him, were there certain things you were looking for?' Oliver replied, 'Well I already had the tape. I spent a lot of time with the tape trying to get him right.' Aside from enjoying meeting him, Oliver did not recall that the meeting with Mates had a significant impact on his work, but rather talked about the DVD in relation to his portrayal. When Jeremy Clyde met Edward Mortimer, as the men went to school with each other, they found themselves at cross-purposes: 'He wanted to talk about our school days. I wanted him to talk about Kofi Annan. I had a very different agenda – what it was like backstage at the UN.' Summarising his meeting with Michael Smith, and expressing a sentiment typical of the experiences in *Called to Account*, Ken Drury noted 'the elements of his character that I did use were straight from the DVD'. He went on: 'I'm not exactly sure what you take away from those meetings. Would my performance have been different had I not met him? I really couldn't answer that.' Indeed, referring to his experiences of previous tribunal plays, William Hoyland stated:

> It is a mistake to meet people before. You get a bit influenced by how they actually are, which doesn't help... You see you can't always trust the real people, because they are not always as self-aware as you think they would be.

Hoyland questions how sincere the person is being, and by doing so suggests that interviews and authenticity do not necessarily go hand in hand. Hoyland's scepticism stands in stark contrast to the *Talking to Terrorists* cast's experiences of their meetings with their subjects. This is no doubt due to the different purposes of the meetings in the processes. In *Talking to Terrorists*, material was generated from the meetings, whereas in Kent's production it existed already. In *Called to Account* the actors' task was rather different: to recreate the testimony that had been recorded. As Rawi stated, 'it was a very specific task: how he gave that testimonial'. Thus, understanding the political significance of the comments was more important than gaining a personal understanding of their subjects. In this light, Hoyland's concern about being 'influenced by how they actually are' can be seen as referring to the temptation to deviate from the delivery of the testimony on the DVD as a result of the actor's new attitude towards the individual created though meeting them. It is also useful to compare these responses to the sentiment articulated by Chipo Chung in *Talking to Terrorists*. With regard to not being able to meet the ex-member of the Ugandan National Resistance Army, she said: 'I was quite, not devastated by it, but quite disappointed.' In *Called to Account*, none of the actors expressed regret at not meeting their subjects in the play's preparation. As a result of the recordings, the meetings were evidently much less central to these actors' experiences than in Stafford-Clark's play.

Establishing the witness's point of view, which was necessitated by the way in which Kent limited the actors' access to the grand narrative of the play, was thus a form of restraint which further foregrounded precision in the actors' processes. As Kent and Norton-Taylor had invented the project, and so could film the cross-examinations, the DVD, despite being a by-product of this approach, came to be the most formative tool the actors had at their disposal.

Restraint in performance

The restraint exercised and imposed in rehearsal by the DVD was also foregrounded in performance. The production was rich with recognisable documentary theatre devices which both encouraged the audience's intellectual involvement and imposed further restraints on the actors' performances. In a style of design familiar from previous tribunal plays, Kent's set (designed by Polly Sullivan) was an evocation of the sort of room in which the original interviews might have taken place. As you can see from the image on the title page of this chapter, the stage was carpeted, with a line of windows obscured by thin office blinds along the back wall which were backlit to suggest daylight outside. Three tables, arranged in a horseshoe formation, were set centre stage, and at them were five chairs. Other set included small filing cabinets and tables. The set was dressed with the usual office paraphernalia, such as water jugs, files and folders.

The oral testimony of the witnesses was also supported by evidence on plasma television screens on both sides of the stage and around the auditorium. The screens constantly displayed the documents to which the actors referred. Their use was consistent with Brecht's comment that:

> The orthodox playwright's objection to the titles is that the dramatist ought to say everything that has to be said in the action, that the text must express everything within its own confines...Footnotes, and the habit of turning back to check a point, need to be introduced to play-writing too. (Willett 1964: 44)

The digitalisation of the documents contributed to the verisimilitude of the theatrical event, and further created a believable look and feel as they were reminiscent of the way in which information is provided for the jury in court. Other signifiers of authenticity included the video camera used to record the interviews, which was positioned stage left, and the conference call machine used to interview Ritter and Valdes, which was brought on by the respective actors. As Derbyshire and Hodson note, *Called to Account* was a 'forensic exercise in which punctilious mirroring of legal process serves to emphasise and implicitly decry the absence of actual legal proceedings' (2008: 201).

At both the beginning and end of the play, devices were deployed which encouraged the audience to invest in the illusion of a real inquiry. When the audience entered, the stage was set, with the lights up. As the play started, there was no lighting change; indeed, apart from the actors' entrance, there was no signal that the play was about to start. The actors chatted casually (this was improvised and not taken from interview) and prepared themselves for their cross-examination, taking out documents and stationery from their briefcases and reading over their notes. Similarly, at the end of the performance, there were none of the usual theatrical signifiers such as a blackout, curtain or bow. Chris Megson's comments about *Justifying War* suggest a very similar performative mode: 'the piece started as a couple of minor officials entered the room preparing for the arrival of Hutton and his team... At the end, there were no bows, no acknowledgment of the spectators, no invitation to applaud' (2005: 370).

Bows in theatre traditionally invite praise from the audience, giving both an opportunity to display their appreciation of the actors' skill and the cathartic release of seeing the actors out of role. By refusing the audience this opportunity, Kent maintained focus on the play's content. Of *Justifying War*, Megson stated that 'Theatricality itself was distinctly downplayed in the production' (2005: 370). However, we must exercise caution with this term 'theatricality'. Patrick Lonergan, writing about *Bloody Sunday*, rightly noted that 'the aesthetic at work here is that there are no aesthetics – the production's creators do all they can to maintain the illusion that we're not in a theatre. Which is of course highly theatrical' (2005: 30). Rather than 'downplayed' theatricality, we might note that the production employed a different kind of theatricality, designed to focus the audience's attention on the accumulation of witness testimony, and to encourage them to view the play as a jury would a trial. To this end, the blocking of the production further restrained the actors' performances. As can be seen in the image, the prosecution sat stage right, with Philippe Sands sitting downstage, and upstage of him, Alison MacDonald. Stage left, sitting directly opposite them, were Julian Knowles and Blinne Ni Ghralaigh, all at right angles to the audience. This meant that both Sands and Knowles looked upstage to ask questions, and that the witnesses sat upstage centre directly facing the audience. As the audience was denied full view of the lawyers, their focus was directed at the witnesses. This blocking also created two head-to-head relationships: the defence faced the prosecution and the witness faced the audience.

Satirising what he evidently identifies as a continuation of documentary theatre's penchant for aesthetic simplicity, in an article in the *Guardian*, playwright David Edgar quipped that the staging conventions in documentary theatre can be reduced to asking 'will it be stools or chairs?' (2008). Although in his polemic he overlooks productions such as *Black Watch* and *Fallujah*, neither of which saw a predominance of occasional furniture, in *Called to Account* the answer was quite definitely 'chairs'. With the exception of the rare moments when Sands stood to help a witness find the correct page, all 11 cross-examinations were conducted with the five participants seated. This was a feature which evidently affected the actors playing the witnesses rather than the lawyers. Roland Oliver noted that:

> It is restricting but also challenging to have so little movement...it does concentrate attention on the text, but also being on the spot as a witness is as daunting for the actor as it probably was for the witness. In rehearsal most of us confessed to feeling as if we were auditioning in front of a panel of severe professional judges.

William Hoyland expressed a similar sentiment when he said:

> You are sitting down all the time – your physicality is hugely restricted. One of the ways you normally get into a character is by thinking how they might walk and the way they might hold themselves, but here you sit and that is all. So it is a little bit more concentrated in a funny way than a normal acting part...it is a different type of acting in that respect...Sometimes you come off and you want to run round the block and shake yourself. You do feel very much imprisoned in the chair behind the desk.

Hoyland's comment that the lack of movement resulted in the performance being 'a little bit more concentrated' is noteworthy. Jeremy Clyde certainly experienced this: 'It is unusual to just do a part that requires you to sit behind a table on a chair...That staging forces it down to an absolute minimum.' Due to the fact that it replicated the pressure the witnesses were under during the interview, this was a feature that evidently specifically affected the actor under cross-examination: neither actor playing a lawyer noted comparable experiences.

In addition, despite the relatively small theatre space, in which the cast could very easily be heard with minimal projection, each actor wore a tie microphone in the cross-examinations and their responses were amplified around the auditorium. Despite being a barely noticeable element of the staging from the audience's point of view, it evidently had a sizeable impact on the actors' performances. Michaels noted: 'Because you are miked, you can't go into sudden theatricality', whilst Hoyland found it 'hard to perform in a theatre when you are being miked. It is very unusual.' Michaels' and Hoyland's observations suggest that the microphones precluded voice projection,

and encouraged a conversational vocal performance that was reminiscent of everyday speech. Clyde noted the benefit of the restraint
the microphones necessitated: 'You don't have to project because you
are miked…I don't like show-off acting. It has become terribly easy
to tear a passion to tatters, but I am not for that.' The microphones
served to enforce a particular discipline and restraint on the actors'
vocal expression. These actors' comments corroborate Kent's description of the primary function of the microphones:

> I've always worked with microphones…the microphones mean the
> actors don't even have to put on a louder voice in order to be heard. The
> hyper-naturalism of everything being very low-key means it is nearer to
> the truth, I suppose. (Hammond and Steward 2009: 156)

Kent's comment that it is 'nearer to the truth' is only true in as much
as by equipping the actors with microphones he relieved the cast of
the need to vocally adapt the interview to fit the bigger space. As they
were able to speak at a conversational pitch, they could more closely
replicate what they saw. Thus, the way in which Lloyd Hutchinson
had to adapt his 'unbelievably soft spoken' interviewee in *Talking to
Terrorists* was not necessary here.

We can thus appreciate that the elements of precision and restraint
were foregrounded in *Called to Account* by the cast's increased
access to the specifics of the original interview made possible by
the DVD recording. These elements prompted quite different challenges from those experienced in the plays examined earlier. In the
actors' working methods in rehearsal, and in the combination of the
static staging and the amplification of their voices in performance,
the cast found innovative and diverse strategies to work on their
roles whilst remaining focused on the political significance of their
subjects' testimony.

Gesture, physicality and appearance

The emergence of precision and restraint as crucial guiding concerns
in the actors' processes is thus clear. This was most prevalent with
regard to the verbal features they identified in the recordings. Given
the dense legal language, and the play's emphasis on the political significance of the testimony, this focus is of little surprise. However,
the DVD recording also allowed the actors to observe their witness's
physical appearance, bearing and gestural range.

Physical selection and adaptation

Terrence Hardiman's and Roland Oliver's experiences regarding gesture are noteworthy in relation to avoiding 'commenting' on the character. However, their experiences depart from the notions of precision we encountered in the actors' attitudes towards verbal features. As noted above, the DVD the actors received contained the full interview, which ranged from an hour to two hours in length. The final edited versions ran at between five and ten minutes. This meant that just as Norton-Taylor chose only certain testimony to include, these actors had to select gestures from the range they had observed. This challenge reveals a rather different attitude towards precision, and complicates our understanding of the term. Hardiman summarised the problem:

> The interview was just over an hour and the final précised version was about five minutes. So that in itself is a problem. The problem of editing. When you edit you select, and in that selection you have to watch out that you are not making a value judgement on the person.

Thus, rather than minutely copy every movement, Hardiman explained:

> I felt that I had to get the equivalent of that cumulative feeling into this very short version, and not over-lard it or lay on another attitude that was not there. I might as an actor think 'oh that would be good and dramatic to do' but it wouldn't fit. You had to avoid it.

Evidently, Hardiman was concerned to avoid expressing anything that was not already present, but which may have appealed to him as a performer. Despite this restraint, the problem with regard to 'commenting' on his witnesses persisted due to his freedom to select certain moments. Oliver also explained that attempting to recreate a specific gesture was unhelpful:

> One move that Mates did a lot was with his right hand. He would put it on his cheek and run it across his forehead and then down over his face, almost as though wiping his face. It looked entirely natural when he did it, and then I started to do it and it looked as though I had chosen a gesture as a way of making a point about him.

It is clear that some gestures did not look natural when included in the edited cross-examination, despite the fact they were copied from the recording. Oliver provided a further example of this issue when he said:

> Some of my friends felt rather miffed on Michael Mates' behalf – they thought I was sending him up a bit, which I can assure you wasn't the case. I mean if you look at the tape, he behaved, at certain points, like an over-grown school boy. He got excited about the camera rolling and pulled a face at it! None of which we did ... I'm playing some of it down. You don't want to look like you are doing a review sketch, even if they did in the interview.

Oliver clearly did not deem Mates' playful performance in the cross-examination helpful in the production, and so had to adapt what he had observed, and yet was still accused of 'sending him up'. In the static staging of *Called to Account*, every move by the actor was viewed as if in close-up. Consequently, in order not to 'colour' their portrayal or 'comment' on the character, the actors considered a straight replica-tion of gestures and behaviour unhelpful. Hardiman noted that 'It can be self-defeating – you try and use some of those idiosyncrasies and the audience say "why did he do that?"' Therefore, unlike the precision they sought in their vocal performances, for these two actors, the notion of 'precision' when working on their witness's physicality was based more on an economy of gesture, specifically designed to avoid 'commenting' on them, than on a detailed replication moment by moment.

This example also provides us with a quite different understanding of the term 'adaptation', which we encountered in Lloyd Hutchinson's approach in *Talking to Terrorists*. Hutchinson needed to make his subject theatrically viable and so adapted the man's quietness to work on stage. Here, however, Oliver had to scale his performance back to be viable within the tone of the production. 'Theatrical viability' thus not only refers to the practical demands of performance (such as being heard), but also to the particular performative mode of the production. Both, in their selective use of what they had observed, created Stanislavski's 'scenic' or 'theatrical truth' in their perform-ances. We tend to understand 'theatrical truth' as making something more entertaining, bigger and more colourful for the stage. However, Oliver's comments suggest that we can also acknowledge that it can constitute a reduction or restraint in order that it fit the particular 'truth' of the production.

Physical appearance

Called to Account was firmly rooted in the be-suited streets of Whitehall and the Inns of Court. With the rare exceptions of Scott

Ritter (blue checked shirt) and Clare Short (red pashmina), costume varied only in the particular shade of suit or colour of tie. Creating the physical appearance of the individual was thus associated with features such as hair colour and style and whether they wore glasses. The cast's comments in relation to these elements were divided. Like Megan Dodds in *My Name is Rachel Corrie*, several actors did not mention appearance at all: Woolley, Hardiman and Rimmer did not recall anything they deemed noteworthy, whilst Drury simply stated 'as far as the appearance is concerned there was nothing to be done about that'. By contrast, for other actors it was clear that creating a strong resemblance was an important component in their portrayal.

I have already noted that Kent cast actors of roughly the right age and ethnicity to play the roles. Rawi felt that the similarity was greater than this when he said, 'It was certainly necessary for the production for the people to look as like their real person as possible.' Similarly, Clyde stated that 'Nick is very good at casting close to the person.' However, we must balance these comments with Hardiman's afore-mentioned statement that 'I don't look like him', and, moreover, that he made no effort to do so. It should be remembered that, with the exception of Clare Short, these were not well-known individuals, rec-ognisable to the audience.

In *Playing for Real*, Roger Allam noted that even when playing an individual as iconic as Hitler, which obviously came with a very strong audience expectation, there were aspects of his appearance which were designed primarily to satisfy the actor:

> on stage you have to be convincing to the audience ... but I noticed that his eyebrows were set lower than mine so I waxed out the top of my brows, keeping the middle and drawing them in lower, and the effect was really quite unsettling. Getting the eyes right made a big difference to me though I don't know that anyone in the audience would have noticed. (Cantrell and Luckhurst 2010: 28)

This was also true of Hoyland's experience of creating a physical like-ness to the men he played: 'If I looked in the mirror before I went on and saw this be-suited and be-spectacled man with different hair looking back at me, it all helps.' Likewise, Rawi stated: 'I had a hair-cut and grew a moustache', and Michaels said: 'I had my hair cut and I dyed it', whilst Clyde found 'the right glasses and the right sweater. We copied what he was wearing.' These actors' comments are consist-ent with Woolley's experience that 'You have a look, you have the voice.' They do not describe attempting to recreate minutely their appearance, but rather they crafted 'a look' of the person, or what Rimmer called 'a reminder'. However, Roland Oliver went further than most to resemble Michael Mates:

> I wore the same colour tie, the same tie pin, same colour shirt, similar suit – although mine is Marks and Spencer's and his is probably Savile Row – and I made up my eyebrows to make them look bushier. But his eyebrows extend a bit across his face and I tried to draw mine to do the same and it didn't work. It may be good for the audience but it doesn't convince me. Whereas if I flicked them up a bit and made them darker, I thought, yes, I look more like him.

As in Allam's description of changing his eyebrows, Oliver also wanted to convince himself, not the audience, that he could create a similarity. Like the approach he took when he worked on Mates' gestures, Oliver evidently adapted what he saw so as to aid his portrayal rather than minutely copy Mates' appearance.

Synecdochic reminders of actuality: Thomas Wheatley

Thomas Wheatley placed by far the most emphasis on physical appearance in his portrayal of Philippe Sands. As he met Sands whilst observing the original cross-examinations, he was able to borrow some of Sands' own belongings: 'I'm using the pens he uses ... I'm wearing one of his own ties, which he has lent me.' The details Wheatley mentions are revealing. They fall under Joseph Roach's category 'accessories' in his book, *It* (2007). Roach's research investigates 'a certain quality, easy to perceive but hard to define, possessed by abnormally interesting people. Call it "it"' (2007: 1). He observes that the English synonyms for *It* are 'charm, charisma and presence' (2007: 7). For actors in documentary theatre, particularly those playing famous individuals (as we shall see in Diane Fletcher's portrayal of Clare Short), capturing their 'presence' is a critical facet of the performance. In relation to Wheatley's experience, Roach's comments on the use of accessories owned by the real person are particularly illuminating. He suggests that an accessory is an object 'that by extension discloses the emerging structures of synthetic experience itself' (2007: 51). It is through this extension that objects owned by the individual can act as a synecdoche for the individual more widely. As Roach notes, 'accessories make meanings under the ever-useful trope of synecdoche – the part stands in for the whole' (2007: 53). For example, Roach analyses the way in which King Charles II's funeral effigy, dressed with the King's own clothes, wig and sceptre, provided the public with a tangible 'living' link to the dead monarch. Wheatley's choice of items certainly appears to have had a talismanic effect on him. They were not of importance to the audience, who didn't need to know, for example, the colour of Sands' tie, and clearly wouldn't know that it actually belonged to him. Instead, these details were of use to Wheatley. They became synecdochic signifiers of authenticity for the actor rather than the audience, providing a tangible link between actor and individual. They allowed him to conjure a presence through Sands' actual possessions. This conjuring has a close association with David Freedberg's writings on *envoûtement* or voodoo in which the individual would dress up the image to be a likeness of their target (1989). Roach notes that it was believed that this 'increases the efficacy of its magic' (2007: 96). Although I'm not suggesting Wheatley employed the dark arts, the presence of Sands' own belongings clearly had a deeper resonance for him. They, he perceived, brought him closer to the man than merely looking like him would allow.

Playing celebrity

Diana Fletcher's experiences are analysed entirely separately because the fame of her subject resulted in her approach being qualitatively different from the other actors whom I interviewed. The experience of portraying Clare Short challenged not only Fletcher's approach to playing a role, but also made her consider the nature of acting and what it constitutes. Although *Talking to Terrorists* featured public figures such as Mo Mowlem and Terry Waite, it was Fletcher who most fully explored the impact of her subject's celebrity on her portrayal. She felt that Short's fame brought with it a profound pressure to capture her with great precision: '[It] terrified me. Some of the characters although you may have heard of them are not known. But everyone obviously knows Clare Short. So I thought if I don't pull this off...' Throughout my interview Fletcher repeatedly echoed this sentiment, describing the experience as one that variously 'frightened' and 'terrified' her, and saying that she had 'never been that nervous'.

Clare Short is a controversial figure. She was Secretary of State for International Development from 1997 until 2003, when she resigned from the Labour Party over the decision to invade Iraq. In an open resignation letter, she stated that she believed Tony Blair was 'engaged in a series of half-truths and deceits to get us to war in Iraq', a view which is now commonly shared (2006). However, to many, her resignation was undermined by her earlier decision not to resign.

Her eventual resignation seemed, therefore, anti-climactic and belated. Short's testimony under cross-examination was arguably the most incisive critique of Blair's leadership heard in the play.

Given the audience's expectations, Fletcher felt that Short's fame meant that 'you couldn't allow yourself interpretation': 'you couldn't invent. You mustn't invent.' Although, as we have seen, all the actors were concerned with precise renditions of their subject, the crucial difference in *Called to Account* is that it was only Fletcher's portrayal that the audience could judge in terms of how successful she had been. Their own memory of Short became a yard-stick by which to measure Fletcher's performance.

Fletcher sought the detail she required from the recording she was given. Her comment that 'you have a lot of work at home – I did a great deal of homework', was something of an understatement: 'I used to play it [the DVD] over and over again ... it was the timing I suppose that I was listening to. I would listen to it and then turn the sound off and then try to match the movement to the voice ... That was the battle.' Rather than using the recording, as others had done, to understand the way in which the individual framed their argument and phrased their answers, Fletcher used it to replicate exactly what she had seen, painstakingly synchronising Short's gestures with her voice and vice-versa. This was an incredibly precise physical and verbal replication in a way we have not previously encountered. Fletcher identified that this process reversed the way in which she usually worked: 'I had always thought of myself as an actor who works out the thought before the physical thing, but this was fascinating as I had to do it the other way round, I had to work out what she was thinking from the way she was moving.'

Fletcher thus attempted to establish explanations for Short's utterances from what she saw. It appears that Fletcher's usual way of working is very much influenced by Stanislavski's early work, in that she focuses on how the psychology and emotion of the character affects her physicality. However, as cited earlier in relation to Bella Merlin's research, Stanislavski also taught how the external can influence internal processes: 'An actor on the stage need only sense the smallest modicum of organic physical truth in his action or general state and instantly his emotions will respond to his inner faith in the genuineness of what his body is doing' (1961a: 150). As Benedetti states, 'physical states can produce mental states' (1998: 69). However, there were points at which this process of psychological justification broke down for Fletcher: 'Sometimes she said things ... where I hadn't a clue why she said it, or why she smiled at a certain time, so occasionally I would have to say, well this is what she did, without knowing why.'

It is clear that the text presented conundrums for which Fletcher felt unable to establish a clear rationale. She went on to give a specific example from the play:

> There was one particular bit where she mentioned Gordon Brown...and she slightly smirked, and I wonder why...perhaps because I don't think they were great pals at all, and she was laying the ground for 'he's just as bad as Blair', I don't know...and the audience can work it out in the same way I did.

When no explanation presented itself, Fletcher elected simply to recreate what she had seen without understanding why it was said. She argued that the audience was then in the same position as she was, trying to establish the motivation behind the comments. It is interesting that Fletcher did not decide on a reason in her own mind, and use it to give motivation to the line. This refusal of a Stanislavskian form of justification meant that she reproduced the original, externally copying what she observed. The DVD recording allowed this approach in a way that was not possible for the *Talking to Terrorists* cast and was clearly impossible for Megan Dodds in *My Name is Rachel Corrie*. By doing so, Fletcher limited colouring or commenting on the utterances. This element of her portrayal was echoed by Jeremy Clyde in his portrayal of Edward Mortimer: 'Yes, there was ambiguity, but then the man is a diplomat so he is used to ambiguity. You don't fill in the gaps. Absolutely not.' In contrast to the *Talking to Terrorists* cast, it appears that these actors more readily accepted the unknown and unknowable when playing a real person, and where some of the actors in Stafford-Clark's production sought a Stanislavskian form of psychological coherency, here the actors were happy to recreate the ambiguities they observed in the DVD recordings.

As Clare Short has a particularly distinctive voice, a large part of Fletcher's work with the DVD involved perfecting her vocal idiosyncrasies. She found capturing Short's accent challenging: 'Her accent shifts all over the place. Sometimes it is very Birmingham, sometimes it has a slight estuary speech, with glottal stops and things. So it confused me sometimes when I was watching it.' This preoccupation with the vocal elements of the performance was one shared by the rest of the cast, but Fletcher's perception of the audience's expectation meant that her approach put a much greater emphasis on a precise replication. This was particularly apparent when I asked whether she consciously adapted anything that she had seen in the recording:

> We did talk about this. Because that was a bit tricky. I did make some changes. She kept her eyes down, although for the theatricality of it I have to lift my head a bit, whereas she only looked at the person asking the question, or away and down.

Although the actor's gaze is critically important in theatre, the degree of adaptation from what Fletcher had observed was evidently minimal. Aside from these subtle changes to Short's eye-line, Fletcher's process was entirely predicated on copying exactly what she had seen.

A parallel concern alongside Fletcher's preoccupation with Short's vocal features was gaining a physical resemblance to her. A close physical similarity was arguably necessary given the audience's familiarity with Short. The production team went to greater lengths than with the other actors to achieve this, which included hiring a wig from the National Theatre: 'I wanted to be as close as possible. I couldn't have done it without the wig. That to me was crucial. Because she has got that very dark Celtic hair. And that's what you think about with her.' The costume was less critical in gaining a physical resemblance to Short. Fletcher described it as being 'just black with that red pashmina'. However, her similarity to Short was uncanny. Ken Drury agreed, commenting that 'she really did look like Clare Short'.

Despite her relentless emphasis on verbal and gestural precision, Fletcher came to reassess her initial reaction to the production: 'At first I thought this isn't acting, this is a different skill you are asking me to do. But then I realised it is of course, this is what we do, we watch people, and then we try to recreate.' Whilst it clearly was acting, and observation is indeed a critically important skill, the way in which actors utilise their observations is rarely done with such an acute emphasis on external detail and precision.

Fletcher found the discipline associated with keeping rigidly to the original interview required a 'feat of concentration' which she found 'exhausting – I think everybody did.' She also felt restricted by the lack of creative input: 'you couldn't allow yourself interpretation … It was like being a butterfly, you were just stuck there, and I always hoped the questions would spark off the answer.' This lack of creativity rendered her unable to develop the role in order to keep it fresh for each performance, sustaining herself creatively throughout the run: 'For me it is the creativity that I lacked in it … because it had to be the same every night, nothing alters.' The process clearly did not release

Fletcher creatively and for this reason she was relieved that the run was quite short: 'I wouldn't have liked to have gone on doing it longer than I did, because my ... acting instinct was taking over a bit ... I'd start to play up to it [the audience response] slightly.' It is interesting that Fletcher obviously felt that her 'instinct' as an actor was a hindrance in this style of performance. This appears to be associated with the degree of restraint she had to apply in performance, particularly with regard to the audience.

Fletcher's frustrations, however, did not temper the success of her portrayal, which was universally praised in the reviews. Comments included: 'Diane Fletcher who deftly catches the tone of ... Clare Short gives an illuminating impression' (de Jongh 2007), 'eerily accurate' (Shuttleworth 2007), 'blazingly accurate' (Clapp 2007), 'spookily accurate' (Brown 2007) and 'her hoarse voice and mannerisms are Short to a T' (Walker 2007). Even Clare Short herself was impressed:

> I could see what a good actress she was, I could see her holding her body or moving her arm in a way that I didn't know I did but when I saw her I realised I did ... She must have watched the video. I was very impressed ... I remember sitting there and knowing that was me, and yet I didn't know that I do those things. It was uncanny ... she felt like a little bit of me. (2008)

Playing such a well-known individual did not liberate Fletcher, however, but rather made profound and lasting demands on her performance, and evidently frustrated her desire for creativity.

Impersonation, imitation and mimicry

The *Called to Account* cast's focus on restraint and precision provokes much more fundamental questions regarding the terms 'impersonation', 'imitation', and 'mimicry' than either of the plays discussed in previous chapters. We have already encountered the term 'impersonation' in the section on Lloyd Hutchinson's approach in *Talking to Terrorists*. Hutchinson identified that although he initially impersonated in the hotseat, his work in rehearsals, due in part to the theatrical viability of the individuals he played and the changes that Stafford-Clark imposed, departed from this. However, he could only impersonate in so far as he could copy selected features that he remembered from his short meeting – which for some actors was conducted over a year before the play opened. By contrast, the cast of

Called to Account could, as evidenced by Diane Fletcher's process, minutely replicate their witnesses' responses in the cross-examinations thanks to the DVD recording.

This issue was given a great emphasis by the cast. In his opening comment in my interview, Hoyland stated that 'There are various, well not exactly rules, but conventions' in the tribunal plays, and 'The most important thing is that you don't imitate.' Similarly, Hardiman spoke of the 'specific challenges' these plays posed, of which 'the main problem was I didn't want to do an imitation of him'. Shane Rimmer also stated that 'Impersonation is not, I think, necessary here ... that was one thing I didn't make a stride towards at all.' In their rejection of these terms, many of the actors referenced performers who are skilled in this area, and from whom the actors differentiated their work. Roland Oliver cited Rory Bremner and Jon Culshaw, whilst David Michaels mentioned Mike Yarwood. Similarly, Ken Drury stated that:

> Most actors are not like Rory Bremner, so you are not going to be able to give an absolute copy of what he did, but the DVD gives you a clearer picture of what the person's behaviour and attitude is like ... It wasn't something I studied and tried to get every nuance, because that is not what we were trying to do really.

It is noteworthy that these actors associated the terms impersonation, imitation and mimicry with comic performers. Although Drury contends that it was his lack of particular skills that precluded him imitating, it is arguably more significant that Bremner, Yarwood and Culshaw all use their skills of replication to parody their subjects. Bremner is particularly associated with his impressions on programmes such as *Bremner, Bird and Fortune*, in which he satirises contemporary politicians to great comic effect. The slightest suggestion that by impersonating the individual the actor might be satirising them clearly dissuaded the cast from using the term.

It is also true that there is a snobbery regarding impersonation, it being viewed as a less noble art than acting. None of the actors in *Called to Account* turned to celebrated portrayals of real people, such as Helen Mirren as Elizabeth II in *The Queen* or Forest Whitaker as Idi Amin in *Last King of Scotland* (both of whom received Oscars for their performances), to offer an example of impersonation. Rather, it appears these terms are considered low-brow in comparison with these performances, which might further explain the actors' reticence in using them. Actor and comedian Jan Ravens – celebrated for her impressions on comedy series such as *Dead Ringers* and *The Big Impression* – has noted this negative distinction between acting and impersonating. In an interview with Derek Paget she stated:

> Michael Sheen or David Morrissey, Helen Mirren [are] all at great pains to say 'Of course, I'm not doing an impersonation!'... there seems to be a sort of an attitude where you don't want to be seen to be doing an impersonation. (Ravens 2008)

Ravens does, however, note the differences between her work as an impressionist (to which we can compare the kind of satirical work referenced by the actors in *Called to Account*) and her other acting work. She states that, due to the immediate topicality and thus quick turnaround on programmes such as *Dead Ringers*,

> You're not so much dealing with a character's inner life as the outer... what they're saying to the world... Because you are the caricaturist, the cartoonist, you are parodying the outer face that these people present to the world. But also, I try to capture... the 'comic spirit' or the 'comic truth'. (Ravens 2008)

In addition to the satiric connotations that Ravens notes, in rejecting these terms, the cast of *Called to Account* also returned to their aim of foregrounding the political significance of their subjects' testimony. Thomas Wheatley stated, 'it is very, very important the impersonation does not detract from what is being said'. Wheatley suggests that impersonation might be linked to indulgence. Rather, the actors had to exercise restraint in order to serve the political narrative. Similarly, Terrence Hardiman asserted that he avoided impersonation in order to privilege Bob Marshall-Andrew's political agenda:

> I don't look like him, I don't sound like him, but I've got to get the essence of what he was saying. That was the big problem to deal with – we all had the same problem... you need to get the audience to listen to the argument. Your other work can't get in the way of that.

This was echoed by Hoyland, who distinguished 'fairness' when portraying the individual from 'accuracy':

> You can't in any way traduce the character you are playing. There is a real responsibility to represent them fairly. I say fairly rather than accurately because again, you don't want to try and give an imitation because that doesn't work, but you want to represent them fairly and give them a fair hearing.

However, although the actors did not describe their approach in this way, they were still working, as Rimmer suggested, 'within certain confines'. This raises the problem of definitions. James Woolley summarised the issue when he said: 'I am not an impersonator as such, I would have a different approach to someone who does mimicking, that is a different take ... but I can't get into the science of where mimicking ends and acting starts.' As Woolley's comment suggests, the terms impersonation, imitation and mimicry do not refer to an agreed set of characteristics or techniques that can be easily distinguished from 'acting'. Woolley's comment was illustrated in the vocabulary David Beames used:

> One doesn't try and do an impersonation of them, but you try and be as much like them as you can ... I tried to sound as like him as I could ... It didn't happen every night, but I did try to copy him to the letter as much as I could.

These definitions are evidently blurred: Beames did not describe his approach using the terms above, but did attempt to 'copy him to the letter', which indicates that it may be more the connotations of the terms that the actors found to be negative rather than the processes involved with them.

This problem raises a critical point. It is clear that Beames and the other actors above struggled to find an appropriate terminology in which to describe their work. When a portrayal is based on precise observation and recreation, as it was here, it appears that these actors believed that the available vocabularies have been appropriated by other forms of performance. Due to their satiric and potentially low-brow connotations, the actors do not happily associate their work with these terms.

Growth and development: 'printing' a portrayal

The DVD recording also raised a new challenge in performance. Closely aligned with the focus on precision, the issue of growth in performance arose repeatedly in my interviews. Although any live event has a freshness and spontaneity, many of the actors felt, like Fletcher, that the run did not evolve in the way they had experienced in fictional plays. David Beames commented that:

> It does change slightly because you are relaxing into it a bit, but because it has to be as true a representation as you can, it can't grow. It is one thing

that Nick comes down on you for: 'The gestures are getting too free and easy' – he tells you to go back to the tape again and do it how it was at the beginning. So in that way it can't grow really.

The recording evidently functioned as a touchstone to which some of the actors returned to ensure precision. William Hoyland also identified Kent's presence during the run as a factor in the play's growth, although he did accept that the performances developed:

You think you've got it right and then two weeks in you realise that you have got better in some funny intangible way. But of course Nick is a great help and gives you notes throughout the run. He might come about two weeks in and say you're getting sloppy in this bit.

Similarly, Jeremy Clyde also noted that Kent was keen to maintain precision with regard to the recording: 'It has been known for Nick to come round after and give someone, myself included, a rocket for spinning it out too much, for enjoying yourself too much.' We have seen in the previous chapter that Alan Rickman, or another member of the creative team, would sit in the audience at most performances, as part of the range of systems put in place to protect Megan Dodds. However, Kent's presence seems to be for a rather different reason. It appears that he monitors the performances to ensure that the actors do not begin to indulge their performances and colour the interviews.

James Woolley called upon vocabularies he associated with his screen work to describe the way in which the limitations on growth affected his performance:

It is more like a 'take' in a film. You have to print exactly the same one each time. In other plays, things develop and change, but in documentary theatre it is more like printing something – it has to be the same each time.

Woolley, unlike Fletcher, did not see this as restricting. He said that 'it is rather satisfying. It becomes a challenge – can I print this the same each night?' These comments on growth and development in performance were not found in the experiences of the *Talking to Terrorists* cast or in Megan Dodds' experience. They were a direct result of the particular working methods and the presence of the recording.

'No acting required'

In *Verbatim: Verbatim*, Kent discussed the performance style in his tribunal plays and made a series of observations regarding actors' approaches:

> For actors it is not like being in an ordinary play. They know they're taking part in something that is to some extent 'history' so they come with such a commitment to the truth and the project that the minute anyone sees anyone else acting, everyone knows – so no one acts; it is like an unwritten pledge that in no way will anyone do anything for effect. So the atmosphere is very restrained. (Hammond and Steward 2009: 155–6)

Kent's comments are initially perplexing, as he turns 'acting' into a negative concept that has to be avoided. Elsewhere in the same interview he states: 'With a tribunal play, if you do anything for dramatic effect it's wrong, you know it's wrong' (2009: 155). It was evident from the actors' recollections that Kent's negative vocabulary in relation to acting was prevalent throughout. Clyde remembered that 'the note to everybody, and Nick always gives it to the newcomers, is "no acting required"'. Similarly, Michaels recalled: 'If you added too much, Nick would say "you don't have to do that. It is not a play".' As with the term 'theatricality', we must be careful to note that this refers to particular dramatic effects, particularly those that were liable to shift the focus from the accumulation of evidence onto individual portrayals. It seems that when Kent sought precise and detailed performances, the short-hand or colloquial language he used to articulate his aims could easily appear to obscure his appreciation of the actors' craft. Once again, this may well be a further manifestation of the suspicion over terms such as 'impersonation', 'imitation' and 'mimicry', and that Kent, like the actors, found that few helpful vocabularies were available. It is obvious that despite the cast's emphasis on precision and restraint, their processes were no less 'acting' than those for an invented part, and yet clearly everyone involved found it difficult to find a vocabulary adequate to describe this.

A similar difficulty regarding vocabularies is evident with regard to the ways in which the actors balanced their role as creative agents in the performance with the need to maintain the audience's focus on the legal thrust and gradual build up of evidence. Michaels stated that:

> One reason that some actors can lose faith with it – I don't mean in our production – is when they try to theatricalise it a bit, without realising that

the strength of it is in the words. An audience will sit and listen. The words explode like little bombs without having to do anything theatrical ... they are waiting to hear the tiny little nuggets that are buried deep in people's speeches.

Michaels refers to the relationship established at the beginning of the play when Knowles informs the audience that they will 'hear' the evidence. As explored earlier in this chapter, the lawyers invited the audience to use the evidence to answer certain questions so as to come to their own conclusions. Whilst Michaels may be right that the audience 'will sit and listen' (indeed these devices directly primed them to do so), I would question how helpful the notion that 'the strength of it is in the words' is for our understanding of these actors' processes. Most would agree that the strength of any dramatic literature lies in the words, and yet the actor still has the primary creative role in giving them life. Rather, Michaels' statement that the actor doesn't have 'to do anything theatrical' again relates to acting 'for dramatic effect', rather than decrying any creative steps the actor might take. Similarly, Clyde commented that 'from an actor's perspective, you can afford to be boring as it has been edited so carefully that whatever you have left to say is going to be quite interesting'. Having analysed the processes involved, we can understand Clyde's comment as relating to the precision the actors pursued in their portrayals, rather than setting out to give a lack-lustre performance. Both the actors and the director are searching for vocabularies to explain the way in which the narrative was foregrounded over individual performances. However, Michaels' comment about the power of the words rather than his own performance, and Kent's negative vocabulary about acting, effectively makes them complicit in obscuring the actors' creativity and skill.

Perhaps more helpful are Clyde's comments in which, like James Woolley, he uses a vocabulary associated with his screen work to illuminate his experiences in *Called to Account*: 'As far as the acting tips were concerned, it was less is more ... you can still do film acting, which is a wonderful thing. I love it.' Clyde acknowledges the benefits of restraint and precision in the production and the effect they had on his performance. These experiences further explain Kent's comments such as 'no acting required'. Rather than dismissing the actors' craft, the emphasis is on scale – which we can also identify in Rickman's instruction to Dodds to avoid being 'showy'. Woolley made a comparable observation when he stated 'There is a lot of emphasis on the subtleties of your answers I think.' Neither Clyde nor Woolley underestimated their creative enterprises; rather, both suggested that the scale of their portrayal was akin to that of a close-up on camera.

CONCLUSION

It is evident from the testimony of the actors in *Called to Account* that the production led to experiences qualitatively different from those encountered by the cast of *Talking to Terrorists* and Megan Dodds in *My Name is Rachel Corrie*. The actors' articulation of their work expands and enriches the range of experience analysed in the previous two chapters, and new terms have emerged which help us understand how actors approach these kinds of roles. Although I have avoided homogenising the actors' processes, and a wide variety of approaches have been analysed, the vocabularies the actors used to describe their preparation and performance in *Called to Account* are more unified, concrete, and less emotional than those in Stafford-Clark or Rickman's production. This appears to be a result of the actors' constant emphasis on the political implications of their witnesses' testimony and the tangible resource the recording provided, which meant that their approaches were based on verbal precision, not on attempting to understand their subject on a personal level. Witnesses were seen in their professional role, not their private surroundings, and thus the testimony was composed of political contributions, rather than of the more personal narratives in Robin Soans' and Rickman and Viner's plays. As a consequence, the actors' processes were predicated not on intangible, ethereal emotions, but on political allegiances, logic and verbal bravado.

Political implications

Although the first three case-studies here were all political projects, the explicitly interventionist nature of *Called to Account* meant that the actors were almost exclusively concerned with the political agendas of their subjects. Given this concern, the cast frequently used a vocabulary with strong Brechtian resonances. The actors' aim was to perform the testimony they had observed so as to foreground the political implications of their subjects' words. In fact, we can see the way in which Kent adapted Brecht's methods for his own purposes: he denied the actors access to the grand narrative of the play which ensured that they focused only on their own role. Although this montage approach is a recognisable Brechtian trope, the way in which it was achieved here was Kent's own post-Brechtian reformulation. While Brecht is helpful at certain points, the actors did not in fact adopt a wholly Brechtian approach to their roles. For example, although the way in which the cast became stimulated by the politics of the play has strong overtones of the way in which Brecht politicised his actors, in *Called to Account* this was designed to increase knowledge and confidence rather than assert the actors' own role as agents of political change. Similarly, we have seen that the actors playing the lawyers directly appealed to the audience and, as in Brecht's theatre, provoked the spectators to stay politically and critically attentive to the political arguments. However, the foregrounding of the DVD in the cast's processes encouraged them to perform their roles as accurately and believably as possible, and thus the actors did not actively aim to interrupt the audiences' identification with the characters.

The DVD recording

It is clear from the actors' testimonies that the DVD recordings were the most formative element in their preparations. Considering just how important the recordings were to their processes, it is noteworthy that prior to this study they have been entirely overlooked. The presence of the DVD gave the actors unprecedented access to the original specifics of their subject's testimony and resulted in an emphasis on restraint and precision. From analysing the actors' experiences, we can be quite specific with regard to the meaning of these terms. The practical consideration of precisely reproducing spoken testimony was evidently a central concern for these actors, unlike for those in *Talking to Terrorists* or *My Name is Rachel Corrie*. In *Called to Account*, the actors found the political intricacies of the text difficult to comprehend and learn, and were constantly aware of the legal requirements to stay close to what they had heard.

The DVD recording provoked further challenges for the actors with regard to physicality and gesture. Here, the critical concern was to avoid 'colouring' their portrayals. To this end, the emphasis on restraint took precedence over precision, as the actors adapted the physical actions of the characters to further foreground their testimonies. In *Talking to Terrorists*, the actors were concerned with making their characters interesting, and so, in accordance with Stanislavski's writings on 'theatrical truth', they adapted what they observed to be more dynamic on stage. Here, by contrast, the actors actively removed the more exuberant moments they observed on the DVD in order to privilege the political agendas of their subjects. The analysis of the actors' work with the DVD illuminates what Kent means by 'no acting required'. Prior to this study, the only comments about performance in the tribunal plays came from Kent and Norton-Taylor. We can now see that Kent's comment refers not to an absence of rehearsal and performance skills, but to the minimalist realism which he promoted in his plays.

In contrast to *Talking to Terrorists*, the actors did not deem meetings with the individuals to be important. As they were working from the DVD recordings, and recreating how a particular testimony was spoken, some actors were openly sceptical about meeting their subjects. The cast of *Talking to Terrorists* used their meetings with the interviewees to learn more about them. As the cast of *Called to Account* were equipped with the recorded testimony, such meetings presented a danger for them, threatening to undermine their dedication to precision and restraint by moving their performance away from the original specifics of the recording.

A further development we have seen in this chapter is the impact of a subject's fame upon an actor's working methods. Diane Fletcher's initial reaction that the production demanded a 'different skill' and that it was 'not acting' suggests the extent to which her experiences of playing Clare Short departed from the way in which she had worked in the past. Her perception of the audience's expectation of her portrayal clearly resulted in a forensically detailed reproduction of what she had observed in the recording. Her decision to imitate moment by moment rather than establish motivations for Short's comments represents a rejection of Stanislavski's teaching, and evidently posed new challenges for Fletcher. However, as with many of her fellow cast members (and arguably British-trained actors generally), there were no other vocabularies to hand for Fletcher to articulate these processes. Although Brecht has emerged as being (at least in part) helpful here, in comparison with Stanislavski his techniques and vocabulary are less familiar to British actors. It appears that Fletcher's initial reaction that it was 'not acting' could be described more accurately as 'not Stanislavskian acting' – and it was this which placed the exigencies of Fletcher's process outside her past experiences or training.

It is clear that, for many of the cast, the 'confines' that Shane Rimmer spoke of with regard to working with the DVD contributed to the departure from using Stanislavski's teaching. In comparison with *Talking to Terrorists* and *My Name is Rachel Corrie*, the foregrounding of the DVD in the actors' processes meant that there was less capacity for invention and interpretation. However, despite the DVD allowing a much closer replication of the original testimony than was available to the others, it is noteworthy that the cast of *Called to Account* were reticent to use terms such as 'mimicry', 'impersonation' and 'imitation'. From analysing their processes, it has become clear that the actors were using the kind of skills these terms refer to, and so we (and the actors) need to divorce those terms from the negative connotations they carry in order to be able to fully explore exactly what they mean. It is critical that these terms are reclaimed if we are to fully understand and articulate the complex nature of these actors' work.

The Girlfriend Experience. Lu Corfield and Alex Lowe (photo by Tristram Kenton)

4

The Girlfriend Experience

INTRODUCTION

Alecky Blythe's play, *The Girlfriend Experience*, directed by Joe Hill-Gibbins, was produced by Blythe's company, Recorded Delivery, and premiered at the Royal Court Theatre on 18 September 2008. The play focuses on four women working as prostitutes in a brothel in Bournemouth over a 14-month period. Set exclusively in the communal/sitting room of the brothel (referred to as a 'parlour' in the play), Blythe recorded the women's conversations in between their 'appointments'. The play also features a string of heard but only half-seen men visiting the brothel. The particular performance methods employed by Blythe are quite unlike anything encountered in the previous case-studies. In both rehearsal and performance, the actors wore headphones through which Blythe's edited version of the original interview material was played. The actors did not rehearse with a written script; indeed, there was no written script until the play was published to coincide with the run. Instead of traditional line-learning, the actors simultaneously listened to the recording in performance and repeated the testimony as precisely as possible, which preserved the characters' vocal tics, repetition, pauses and illogicalities.

An actor's usual task is interpreting a role and bringing it to life on stage. As the use of headphones requires the actors to repeat the audio they hear, the process provokes performance questions of a different nature from any of the previous case-studies. Christopher Innes, in one of the very few studies to refer to Blythe, states that the process allows actors only 'a modicum of interpretation' (2007: 436). Innes assumes that the use of headphones severely limits the actors' capacity for interpretive interventions. However, the picture is more complicated than this and evidence from the actors in *The Girlfriend Experience* does not support his contention. This case-study focuses on how actors worked creatively within such unusual and prescriptive performance conditions.

The development of the Recorded Delivery approach

Despite now finding herself best known as a documentary theatre-maker, like all the writers of these plays, Blythe's background was not in playwriting. Rather, she was an actor who came across documentary theatre by chance:

> The way I came to it was as an actor looking for work. I was doing some workshops at the Actors Centre, and one of the workshops I did was run by a director called Mark Wing-Davey...I did his workshop not through any worthier reason than I was trying to get an agent – I didn't know what verbatim was, it wasn't called a verbatim workshop it was called 'Drama Without Paper'.

This workshop was to have a far-reaching impact. Roslyn Oades, the Australian documentary theatre-maker mentioned in this book's introduction, also attended Wing-Davey's workshop, and has used the headphone technique to great effect in her own productions.

As I explored in the introduction, the use of headphones in documentary theatre was developed by the American actor, writer and academic Anna Deavere Smith. Mark Wing-Davey, who ran the workshop that Blythe and Oades attended, directed and developed Smith's 1997 solo play, *House Arrest: A Search for American Character In and Around the White House*. Smith interviewed individuals and edited their testimony on audio files, and rehearsed using headphones through which the interview was played. In performance she worked without the audio, relying on her memory of the recording to recreate speech patterns, accent and emphasis. In a modification of Smith's technique, Mark Wing-Davey experimented with keeping the headphones on in performance in his workshop at the Actors Centre.[1]

The actor and the role: Recorded Delivery's productions

The Girlfriend Experience was Alecky Blythe's eighth play with her company. As Blythe recalls, she developed her first production, *Come Out Eli* (2003), at the Actors Centre before its premiere at the Arcola Theatre, following her involvement in Mark Wing-Davey's workshop. The play was based on interviews surrounding Britain's longest siege, over 16 days in Hackney, North London. The final play featured testimony from 41 individuals, who were all played by a cast of five, including Blythe. Blythe was herself portrayed by fellow actor Miranda Hart. Blythe has noted her interesting approach to casting the production:

> I made a point of casting against type. I played a 70-year-old West Indian grandma, and Don Gilet who is a black actor played a 60-year-old white man, and the reason for that was that it actually made their words more powerful – you wouldn't expect those words to come out of me, and so it just made sense to play away from type. It made the technique even more extraordinary.

Casting against type is also a feature of Roslyn Oades' headphone productions. Paul Brown writes that: 'By preserving the voiceprint and mismatching the voice with a speaker of a different gender, age or racial background, she offers her audience the opportunity to hear community-based stories from an alternative perspective' (2010: 84). Blythe's interest in multi-rolling continued in her next productions. These included *Strawberry Fields* (2005), which explored the employment of migrant workers on a large strawberry farm in Herefordshire, and the resulting tensions within the community; and *All the Right People Come Here*, which was based on her own adventures as a spectator at the Wimbledon Tennis championships, and included Blythe playing herself as the interviewer. Later in 2005, Blythe created and directed *I Only Came Here for Six Months* in Brussels. Following an invitation by the British Council, Blythe interviewed British and local people living in Brussels about issues regarding identity and integration. In 2007, Blythe worked with director Matthew Dunster at the National Theatre Studio, producing *A Man in a Box*. The play followed Colin, an autograph hunter, and used the backdrop of illusionist David Blaine's stunt in which he lived in a Perspex box suspended over the River Thames for 44 days in 2003.

In her next two plays, *Cruising* and *The Girlfriend Experience*, Blythe shifted her focus from creating narratives generated from the breadth of testimony to look in more detail at fewer individuals: 'there are two types of play I've done: community plays and plays that are more like the typical drama about an individual.' For example, her play *Cruising* (Bush Theatre, 2006), explored the love lives of the over-50s; only 11 characters appeared, and Miranda Hart only played one character (Maureen, the protagonist). In *The Girlfriend Experience*, Blythe cast the play much more closely to type than in previous productions:

> I realised to do that [cast against type] with characters you followed all the way through the piece may be not so successful, and so I cast to type. It became less about the technique and more about the story. So with *The Girlfriend Experience* I tried to cast women who were the same age and size.

In this way, Blythe stated that, at the time of my interview, '*The Girlfriend Experience* is the furthest removed of all my plays from the formula established by *Come Out Eli*.' *The Girlfriend Experience* saw the multi-character narrative 'formula' to which she alludes, which foregrounded the process by emphasising the discrepancy between the actors and their roles, replaced with through-characters played by actors who were cast for their similarity (in terms of age, physical appearance and ethnicity) to the character, rather than their distance from them.

However, Blythe has not suggested that her work has followed a linear progression of form or style:

> The way I am working at the moment is very different from the way I started, but that doesn't mean I won't go back to it. Because everyone goes on a bit of a journey... the subject matter will always dictate what the production values will be.

This statement was certainly true, as in her play, *Do We Look Like Refugees?!* (Edinburgh Fringe, 2010), Blythe returned to her multi-character narrative approach. A cast of five Georgian actors played dozens of characters. Again, the Recorded Delivery headphone approach was used, but in a departure from her previous productions, the actors frequently spoke in their native tongue, with the text translated on subtitles. This was followed by the immensely successful *London Road* (National Theatre, 2011). This project marked a further development of her technique. Blythe worked with the composer

Adam Cork, who, using interviews Blythe had conducted following the arrest of Steve Wright for the Ipswich murders, composed an entire musical based on the speech cadences caught on the audio.

The Girlfriend Experience

The Girlfriend Experience was first produced as a 'Rough Cut' which opened on 3 July 2008 and ran for three performances at the Royal Court Theatre Upstairs. The fully-staged production opened in the same space on 18 September 2008, where it played for three weeks before a two-week run at the Drum Theatre, Plymouth. The production was remounted with the same cast for another three weeks in July 2009 at the Young Vic Theatre.

Recording processes

An attraction of interviewing the women in the brothel was that Blythe could 'escape the confines of retrospective story-telling and include action that takes place in the present' (Hammond and Steward 2009: 92). This is a useful distinction. All of the previous case-studies were predicated on the interviewees' memory of past events (even if these were very recent events for Rachel Corrie). By contrast, in *The Girlfriend Experience*, the women frequently react to events as they happen. However, the testimony and events are, of course, not unaffected by Blythe's presence – quite the reverse, there are moments of open suspicion in the play. Cast member Beatie Edney stated: 'I think that they were rather suspicious of what she [Blythe] was doing.' Given the nature of the women's occupation, Blythe's presence had a significant impact on the material she recorded. Interestingly, though, in a move which is totally different from any of the previous productions, Blythe stated that 'When I'm unable to be at the parlour myself, the girls have agreed to record themselves in my absence' (Hammond and Steward 2009: 93). Questions abound from Blythe's decision to allow this recording. To what extent did the subjects craft and manipulate material? What are the ethics of using this testimony? This means that the status and credibility of the testimony is much more problematic to ascertain.

There are further sensitive ethical questions raised by Blythe's working methods on *The Girlfriend Experience*. As we have seen, all the women working as prostitutes agreed to be interviewed, and their names were changed in the production. In addition, one of the women, Suzie, was invited into rehearsals and on one occasion the cast were invited into the brothel during the rehearsal period, where they met Tessa, Suzie and Poppy, three of the women working there. All the women thus knew the purpose of the recording. By contrast, the male clientele did not know that they were being recorded, and thus did not give their permission, and yet their testimony appeared in the production. Blythe recorded their conversations with the women covertly, capturing their words in the hallway of the brothel from inside the sitting room. Alex Lowe stated: 'When I think about the risks Alecky took – one arm outside the living room trying to record it. You can imagine it could have turned nasty if anyone had seen she was recording.' Using the recordings of the men without their permission is concerning. All of the people who appeared in *Talking to Terrorists* and *Called to Account* knew the purpose of the interview, and Rachel Corrie's parents had given Rickman and Viner permission to use their daughter's writing. Blythe makes no reference to the use of the men's words in her introduction to the printed text of the play (which also functioned as the programme). It is not clear how Blythe and the Royal Court negotiated the legalities of including material that had been recorded without the subjects' knowledge or consent.

In addition to the lack of consent regarding their testimony, the men are a source of ridicule and derision in the play. They are known by the women's nicknames such as Dick-brain, Groper, Viagra Man and God's Gift. Whilst this may provide anonymity, their nicknames indicate Blythe's agenda, which was clearly to evoke sympathy for the women and to deprivilege the men, depicting them as pathetic caricatures. Michael Billington commented that he 'wish[ed] Blythe could have told us more about the clients who remain shadowy figures' (2008). The women's testimony was thus given a totally different status from that of the men, who were prejudged from the beginning. This ethical dilemma is further complicated by Joe Hill-Gibbins, the director, who suggested that the lack of consent was an attraction for the audience: 'There is a voyeuristic thrill of listening to those men who don't know they're being recorded.' The legitimacy of this voyeurism must be questioned, as must the fact that anyone who does not know that they are being recorded behaves differently from those who do. The women are therefore cast as privileged performers and the men are used as fodder in the play.

Editing processes

Blythe recorded all her visits to the brothel and edited and constructed the play from these recordings. Over the course of 14 months, she amassed many hours of testimony. Rather than transcribe the material, she edited the audio file using computer software, so the play did not exist in written form before the play opened.

The cast received an audio copy of the edited recording about a week before rehearsals commenced, though Blythe continued to re-edit throughout rehearsals, during which *The Girlfriend Experience* was transformed from a two-act play with an interval to one act with no break. The scope of the editing process was increased by the fact that the actors did not have to learn lines, as cast member Alex Lowe stated: 'Thank God it was on audio, if they were cutting a text each night, it would be impossible.' However, this process was evidently still difficult, as Beatie Edney recalled:

> It really changed. Loads of cuts. We were in tears, it was rather dramatic. But we didn't have an excuse because we didn't need to learn any lines, so they could just cut scenes. It was difficult ... I remember telling them 'you are shuffling it in my head'. This was the day before we opened.

Central to Alecky Blythe's approach is the belief that an individual's speech reveals their character. Blythe saw this in Anna Deavere Smith's work: 'Crucially, her work demonstrated that language is the root of character' (Hammond and Steward 2009: 80). As we have seen, the working processes on *Talking to Terrorists* placed the final testimony spoken by the actors at several removes from the original speakers' words, and *My Name is Rachel Corrie* was never designed as spoken testimony. In comparison to *The Girlfriend Experience*, the testimony in *Called to Account* was notably free of verbal tics, overlaps and idiosyncrasies. Presumably, this was because those interviewed in Kent's play were experienced public speakers. Although the content was repeatedly re-edited and re-ordered by Blythe, she chose to include these features. The material is so full of circumlocutions, hesitations, and half completed phrases, that some sections of the script are rendered almost unreadable. Consider, for example, the following extract from a speech by Tessa:

> This is a business – where – i-it *is* a business where iss (*Beat.*) – ah-I *want* a give the best I *can* (*Beat.*) – and make people *happy.* (*Beat.*) I was so fed up – wiiith (*Beat.*) – being told what to do and how to do it (*Beat.*) – w-workin' for someone *else* ... (Blythe 2008b: 12)

Indeed, such was the atypical relationship between the play and the published script, that actor Debbie Chazen remembers 'we saw the published version once we had opened, and we all had a look at it and thought "Oh, is that what she said?!"' Chazen's comment reinforces the fact that the written transcription cannot render the exact sounds and emphases caught on the audio versions.

Although the vocal features may have been preserved, a series of ethical questions are raised by the relationship between the editing process and the action in the play. This is particularly apparent in comic moments. Chazen noted that 'You have to do their comic timing. Fortunately [Tessa] is funny without always knowing it. There is a lot you can do physically – a raised eyebrow at the end of a sentence.' Chazen's comments prompt several concerns; firstly, the comic moments she heard on the audio were edited by Blythe, and may not have been the intention of the original speaker. For example, near the beginning of the play, Blythe and Hill-Gibbins manufactured a comic moment by removing it from its original context. On Tessa's line, 'I *love* the nineteen-thirties, I *love* Art Deco, I'm *very* old-fashioned, I'm I'm sorry I am / I'm not modern' (Blythe 2008b: 8), Tessa was folding a pair of large black leather knickers. I asked Debbie Chazen about this moment:

> That was invented... There were a lot of bits like that. But we tried to make sure it was as true life as we could. In some cases it was funnier just to be real. You didn't have to invent much. I mean that line is funny anyway. We just enhanced it.

This throws into question the claims to validity with regard to the audio testimony given that its meaning could be altered by the actions of the characters. Chazen's comment that a raised eyebrow could provide comedy also suggests that the actors could comment on their characters to the audience, and thereby cast a judgement on their subjects.

Chazen's statement also provokes questions from another point of view. At the beginning of the play, Tessa and Suzie discuss a light fitting that Tessa bought in Wilkinson's. The moment was received with a great deal of laughter. Alex Lowe voiced his concerns:

> Alecky recorded these women and they don't have particularly nice lives, and we're all here in Sloane Square, with media London types thinking 'isn't this hilarious'. I know all this is voyeuristic in a way, but occasionally I think 'why do you find that so funny?' it is tragic and I think 'oh god what are we doing?' It is like the line 'where did you get that lamp?' and she says 'Wilkinson's' and Wilkinson's is a cheap DIY store, and that gets a huge

laugh and I think, 'what, is that funny just because she can't afford to go to a posher place?'

Although Lowe directs his unease at the audience, this moment was clearly included by Blythe for comic effect. Reviewer Michael Billington experienced a similar anxiety about the audience's response: 'I was struck by the sadness of the milieu depicted, unlike the rest of the audience who seemed to find the notion of an old man with prostate trouble needing sexual assistance hilarious' (2008). Lowe clearly had ethical concerns about the way in which the play satirised aspects of the women's lives, and the voyeurism inherent within it. The comedy in the play was thus not always generated by the subjects themselves, but by the editing processes.

Staging Blythe's 'point of view'

The mode of delivery in *The Girlfriend Experience* cast the audience as Blythe, in much the same way that *Called to Account* cast the audience as the jury. The actors often spoke directly to the audience on lines such as:

> TESSA (*to audience*). If anybody asks, you're the lady who does the
> phones, okay?
> SUZIE. Jus' say – jus' say you're the maid. (Blythe 2008b: 7)

Debbie Chazen stated that:

> The first scene is like the introduction. It was Suzie introducing the audience – who is Alecky – to Tessa. So at the beginning I was a bit more shy and a bit more reticent. But then the audience and Alecky become a friend, just someone who is there in the parlour.

We must problematise Chazen's comment. Although in performance Chazen may have viewed the audience in this way, her comment that Blythe became 'a friend, just someone who is there in the parlour' is a romanticised view – she was a theatre-maker with a recording device.

The way in which the unwitting men appeared in the play also foregrounds Blythe's point of view. Like her, the audience was denied full view of the male clientele. They appeared stage right along a semi-boarded corridor (seen in the background of the photograph at the beginning of this chapter). As Alex Lowe recalled:

> I never go into the main body of the stage. I always appear in this corridor.
> It is deliberately obscured from some of the audience, just to get the feeling

of what Alecky could see. She couldn't quite see these guys, she certainly couldn't go and have a good gawp, so she would only catch glimpses of these guys passing.

Thus, the way in which Blythe constructed her material served as a self-reflective reminder of the process. Her presence was constantly foregrounded, in contrast to the way in which Norton-Taylor and Soans strived for absence.

Casting and rehearsals

The Rough Cut, in July 2008, featured three actors, as only one scene was presented. Debbie Chazen played Tessa, the owner of the par-lour, Beatie Edney played Suzie who worked there, and Jason Barnett played the men who visited the brothel. In the full production at the Royal Court, Edney and Chazen reprised their roles, and were joined by Esther Coles playing Amber and Lu Corfield, who played Poppy.[2] The men were all played by Alex Lowe. All cast members were expe-rienced comic performers. They rehearsed for four weeks at the Royal Court's rehearsal rooms in Sloane Square.

The decision to cast actors who were physically similar to their roles was driven by the nature of the women's profession, as the play is punctuated by phone calls in which they are physically described:

> SUZIE: He-*llo*? (*Pause.*)...we have Tessa – she's thirty-nine – five foot six, she has long dark hair brown eyes – very busty, thirty-eight double-F curvy dress size- fourteen-very lovely lady...– we also have Suzie – she's thirty-seven, five foot two auburn hair blue eyes – very busty forty double-D – and curvy dress size eighteen to twenty... (Blythe 2008b: 13)

Evidently, this brought the issue of casting to the fore, as any departure from these descriptions would be repeatedly emphasised throughout the play. The physicality of the women was also foregrounded by the costumes the actors wore. For most of the play, the cast wore lingerie and revealing clothing. Of her casting decisions, Blythe explained:

> I just felt we couldn't do this with skinny little size eights. It just wouldn't have worked. When I met these women I thought how brilliant to get women like this on the stage. The material just seemed to suggest how to bring it to life.

Blythe and Hill-Gibbins thus cast actors who were similar in size and age to the women described in the phone calls. These casting choices clearly reduced the distance between the actor and the role that had characterised Blythe's early plays.

'An alienating effect': *The Girlfriend Experience* in performance

The director, Joe Hill-Gibbins, developed a number of techniques in the staging of *The Girlfriend Experience* to remind the audience of the source of the testimony. He told me:

> If you are in *Come Out Eli*, and you are playing a Jamaican grandma, and you are a young white male, it is clear by casting against type that these are real people's words...so it has an alienating effect. [In *The Girlfriend Experience*] how do you create the alienation? We used to have these in-ear headphones, and one rehearsal the lighting designer came in and he couldn't see whether they were wearing them. I thought that that could ruin the whole thing. You have to have the alienation...If you make it clear that they are actors and this is a recreation, it becomes more real in sense because you become aware of the process and that there were real people out there saying these words. So we put the sound desk on stage, they declared the technique by putting the headphones on onstage. With the set...we had it completely crudely done, with the bare wood. Absolutely saying to the audience this is not the real thing, but it is a recreation of a real thing.

Hill-Gibbins' comments are interesting as he provides a reflective account of his decisions and recognises the tensions in this process. However, there are a number of assumptions in his statement which deserve scrutiny. The main point of confusion is over alienation and its relation to truth. Alienation techniques highlight distance and the materiality of production. As Hill-Gibbins rightly notes, they draw attention to the process; however, they do not inherently make the process more real. His assertion that 'it is clear by casting against type that these are real people's words' is spurious: it may be intended to alert the audience to the fact that the speaker on stage is not the original speaker, but it does not logically follow that they were spoken by real people rather than fictional characters. It is clear, however, that Hill-Gibbins felt that reminding the audience about the artifice of the theatrical event was absolutely integral to the success of the production.

His choices with regard to the *mise-en-scène* saw the mechanics of the theatrical event brought into full view of the audience. Blythe notes that they wanted 'To remind the audience that this is a performance. They are not the prostitutes. You are in a theatre. So we avoided a naturalistic set.' The walls of the set were half-finished, with the wooden trusses and supports visible to the audience, evocative of a rehearsal room mock-up.

In addition, the audience entered the auditorium through the set, past the props table and costume rails. Downstage left was the lighting desk and downstage right was the sound desk, from which the headsets were operated. Similarly, though Blythe has noted that advances in technology 'helped to disguise the practicalities of the recorded delivery technique' (Hammond and Steward 2009: 99), in *The Girlfriend Experience*, Blythe and Hill-Gibbins decided on conspicuous headphones. Blythe stated:

> Compared to previous shows when I haven't been as obvious about pointing out the technology and spelling out the ear phones – you see now you can have tiny inner ear pieces – Joe and I felt that if we had the opportunity to tell the audience, how we could tell them that these are actors taking on these parts and the words are being fed to them.

This was made absolutely clear for the audience at the beginning of the play. Chazen and Edney entered, out of role, with the headphones in their hands. They put on the headsets and indicated to the sound desk that they were ready. The play opened with an audio prologue in which the audience heard Blythe telling the women about the process:

> I kindof make (*Beat.*) – um (*Beat.*) – they're sortof documentary plays. (*Pause.*) But – I don't –*film* anything (*Beat.*) – I just re*cord* – hours and hours of-of – audio ... (Blythe 2008b: 5)

As the women on the audio replied to Blythe's introduction, the actors repeated their words, so that the audience heard both the actual women and the actors' voices. As the play began, the auditorium speakers faded down. The last line heard from the actual subjects was 'It is all getting very real now!', until only the actors' voices could be heard. The decision to stage the moment at which the actors stepped into the role very clearly created an alienating effect. It was designed explicitly to demonstrate to the audience that the actors were repeating the words they were hearing via headphones. However, Hill-Gibbins' and Blythe's contention that wearing headphones is a constant reminder of the real subjects is problematic. This is not proven: alienation cannot be a constant – of necessity alienation amounts to a set of devices which interrupt audience identification. The constant wearing of headphones simply becomes a convention, and in fact, after a time, the spectator accepts it as the norm. There is no evidence that they functioned in the Brechtian manner that Hill-Gibbins describes, as they did not interrupt the audience's identification with the action or the actors' portrayals. In fact, almost all reviewers felt that the headphones were unnecessary. Alice Jones' review in the *Independent* is typical:

> I'm not convinced by this device – audiences have seen enough verbatim theatre to understand the concept, and the actors could just learn the lines, which they appear to have done. In any case, the excellent cast deliver the warmest and most engaging of performances. (2008)

Most reviewers expressed both their suspicion about the efficacy of the headphones and their admiration of the actors' technical acting skills. Karen Fricker observed:

> It's not clear...what is gained by having the actors listen to headsets and repeat back the recorded voices of their subjects as they perform...Given the strength of material and performers, having the actors wear headsets feels like a gimmick, particularly since their delivery is so polished it's hard to believe they haven't memorized the lines. (2008)

For this critic, the headphones evidently had the reverse effect of that intended by Blythe and Hill-Gibbins. Similarly, Nicholas de Jongh wrote of the 'pedantic over-emphasis on what is pretentiously termed "The Recorded Delivery Writing and Performance technique"...None of the four fine actresses needs such stimulus' (2008), and Caroline McGinn noted 'Its integrity doesn't stem from the headphones' (2008). It is evident that whilst reviewers were impressed by the actors, they had profound misgivings about the device, and did not equate the headphones as a piece of machinery with any great 'authenticity' in the production.

The question prompted by the critics is whether the headphones bring anything new to the audience experience. From the audience point of view, there is nothing to suggest they bring a radically new meaning to the performance of documentary material. This is due, in part, to the fact that as the audience could not hear the audio, they could not judge the precision, or indeed be sure that the actors were hearing any voice at all. If anything, the spectator questions what the relationship might be between the actor and the headphones, and does not assume that this relationship is unproblematic or straightforward. However, most importantly for this study, the actors found that the headphone approach set new challenges and enabled new processes in their approach to the play. Cast member Esther Coles expressed frustration that the critics praised their 'truthfulness' and 'engaging' performances at the same time as rejecting the headphone approach. For her the two were not mutually exclusive, but rather were utterly reliant on each other – the strong performances were attributable to the headphone approach:

> I think it is essential we have the headphones. It means no matter what happens, it stays the same. Without the headphones it would change and end up not being at all the same. You wouldn't speak over each other, you'd wait, you'd fall into your own intonations, you'd start doing it your own way. There have been criticisms about the headphones from the press, but I think that is because of the lack of understanding about the technique.

As we shall see, Coles' comments are not straightforward, as the delivery of the testimony did not necessarily 'stay the same'. It is clear, however, that the actors found that the headphone approach was critical in creating their much-praised portrayals.

ACTING PROCESSES

The practical challenges of the Recorded Delivery process

I interviewed the cast of *The Girlfriend Experience* between 10 October 2008 and 16 January 2009.[3] Despite the fact that three of the actors met the women they played, by far the most formative element of the production for all the actors was the use of the headphones. I will first explore the practical challenges of the process before analysing how the actors developed their roles by working with the headphones in rehearsal.

All the actors wore headphones in both ears, through which the audio was wirelessly received. Each actor heard all the audio recording, not just his/her own parts. The cast were instructed to turn the volume on their headphones to maximum, to avoid them being able to hear the other actor, the audience, or indeed themselves. This is quite unlike any of the performance practices seen in the previous case-studies and, unsurprisingly, led to particular difficulties. Debbie Chazen noted that:

> When we were all on stage, I couldn't hear the others, as I didn't want to. I wanted to be able to concentrate on my audio. That is what you are supposed to do. That is the way the technique works – you turn it up so high that you can't hear the others. So I had to concentrate on lips to ensure that I didn't answer a question before it was asked ... The whole of the first week

was spent listening to the audio, and trying to sort out whose voice was whose, and what it was they were saying ... It took literally a whole week of really intensive listening to sort those strands out.

Practically establishing what was said and by whom was thus a time-consuming element of the rehearsal process. Once the issue of actually establishing the words of the subject had been overcome, the actors were faced with further problems in rehearsal. Unable to hear their own voices, the actors often struggled to find an appropriate volume. Beatie Edney stated:

One technical thing with the headsets which was difficult is that I have a very loud voice, I don't need to project really, it just rings out. Joe kept telling me to be quieter. My main difficulty was trusting that I could be heard. That was really hard with the headphones.

Esther Coles found the opposite: 'Joe kept telling me to be louder, as I always had the headphones on full through the rehearsal, I couldn't actually hear how loud I was.' Timing was similarly problematic. The actors repeated the words very shortly after hearing them. Naturally, this delay varied from actor to actor, as Lowe pointed out:

The thing I find most difficult is when you get way behind the other actor, because everyone works at different speeds. I was on with one of the other actors the other night, and we ended up about ten seconds behind. I thought come on! Hurry up!

The technique of speaking the words moments after hearing them was called 'trailing' by the actors in Stuart Young and Hilary Halba's play *Hush: A Documentary Play on Family Violence*, which they produced in New Zealand. Like Blythe's actors, the three performers wore headphones. However, when I spoke to them about the process, a significant difference became apparent. The actors in *Hush* spoke in time with the voice they heard, not trailing it. Thus, they learnt the piece completely, and used the tape to gain the pitch of the voice. Cindy Diver, one of the actors, spoke of 'breathing alongside her subject' (Diver 2010). Questions abound from this process, which, as the actors speak simultaneously, is not based on listening in performance to the same degree as Blythe's work.

A further complication for the cast of *The Girlfriend Experience* in relation to timing was the comedic nature of much of the material. Edney stated: '[The audience] can't interrupt the action by laughing, we just plough on! For Debbie and I who are both comedians that is bloody hard...I used to lose my laughs left, right and centre.' The audio, to some extent, denied the cast the opportunity to vary their delivery so as to prompt or ride the laughter. However, Lowe noted that once the actors became familiar with the material, a degree of adaptation took place:

> If I'm entirely honest there is a little bit of that that goes on...I play the old guy who can't hear them very well, and he has this great line 'I like the feel of your paddles on my bare arse'. Now right over the line there's a dog bark, but I wait until after so the audience can hear the line. So you can time it a bit. I've noticed the others do it, although they probably say they don't. But really you can't pause for the laughter. You can't ride it.

Lowe's admission is fascinating in that his clandestine tone suggests that although the actors bent the rules, they wanted to preserve a party-line about their use of the headphones. It is evident that the actors' timing did alter in performance, but as they could not pause the recordings, the extent to which they could do this was limited.

The concentration needed to master using the headphones became clear when Lowe stated:

> It is quite a hard technique because you have one ear on what you're hearing...one ear on the other person, so you can make sure you don't answer a question before it is asked – that's a fear, and another ear on whether you are being too loud, and one on your own diction and enunciation. So there are four things going on, and I've only got two ears.

We can thus more fully start to understand how the approach functioned, and the way in which, when trying to master the process, the actors' minds were entirely focused on the task in hand. A critical result of this demand was that as listening to the headphones was so engrossing, the actors were faced with a quite different set of concerns from those in productions without headphones. Edney stated:

> You are just listening, which is basically what you want as an actor. If it is working, what you want to be is in the moment and listening. And that is what this makes you do...you are not policing yourself all the time about what you are doing. You haven't got someone on your shoulder saying you don't sound like her, you missed that, etc. You don't come outside of yourself.

The exigencies prompted by the headphones thus altered Edney's stage awareness. As she was so preoccupied with listening, she had less ability to 'police' herself. This can be seen as an extreme form of alienation, in which the actors are alienated from themselves, which goes well beyond Brecht's writings on the subject. It is evident from Edney's comment that this was a very positive aspect of the process. She noted that 'not policing yourself' had two particular outcomes in performance: the lack of both nerves and self-consciousness. Nerves were a notable feature in the previous case-studies. Here, however, none of the actors recalled feeling nervous. Edney stated: 'The great thing about the technique is that you don't get nerves...I think it is to do with not having to remember lines. You are just listening...It forces it upon you, and so you are not nervous, it is extraordinary.' With reference to the lingerie that the women wore, Edney continued:

> It takes all your self-consciousness away. We were four middle-aged women, and my god what we were wearing – I got away lightly. There was no self-consciousness. Because the brain is only engaged in the voice you are hearing.

It appears that the headphones created an alienation from self and functioned as a mental 'fourth wall' for Edney. Although she frequently spoke to the audience (and so broke the fourth wall in the traditional sense), the headphones and the associated concentration appeared to remove her from a direct relationship with the audience. Her attention to the audio and the freedom from having to remember lines evidently reassured her.

In contrast to the critics' suspicions, and despite a familiarity with the script, Edney maintained that she did not learn the audio: 'I once went on stage without my headphones, and it was late on in the run and I couldn't do it. It shows that you need the audio. We are not just pretending to listen. It proved it to me.' As the critics noted, in the run of the play it is hard to believe that the actors didn't learn their lines (albeit through constant repetition rather than conscious endeavour), but this is a very interesting aspect of Blythe's process. Chazen was clear that 'You don't learn it, because you just can't as the performance is such that your brain doesn't work in that way, but at the beginning because I didn't know what was coming next, it really was fresh and spontaneous.' This may account for her further comment that 'It is quite an amazing thing to feel on stage, so free and saying whatever came out of your mouth and not thinking several lines ahead.' However, it is clear from her statements that although Chazen didn't learn the audio, familiarity with it changed her portrayal throughout the run. These comments appear to contradict the earlier statements about the complexity of the process. This is further problematised by Blythe's observation:

> I find towards the end of a four-week run, the actors weren't as good to my mind as they were at the beginning. They knew it too well, so they could play little moments. They were also talking in time with the text or ahead of the text, they stopped listening. The more they know the more they can talk with it, but if you keep behind it there are always little details. They stop working a bit and become a bit self-conscious.

Blythe's comments are in contrast to her statement that 'Because the listening takes so much concentration, part of your brain is already busy, so there is less room for actor's thoughts – going "oh they liked that line I think I'll push that one a bit more"'. It is evident that, through the repetition, the challenge associated with the audio testimony eased throughout the run. The actors' comments about complexity are thus perhaps attributable to the early stages of the performance, when the process was an extremely difficult technical skill to master. It was only at this point that the actors experienced what I have called 'alienation from self'. As Blythe suggests, as the actors became proficient in these new skills, they were able to develop and inflect their performances.

Like in the previous case-studies, it appears that the rhetoric surrounding the working processes on the production was designed to support and further Blythe's claims of authenticity. Her headphone approach is predicated on the actors' complete concentration on the minutiae of the utterances they hear. As she has stated:

> [In documentary productions without the headphones,] once actors have memorised their lines, they stop listening to how they were actually spoken in the first place, and this is when they start deviating from the original intonation and embellishing it. I have continued to work with earphones precisely to prevent this from happening. I do not deny that actors are highly skilled at interpreting their lines, but the way the real person said them will always be more interesting. (Hammond and Steward 2009: 81)

However, my interviews have demonstrated that this is not the way all the actors functioned in performance. The contrasting statements from the actors and from Blythe herself suggest that through repetition, the actors relied less on the headphones and developed their roles. As in *Talking to Terrorists* and *My Name is Rachel Corrie*, the actors' assumption appears to be that this development ran counter to claims of authenticity, and the actors feared that this undermined the validity of Blythe's approach. However, questioning the veracity of the headphones should not overshadow the fact that their use was entirely new to the actors and prompted particular challenges in their processes.

Rehearsal processes: 'outside-in' and Stanislavski's Method of Physical Action

The order of my investigations here reflects the structure of the rehearsal period. Hill-Gibbins stated:

> [The actors'] first job was to sound like the audio...the discipline is to replicate that perfectly...So what you are doing at the beginning is very technical...Then we work out the psychological and emotional lives which sit beneath that. But all that comes later.

Once the actors had mastered the initial technical demands outlined in the previous section, they were able to develop their portrayals. Hill-Gibbins stated that he used Stanislavski's later teaching to do this:

> Normally I would start in a Stanislavskian way, so one of the first things you are thinking about is intentions and dramatic action. What does Character A want from Character B, and what tactics are they using to get what they want. You think about their psychology, and you use that as one of the central guides to thinking about the way they speak and move. It is different in *The Girlfriend Experience* because you start with the voice. You work outside-in rather than inside-out. A lot of Stanislavski teaching is based on early- to mid-Stanislavski which is inside-out, and this is very different, it is outside-in, which he looked at later.

Again, Hill-Gibbins' cogent articulation of the influences on his work with the actors in the play is helpful. The specificity with which he identifies a particular period of Stanislavski's teaching provides an interesting frame of reference.

The Method of Physical Action

Hill-Gibbins' comments about Stanislavski's 'later work', which was 'outside-in', refer specifically to the Method of Physical Action. Frustrated with misunderstandings and misapplications of his system,

in the last three years of his life (1935–38), Stanislavski worked
with 11 hand-picked directors and actors at his new theatre, the
Opera-Dramatic Studio in Moscow. Stanislavski's frustrations were,
in part, a result of Soviet censorship of his work, as Sharon Carnicke
has outlined:

> By 1934, when Socialist Realism became the only lawful artistic style, gov-
> ernmental control turned into a stranglehold...By focusing on his early
> career and wilfully ignoring his experimental interests, the press of the
> 1930s turned Stanislavski into a model for theatrical Socialist Realism.
> (2010: 5)

However, Stanislavski turned this 'stranglehold' into a strength in his
late work. He was subject to Stalin's policy of 'isolation and preser-
vation', which put Stanislavski into 'internal exile' (Carnicke 2010:
6). According to Carnicke, 'He left his home only for brief visits to
doctors...Ironically, Stanislavski conducted his most non-naturalistic
work during these last years' (2010: 6). Thus, his state of house-arrest
meant, paradoxically, that he was free to develop his theories, which
his small group of practitioners recorded through copious notes.[4]
Stanislavski called this work 'the new secret, the new aspect of my
technique' (2010: 68). Jean Benedetti has gone as far as to suggest that
'The work of the Opera-Dramatic Studio is Stanislavski's true testament' (1998: xii).

The critical development of Stanislavski's theory was with regard
to the centrality of physical action within the given circumstances of
the play.[5] As Hill-Gibbins noted above, in his early and mid-career
writings, Stanislavski saw physical action as emerging from work on
emotion and psychology: 'In the classical model of MXAT [Moscow
Art Theatre] rehearsal, physical action came last. It was the bait with
which to "lure" the required feelings' (Benedetti 1982: 68). In the
Method of Physical Action, by contrast, rehearsals started with establishing the character's actions:

> if you are logically consistent in your reasoning and actions, if you bear
> in mind all the situations in the role...You will feel much that is close to
> the role...and some of the character's experiences will come alive in you.
> (Benedetti 1982: 60)

Stanislavski thus came to identify that rather than being the product
of psychological states, simple physical tasks could actually prompt
inner feeling in the actor, which Hill-Gibbins called the 'outside-in'

approach. Stanislavski also used this term: 'You probably know from your own experience the link between physical action and the inner causes, impulses, efforts it causes. This is from the outside in' (2010: 79). In his translation of the notes of one of Stanislavski's assistants from this period, Benedetti writes that 'Physical action is the foundation on which the entire emotional, mental and philosophical superstructure of the ultimate performance is built' (1998: xv). He goes on: 'By finding out what happens and deciding what I would do physically in any situation, and believing in the truth of my actions, I release my creative energies and my natural emotional responses organically' (1998: 4).

It is thus clear why Hill-Gibbins used Stanislavski's late teaching in his direction of *The Girlfriend Experience*. The exigencies of the Recorded Delivery technique necessitated the director and actors working backwards from the voice and physical actions, as Hill-Gibbins noted:

> *The Girlfriend Experience* taught me a lot about acting. Because you have a structure already in place, it is much more like directing music or dance. With a normal play you have lines of text and some stage directions, so there is the question of how you say the lines and there's also the question of staging. But in *The Girlfriend Experience* the structure is all there ... Where I earn my money a bit more is then working out the psychological and emotional elements which sit underneath that.

Like many other interviewees in this study, Hill-Gibbins stated that he had not worked in this way before: 'it was new to start with the body and the voice and go outside-in'. Although he asserts that the 'structure is all there', in identifying the 'actions' in the play, we shall see that this is not in fact true of the way in which he worked on the production.

Sources of 'actions' in *The Girlfriend Experience*

It is informative to establish what constituted 'actions' in *The Girlfriend Experience*. From Hill-Gibbins' and the actors' experiences, it is clear that they existed in three forms. Firstly, they were present on the audio. Hill-Gibbins noted the amount of physical action that could be heard on the recording:

> Not only on the tape do you have the verbal, musical structure of what they say, and exactly how they say it, you also have the physical structure as well ... There is so much of the physical life of it that is contained there. You can hear when they move, and you can hear what they are doing. You

can hear when they are eating something, or using a hair dryer or brushing their teeth or sitting down.

It is surprising that these moments still existed on the audio given the extent of Blythe's editing and re-ordering. This element of physical action was also supplemented by Blythe herself, who had witnessed most of the events caught on the audio, as Hill-Gibbins also noted: 'not only do you have that, you have Alecky Blythe, who tells us she sat there and did this or that, because she has quite a vivid memory of it'. However, we must also remember the actors' accounts in the earlier section, where they noted that actions not present on the audio were added. This implies that where the cast and director deemed the actions appropriate they were included, and if not, others were invented.

Secondly, the action was the voice itself, captured on the audio recordings and played through the headsets. With regard to voice in the Method of Physical Action, Sonia Moore, one of Stanislavski's actors, stated: 'The physical action is the "bait" for an emotion. It is, however, important to understand that Stanislavski also considered the spoken word a physical action' (1965: 92). Similarly, Toporkov writes of the text as 'verbal action' (1979: 91). Finally, physical actions were developed by the actors through Hill-Gibbins' improvisations, which will be explored below. As we shall see, the actors used a combination of these three sources of 'action' in their preparation for the play.

Voice – physicality – psychology

A remarkable feature of the actors' articulation of their processes in *The Girlfriend Experience* was their emphasis on using the voice to work on both physicality and, finally, psychology. This section will explore this journey for the different actors. The lack of information about his subjects made this a particularly interesting process for Alex Lowe.

Lowe played all the men who visited the brothel. Aside from the recording and a small amount of information from the women, there was no other material to assist him. His only resources from which to develop physicalities for his roles were thus the voice and his imagination:

> There is this guy, Dick-brain, towards the end, and he has a voice with a
> very open back to the throat, so I felt that would make him stand with his

head jutted forward to lengthen the neck. So you get the open back of the throat on the line 'I'm all keyed up to go.'

In my interview, Lowe vocally recreated the line he quotes above. He was very clear that to recreate the tone of voice on the audio he needed his larynx low in his throat and the pharynx open and stretched. In order to do this, Lowe adapted his stance. An integral aspect of his process was thus experimenting with his own posture and body shape to reproduce the sounds of the voice he heard. However, he then developed this further by exploring what this physicality might reveal about the individual's psychology: 'These physicalities come from the content of the audio. They suggest a sort of insistence, leading with the head. He is not entirely comfortable about being there.' This was a product of Lowe's imagination, developed from how he felt when he held his body in a particular way, and his own projection of unease onto the subject. Lowe was aware that this was based on little more than his imaginative response to the voice he heard: 'I don't know whether he really was like that, but his voice suggested that to me.' The way in which a particular physicality suggested a mental state to Lowe echoes the approach that Stanislavski endorsed in the Method of Physical Action: 'As the actor discovers and follows...his line of physical actions, involuntarily and, possibly, unnoticed by himself, he finds the features of his outer characteristics' (Toporkov 1979: 203).

Although Lowe developed the 'outer characteristics' from the voice, his physical manifestation, unlike the process described in Stanislavski's comment, was not subliminal, but rather an active and conscious endeavour. In addition, Stanislavski looked for detailed inner psychology. As Lowe had so little on which to base his work, this kind of detail was impossible for him to achieve. Indeed, Lowe was aware that he was extrapolating a physicality based on only extremely limited testimony: 'You have of course only got what you're hearing to go on, so I dare say if there is more audio she had, that might throw everything, as you've gone purely on what is in the play.' Lowe's challenge was different from many of the actors whose processes I have analysed across my case-study productions. The first chapter explored the ways in which Catherine Russell, Chris Ryman and Alexander Hanson learnt more about their subjects' lives through their meetings, and thus were able to contextualise the testimony in the play. Similarly, Megan Dodds had the 184-page document of Rachel Corrie's writing, and the *Called to Account* cast were able to research the individuals they played to provide supplementary information. Here, by contrast,

Lowe had few other resources aside from the recorded words, and thus rather than claiming to understand or empathise with his subject, he was very clear that his portrayal of Dick-brain was predicated on a combination of the physicality suggested in the voice, a few comments by the women, and his own imagination.

Once Lowe's work on physicality had begun, Hill-Gibbins, in line with Stanislavski's Method of Physical Action, worked on the actors' psychological rendering of their subjects. Hill-Gibbins outlined this journey:

> Psychologically, you want to make it [the portrayal] as intense or as deep as possible. On a deep level it is as felt as it can be. So we would do work to achieve that...Doing that off-audio work is all about developing the sense of empathy between the actors and characters, and giving them a lived and felt experience. We did quite a bit of that. It always paid dividends.

It is intriguing that in order to develop the psychology of the character, Hill-Gibbins worked 'off-audio' with Lowe. This strongly suggests that it was not possible to work on the character using their testimony alone, but rather that cultivating the actors' invention was a crucial element in Hill-Gibbins' process. This further problematises his comments about the fixed structure on the audio, and indeed his outside-in approach. Lowe's comments about a particular improvisation illustrate the contradiction:

> We did a fantastic exercise...where I went out and chose one of these punters, Dick-brain, and I walked round Sloane Square – we tried to do it in real time to try and evoke a sense of how the punter feels turning up and how the working girl feels about him turning up. We did it from 15 minutes before, with them knowing this guy is going to turn up from the streets.

This exercise evidently prompted Lowe to probe within himself the psychology of the individual he played:

> Doing that, and me living as the character round Sloane Square and thinking lines like Dick-brain's 'I'm all keyed up to go', was very helpful. One of the women in the parlour told me Dick-brain was married. I mean if you think about that, he is going to somewhere that is clandestine, you're nervous, you have to get away from your wife to do it, and come up with some vague excuse (which presumably he has been doing for years), how do you square that with yourself? Years and years and years of excuses. Presumably your wife knows and you know she knows? Literally to act this out as an exercise, rather than having it down on paper 'he's married'

was extremely helpful. So doing it as an exercise away from the audio and seeing the place that it happened really gives you a sense of what that's about.

Lowe's work on physicality was thus supplemented with off-audio exercises. His description of how helpful this was reinforces the fact that the audio itself was not sufficient. This raises the question as to whether this process was, as Hill-Gibbins noted, 'outside-in'. It was certainly not a linear journey for Lowe; rather his development of a physicality based on the voice was assisted by exercises in which he did not use his subjects' words at all.

However, the main departure from the Method of Physical Action was in the lack of given circumstances available to Lowe. Stanislavski states: 'You cannot act without feeling, but it isn't worthwhile to worry and fret about it. It will come of itself as a result of your concentration on live action in the given circumstances' (Toporkov 1979: 202). The question as to what constituted the given circumstances for any of the men is a real problem. Lowe had access to only one fact: that one of them was married. However, this circumstance was not in the play, but was a piece of unsubstantiated information from the women.

This lack of given circumstances was also a critical element in Esther Coles' process. Coles played Amber who worked in the parlour. Amber appeared to be much more guarded than the other women about her involvement with the production, as Coles observed:

> My character is a bit different from everybody else's as she didn't really want to be part of it, she didn't really give anything away. Whilst the other women were happy to chat to Alecky and tell her everything, my character didn't do any of that at all.

It appears Amber exercised the most caution in her involvement in the play. Coles stated that her approach was predicated on two particular elements:

> I built up the character from the facts I knew about her. I found out that she was a district nurse before, so from that I suppose I learnt that she was a caring person, but also, it made me wonder how she went from a having a good job to being a prostitute. Those things also helped. I built the character from the voice and the facts.

It is important again to contest this identification of 'facts'. Despite her comment, it appears that at the centre of Coles' portrayal were not facts, but quite the opposite – the apparent mystery of Amber's professional background. Like Lowe, the lack of information prompted Coles to focus on her subject's voice:

> I think what is really interesting about what you hear is that the more you listen to the voice, in a way, you can actually start to understand the character. Just hearing the voice over and over again, you hear the range of intonations, the moments at which they stumble, and it all gives you an idea of their psychology.

This was a feature that Hill-Gibbins also foregrounded in the rehearsal process he devised:

> It is absolutely shocking the amount we give away about ourselves from the way we speak, not what we say but how we say it … I'm not a speech specialist, but when you repeatedly listen to something, it is mindboggling the amount you reveal about your psychology. Where you hesitate, where you mis-speak. That is what is interesting, and then drawing the actors' attentions to what might be going on. So once you have the physical and vocal structure there, psychologically you are creating the drama.

Although they were not conversation analysts, the personal nature of the testimony in the play evidently led both Coles and Hill-Gibbins to believe they could ascertain a great deal about the character from the way they spoke. Whilst accepting that caution must be exercised as the testimony was not only affected by Blythe's presence but also highly edited and re-structured, this focus is entirely explicable, as it was all the actors had. Coles' lack of information prompted her to develop different analytical skills. She evolved a new understanding of character-study through intense listening.

However, Coles found that her reliance on the recorded material alone was an insufficient stimulus, and that in rehearsal the headphone technique was inhibiting her process. She stated that:

> Towards the end of the rehearsal period I just wanted to put the headphones down, learn it and do it without them. Be able to go somewhere with the character. I'm not sure if that is because I only had a small part or whether it was slightly restricting.

Coles' comments suggest that using the headphones meant there was little chance of developing a psychological journey. But interestingly, she did not experience this in performance:

> Through the process of performing, I haven't really felt like that – it has felt very alive every time. I think that is something to do with the process.

You have to listen, and in the course of doing that, something has happened and I have become a character. But I can't really say that I tried to find a way with that, but rather that it has developed from just really trying to listen.

Coles' comments are surprising. It is clear that she found that the frustratingly prescriptive and technical rehearsal demands finally released her creatively. It was not the development of a deep understanding or emotional affinity that released her, but a much less definable process of rote-learning and an intense attention to absolute precision.

Flexible psychology and multiple truths

Debbie Chazen most fully explored how she developed her role using the audio she heard. Her comments are also highly pertinent with regard to the complex relationship between the Method of Physical Action and Stanislavski's reformulations of emotion memory.

Chazen found using the headphones difficult. Her early experiences of the play's run highlight the fundamental challenge of the Recorded Delivery process:

> The technique is incredibly freeing in many ways, but it is also quite restricting in others. It is the same thing every night, and you can't ever put a spin on it. In a normal play with a script you can say the line in a different way every night if you want to. In this one you can't. After about a week of performance I was going to the theatre and I thought 'Shit, it is going to be exactly the same tonight as it was last night.' I had this fear that I was going to get so bored over the five week run.

However, Chazen experienced a crucial breakthrough in performance:

> I did the show that night and something clicked. I realised that although I had to say the lines the same, the meaning behind it could be completely different. It changed everything. You sort of unravelled it backwards. When anyone says anything, there could be a hundred different readings behind it. If I say to someone 'You look nice today' it could mean you do look nice, or you look awful, and it can mean both of those things without changing the way you say it. So I could play many meanings, and all could be true. By doing that I was able to keep it fresh each night.

Chazen was the only actor across my case-studies to articulate this particular understanding of 'truth'. Although her delivery was fixed (at least within the slight deviations investigated earlier), Chazen found a creative role in the play by changing the thought which prompted the utterance. Considering her worries during the early performances, this was evidently a hugely releasing and satisfying intervention. Her realisation that the psychology is unstable and fluid, and can change in each performance, represents a departure from a Stanislavskian view of character, which seeks psychological coherency and stability in the actor's portrayal. Chazen's understanding of character was, therefore, different every night, which is a radical intervention for an actor to make.

One of Chazen's ways into creating this psychological background was through Hill-Gibbins' use of improvisation: 'That is where the improvisations came in really useful. You had to dig deep beneath the lines to find the character. Only then can you start to establish what the lines mean.' In analysing her utilisation of these techniques, Chazen focused particularly on a monologue by Tessa, in which she recounts her decision to close the brothel for three days:

> This past – few weeks (*Beat.*) – I mean, we closed for three days. (*Beat.*) Oooh. (*Beat.*) Oh, I was gonna – stop everything. I'm looking through the paper looking for a fucking job. Bad. (*Beat.*) I needed a break. (*Beat.*) Just with everything, with Mike, with these dirty old men. Ohh, I just couldn't handle it. It was like 'wooh' put up the barriers quick. (*Laughs.*) (Blythe 2008b: 62)

This is perhaps the most personal moment for Tessa in the play, as Chazen explains:

> The whole monologue is perhaps more truthful than she is being anywhere else in the play. We worked on that intensively. We did this whole improvisation where I was doing what I thought she did in those three days when she went off. She hasn't told anyone what she did. I asked her and she said she couldn't tell me. So for the character I acted out what I imagined she might have done. That was fantastic. That changed the monologue every night as I tried to remember how I felt doing the different bits of the improvisation, which changed the background.

Chazen's improvisations started with what she imagined Tessa *did*, not how she *felt*, which then evidently prompted feelings. This was also Stanislavski's emphasis: 'ask yourself what would you do – not what you would feel – what physical actions you would perform' (Gorchakov 1954: 378). Like Lowe's and Coles' approach, Chazen's experiences are attributable to the lack of information she had about Tessa. It appears that it was not, as she stated, digging 'beneath the lines' that was freeing for Chazen, but rather imagining the unknown circumstances that her subject refused to clarify. The women were evidently guarded and careful about what they revealed. Thus, in contrast to the previous case-studies in which the actors used their research to help them, here the actors used their own invention to a greater extent.

The improvisations were designed to enrich the unknown background to the testimony. We might compare Chazen's comment that 'This made quite a difference, I could fill in the gaps' with *Called to Account* cast-member Jeremy Clyde's statement that 'You don't fill in the gaps. Absolutely not.' These contrasting attitudes are a product of the different scope of the plays: in the politically nuanced testimony of *Called to Account*, psychology was subsumed to precision and restraint, whereas in *The Girlfriend Experience*, the sex workers' attitudes and interactions were foregrounded. In addition, in *Called to Account*, much more could be researched about the individuals, whereas in *The Girlfriend Experience*, as the actors had so little information, inventing a history was a valuable exercise for them.

Not only did Chazen change the psychological and emotional stimuli for Tessa's comments, she also used a form of emotion memory to remember how she felt in different moments of the improvisations. Rather than use her own experiences to provide analogous feelings, these emotions were a product of the improvisations. In his final writings, it is evident that Stanislavski had changed his attitude towards emotion memory: 'the truth of physical actions and belief in them...can evoke the psychological experiencing of the role naturally, automatically, so that we do not assault our feelings' (2010: 66–7).

Stanislavski thus identified that physical actions, not an 'assault' on feelings, could provide the necessary emotions for a role. From Stanislavski's own writings, and from those who worked with him, it is evident that his views changed considerably.[6] In one of his last writings, written three weeks before his death, he laid out a 25-point plan for the Method of Physical Action entitled 'The Approach to the Role', in which emotion memory was not even mentioned. The way in which Chazen employed the emotions engendered through her physical rendering of the role in improvised scenes thus bears resemblances to Stanislavski's Method of Physical Action. Her work still involved a personal input, as the improvisations were predicated on her own invention. However, despite some commonalities, her identification of a fluid psychology which could change with each performance moves her work away from Stanislavski's teaching.

CONCLUSION

This chapter has explored one of the most unusual documentary performance approaches, and has found a quite fascinating new mode of character creation. This process is predicated on a radical reworking of Stanislavski's Method of Physical Action which places intense and detailed listening at its centre. Like a linguist or conversation analyst, the actors in *The Girlfriend Experience* found innovative ways to begin to understand their characters and develop their portrayals based almost exclusively on what they said and how they spoke.

I have highlighted a set of problematic assumptions which are a result of the lack of investigation into the use of headphones, and have put some of the rhetoric associated with the headphone approach under the microscope. As the writing, directing and acting processes associated with headphones are uncharted in the academy, it has been critical to locate the actors' work within the context of these atypical working methods.

Hill-Gibbins' description has proved interesting as he identified both Stanislavskian and Brechtian influences on his processes. His staging decisions were clearly inspired by Brecht. However, though Hill-Gibbins was concerned with alienating the audience, and attempted to achieve this through the use of headphones, in fact it was the actors themselves who experienced a profound form of alienation. Although we have seen how this developed as they mastered the technical demands associated with using the headphones, it is evident that the actors' focus on stage was quite different from their work without headphones. They were alienated from both their own self-consciousness as actors, and from a complete immersion in the role. Alienation was thus achieved in the actors' performances in a way that it wasn't for the audience: the headphones did not function as alienating devices for the spectators, but rather became a convention in performance and did not necessarily interrupt the narrative flow or the audience's identification with the characters. As we have seen, however, they prompted a quite different set of processes in the actors.

It is clear why Hill-Gibbins evoked Stanislavski's late teaching in his articulation of his processes in the play, and it has been a useful lens through which to interrogate the actors' work. The movement from external action to internal processes was prescribed by the Recorded Delivery approach, and thus Stanislavski's emphasis on action, rather than on emotion or psychology, was evidently a useful reference point for Hill-Gibbins. However, by examining the actors' processes in detail, and interrogating Stanislavski's late work, it has become evident that the cast did not wholly follow that work in the manner laid out in the Method of Physical Action, but rather re-imagined it in the context of their work here. The main departure from Stanislavski's Method of Physical Action was the lack of given circumstances in the play. For Stanislavski, the given circumstances became more central in his later work than they had been earlier in his career. These were the subject of intense scrutiny and research by his actors, and were critical in creating a context within which to develop the character's 'actions'. In *The Girlfriend Experience*, by contrast, the almost complete lack of given circumstances, and the questionable veracity of those that were given, made this a very different enterprise. The fact that these women keep their identity a secret in their work means that they are cautious by habit. *The Girlfriend Experience* cast's processes, therefore, frequently developed in ways that were a direct result of their lack of information about the people they portrayed. The mystery about the professional life of Coles' character, and the enigma surrounding Tessa's actions over the three days, are both testament to the lack of circumstances given in the play, and further foregrounded the audio as the most significant resource the actors had at their disposal.

It is, however, critical to note that whilst the lack of circumstances might have entailed a move away from Stanislavski's teaching, it did not mean that the actors suffered, or that this was to the detriment of their portrayals. Rather, it prompted the innovative work they carried out through the emphasis on listening; work which bore rich fruit for the actors. We can see that listening took the place of given circumstances in their rework of the Method of Physical Action.

The headphone approach is so unusual that it challenges assumed notions of character, such as: What is a motivation when an actor is repeating words from a recording? What constitutes a given circumstance when subjects do not share personal information? In response to these fundamental questions, this chapter has outlined the ways in which, through listening, the actors were able to develop a different set of analytical skills.

Active formulations

In contrast to the previous chapters, in which actors frequently described their processes in passive terms, on the whole, the actors in *The Girlfriend Experience* were most open in their articulation of the creative interventions they made. As I have explored, it appears that the actors in the previous chapters felt that to acknowledge their own interpretations would leave them open to accusations that they were not accurately portraying what they had observed. However, in *The Girlfriend Experience*, as the headphones spelt out the approach to the audience, and suggested (or, as we have seen, over-emphasised) the limitations on the actors for the audience, the cast more readily investigated how they functioned creatively, and how they adapted their character-building skills in response to the specific demands of the production.

Notes

1 Talking to Terrorists

1. In 2003, Elworthy founded Peace Direct, which supports peace work in conflict areas. She has constantly returned to theatre as a medium to explore the issues surrounding her political work. For example, whilst chairing Kupugani, a nutrition education organisation in South Africa, she helped found the Market Theatre in Johannesburg in 1976. During the London transfer of David Edgar's play *The Prisoner's Dilemma* (RSC: Stratford and London, 2001) at the Barbican, Elworthy organised a two-day seminar entitled 'Theatre of War, Theatre of Peace' (31 January–1 February 2002). In a real-life precursor to *Talking to Terrorists*, the event brought onto the same stage Pat Magee, the Brighton bomber, and Jo Berry, whose father was killed by Magee's bomb.
2. The researchers involved with the first research phase of *Talking to Terrorists* were: from *The Permanent Way*, actors Lloyd Hutchinson, Kika Markham, Bella Merlin and Ian Redford, assistant director Naomi Jones, and sound designer Philip Arditti. They were joined by Nathalie Armin, Chipo Chung, Sidney Cole, Matthew Dunster, Nabil Elouahabi and Chris Ryman.
3. The actors' training was as follows: Chipo Chung and Lloyd Hutchinson trained at RADA, Jonathan Cullen, Chris Ryman and Alexander Hanson at Guildhall School of Music and Drama, Christopher Ettridge at Drama Centre, Catherine Russell at Central School of Speech and Drama and June Watson at Edinburgh College of Drama. None of these schools has a commitment to a single theorist, but all introduce actors to aspects of Stanislavski's work.
4. For example, David Richard Jones, in his research into Brecht's model-book for *Mother Courage* (the 'Couragemodell'), noted that Brecht's actors used their imagination within the 'given circumstances' to build their characters: 'They attempted to approximate premature ageing by actively imagining the background: child abuse, hard labours, rapes, disfigurements, having to lick boots of many colours. With the character thus far along, they attached behavioural specifics' (Jones 1986: 87–9).

2 My Name is Rachel Corrie

1. Though many documentary productions focus on death, rarely do we hear the words of the dead individual on stage. As Carol Martin states, 'more

171

often than not documentary theatre is where "real people" are absent – unavailable, dead, disappeared' (2006: 9). Thus, at the centre of many plays is an absence. Several plays focus on the death of a particular individual – among which we might list *The Colour of Justice* (Stephen Lawrence), *The Laramie Project* (Matthew Shepherd), and *Justifying War* (Dr David Kelly). However these do not use testimony from the dead individual, and they are not portrayed on stage. By contrast, although both Gregory Burke's *Black Watch* and Tanika Gupta's *Gladiator Games* (2005) depict people who have died, the writers use invented scenes to transport the audience back to Iraq and inside the cell in Feltham Young Offenders Institution respectively.

3   Called to Account

1. In all previous tribunal plays, Norton-Taylor has not altered the order of the material, maintaining the chronology of the evidence. There is only one exception to this rule. In the foreword to *Justifying War*, Norton-Taylor states that he moved the evidence given by Janice Kelly, Dr David Kelly's wife, so that it was the final interview. 'The evidence is presented chronologically, with the exception of that of Dr Jones. He gave his evidence two days after Mrs Kelly. It is presented here before her evidence' (2003: 7). There is little doubt that Norton-Taylor positioned Mrs Kelly's evidence at the end of the play to give the piece an emotional punch, as it is the play's most heartfelt and shocking interview.
2. The Downing Street Memo is the transcript of a top ministerial meeting held on 23 July 2002, which outlined America's intention to remove Saddam Hussein from power over a year before the invasion began. It was leaked to the *Sunday Times* on 1 May 2005.
3. The cast's previous experiences of the tribunal plays are as follows: William Hoyland and Thomas Wheatley have appeared in all but *Tactical Questioning*; James Woolley has appeared in all but *Half the Picture* and *Tactical Questioning*; and Jeremy Clyde has appeared in all but *Justifying War* and *Tactical Questioning*. David Beames appeared in *Justifying War* and *Bloody Sunday*; Ken Drury appeared in *The Colour of Justice*; Terrence Hardiman appeared in *Bloody Sunday*; David Michaels and Roland Oliver appeared in *Justifying War* and Raad Rawi appeared in *Half the Picture* and *Nuremberg*. Only Shane Rimmer, Diane Fletcher, Morven Macbeth and Charlotte Lucas were new to the tribunal plays.
4. For example, on 10 May 2007, during the play's run, a major story broke when David Keogh and Leo O'Connor were convicted of breaking the Official Secrets Act for leaking the Downing Street Memo, which Michael Smith then published. The publicity the story generated arguably shifted attention onto Ken Drury's cross-examination as Smith.

4   The Girlfriend Experience

1. Although Blythe is the only British documentary theatre-maker to employ headphones in performance, they have also been used in fictional plays. Rotozaza is a theatre company which specialises in working with the 'unrehearsed' performer. Their production of *ROMCOM* experimented with performers reacting to a voice on headphones. In this play, like in Blythe's work with Recorded Delivery, the actors repeated the words they heard. Writer-performer Tim Crouch has made similar experiments. His play, *An Oak Tree* (2006), is a fictional hypnosis act between the father of a girl killed in a car crash and the hypnotist who was driving the car. Both actors hear the play through headphones, and repeat the words as in Recorded Delivery's productions. In all performances, Crouch played the hypnotist and so knew the words and the story. The father was played by a different guest star at each performance, who knew nothing about the play, the plot or the character; they simply reacted to the words they heard and the unfolding story. The difference between Crouch's and Rotozaza's approaches and Blythe's is that they are predicated on the performer knowing very little, if anything, about the event. By contrast, in Recorded Delivery's productions, the actors rehearse with the audio and thus become familiar with it.

2. The actors' training was as follows: Esther Coles and Lu Corfield trained at RADA; Debbie Chazen at LAMDA; Beatie Edney studied English and Drama at Leeds University; and Alex Lowe at The Studio School and Leicester School of Performing Arts.

3. I was unable to secure an interview with Lu Corfield, who played Poppy.

4. The notes of the assistants tasked with recording his 'new aspect' have not been drawn together. Instead, we have some writings from this period by Stanislavski himself, included in *An Actor's Work on a Role*, and books by two of his assistants: actor Vasily Toporkov's *Stanislavski in Rehearsal: The Final Years* (translated in 1979), and director Nikolai Gorchakov's *Stanislavski Directs* (translated in 1954). Jean Benedetti based his book, *Stanislavski and the Actor* (1998), on the notebooks of Irina Novitskaya, another of the assistants who worked with Stanislavski during this period. Also see Sharon M. Carnicke's chapter on Maria Knebel, also an assistant during this time, in Hodge (2010: 99–116).

5. To see this as a reversal of the system would be a mistake. Quoting G. W. Kristi, who edited the eight-volume Russian edition of Stanislavski's works, Coger has noted: 'The use of physical actions seems like a reversal of the system where the role is created through analysis and exercise and then applied to the play's circumstances. But Stanislavski never intended to emphasise one part of his work at the expense of the other. As Kristi points out, "the psychological action and the physical action are two parts of one procedure". What happened was that Stanislavski used

physical actions to create the need for that inner life which permits the actor to realise the external action' (Coger 1964: 67). Only those for whom Stanislavski's teaching began and ended with *An Actor Prepares* would see this as a complete reversal. What was new in Stanislavski's teaching was the direct effect of physical action on psychological states.

6. Toporkov quoted Stanislavski: 'Don't think of the character, of the emotional experience. You just have a series of episodes' (1979: 126). Similarly, Gorchakov noted that 'physical action is the best channel-conductor to the emotion' (1954: 395).

Bibliography

Adams, G. (2004) 'Rickman Stages Show of Anger at Israel's Strong-arm Tactics', *Independent* (7 December).

Adler, S. (1988) *The Technique of Acting* (New York: Bantam Books).

Adler, S., Soloviova, V., Meisner, S. and Gray, P. (1964) 'The Reality of Doing', *Tulane Drama Review*, 9, 1 (Autumn) 136–55.

All Voices (2010) 'Remembering Rachel Corrie – the Martyr of Peace in Gaza', *All Voices* (2 June), www.allvoices.com/contributed-news/5974602-remembering-rachel-corrie-the-martyr-of-peace-in-gaza, accessed 10 March 2010.

Anderson, L. (2004) *The Diaries* (London: Methuen).

Aragay, M., Klein, H., Monforte, E. and Zozaya, P. (eds) (2007) *British Theatre of the 1990s: Interviews with Directors, Playwrights, Critics and Academics* (Basingstoke: Palgrave Macmillan).

Arcola Theatre (2009) *Past Productions: Come Out Eli*, 2005, www.arcolatheatre.com/?action=pasttemplate&pid=94, accessed 10 August 2009.

Arnold, H. A. (1980) 'The Other Tradition: A Brief Anatomy of Modern German Drama', *Theatre Journal*, 32, 1 (March) 43–53.

Aston, E. and Reinelt, J. (2001) 'Building Bridges: Life on Dunbar's Arbor, Past and Present', *Theatre Research International*, 26, 3 (October) 285–93.

Bai, R. (1998) 'Dances with Mei Lanfang: Brecht and the Alienation Effect', *Comparative Drama*, 32, 3: 388–433.

Banks, G. (2005) 'Parents Speaking Out to Keep Alive Memory of Child Killed in Gaza', *Pittsburgh Post-Gazette* (2 December).

Barish, J. (1981) *The Anti-Theatrical Prejudice* (Berkeley: California University Press).

Barker, C. (2010) 'Joan Littlewood' in A. Hodge (ed.) *Actor Training* (2nd edn) (London: Routledge) 130–43.

Bartram, G. and Waine, A. (eds) (1982) *Brecht in Perspective* (New York: Longman).

Bassett, K. (2007) 'You Can't Handle the Half-truths', *Independent* (29 April).

Baugh, C. (2006) 'Brecht and Stage Design: The *Bühnenbildner* and the *Bühnenbauer*' in Sacks, G. and Thompson, P. (eds) *The Cambridge Companion to Bertolt Brecht (*2nd edn*)* (Cambridge: Cambridge University Press), 259–77.

Beames, D. (2009) Telephone interview with author (28 April).

Benedetti, J. (1982) *Stanislavski: An Introduction* (London: Methuen).

—— (1998) *Stanislavski and the Actor* (London: Methuen).

Bentley, E. (ed.) (1964) *The Storm over The Deputy* (New York: Grove Press).

Bial, H. and Martin, C. (eds) (2000) *The Brecht Sourcebook* (London and New York: Routledge).

Billington, M. (2005) Review of *My Name is Rachel Corrie*, *Guardian* (14 April).

—— (2007a) Review of *Called to Account*, *Guardian* (24 April).

——(2007b) *State of the Nation* (London: Faber).

——(2007c) 'Theatre Wants Your Vote', *Guardian* (18 April).

—— (2008) Review of *The Girlfriend Experience*, *Guardian* (25 September).

Blank, J., and Jensen, E. (2004) *The Exonerated* (New York: Dramatist's Play Service).

Blumberg, M. and Walder, D. (eds) (1999) *South African Theatre as/and Intervention* (Amsterdam: Rodopi).

Blythe, A. (2006) *Cruising* (London: Nick Hern Books).

—— (2008a) Interview with author, London (11 January).

—— (2008b) *The Girlfriend Experience* (London: Nick Hern Books).

—— (2009) Telephone interview with author (22 January).

—— (2011) *London Road* (London: Nick Hern Books).

Boenisch, P. M. (2008) 'Other People Live: Rimini Protokoll and their Theatre of Experts – An Interview', *Contemporary Theatre Review*, 18, 1: 107–13.

Boleslavsky, R. (1933) *Acting: The First Six Lessons* (London: Theatre Arts Book, Routledge).

Boon, R. (ed.) (2007) *The Cambridge Companion to David Hare* (Cambridge: Cambridge University Press).

Borger, J. (2006) 'Rickman Slams "Censorship" of Play About US Gaza Activist', *Guardian* (28 February).

Botham, P. (2008) 'From Deconstruction to Reconstruction: A Habermasian Framework for Contemporary Political Theatre', *Contemporary Theatre Review*, 18, 3: 307–17.

—— (2009) 'Witnesses in the Public Sphere: *Bloody Sunday* and the Redefinition of Political Theatre' in Haedicke, S. C., Heddon, D., Oz, A. and Westlake, E. J. (eds) *Political Performances* (New York: Rodopi) 35–53.

Bottoms, S. (2006) 'Putting the Document in Documentary', *Tulane Drama Review*, 50, 3 (Fall) 56–68.

—— (2005) 'Solo Performance Drama' in Krasner, D. (ed.) *A Companion to Twentieth-Century American Drama* (Oxford: Blackwell) 519–35.

Bradby, D. and Capon, S. (eds) (2004) *Freedom's Pioneer: John McGrath's Work in Theatre, Film and Television* (Exeter: Exeter University Press).

Brantley, B. (2006) 'Notes From a Young Idealist in a World Gone Awry', Review of *My Name is Rachel Corrie*, *New York Times* (16 October).

Brecht, B. (1997) *Mother Courage and Her Children*, trans. Peter Thomson (Cambridge: Cambridge University Press).

—— (1965) *The Messingkauf Dialogues*, trans. John Willett (London: Eyre Methuen).
Brenton, H. (1977) *Epsom Downs* (London: Methuen).
Brittain, V. and Slovo, G. (2004) *Guantanamo: 'Honour Bound to Defend Freedom'* (London: Oberon).
Brooker, P. (2006) 'Key Words in Brecht's Theory and Practice of Theatre' in Sacks, G. and Thompson, P. (eds) *The Cambridge Companion to Bertolt Brecht* (2nd edn) (Cambridge: Cambridge University Press) 209–24.
Brown, G. (2007) Review of *Called to Account, Mail on Sunday* (29 April).
Brown, P. (1993) *Aftershocks* (Sydney: Currency Press).
—— (2009) Interview on Currency Press website, www.currency.com.au /PaulBrown.aspx (not currently available).
—— (2010) *Verbatim: Staging Memory and Community* (Sydney: Currency Press).
Bruzzi, S. (2006) *New Documentary: A Critical Introduction* (2nd edn) (London: Routledge).
Bull, J. (1984) *New British Political Dramatists* (London: Macmillan).
Burke, G. (2007) *Black Watch* (London: Faber & Faber).
Callow, S. (1984) *Being an Actor* (London: Penguin).
Cantrell, T. and Luckhurst, M. (eds) (2010) *Playing for Real: Actors on Playing Real People* (Basingstoke: Palgrave Macmillan).
Carlson, M. (2001) *The Haunted Stage: The Theatre as a Memory Machine* (Michigan: University of Michigan Press).
Carlson, M., Heilpern, J., Shinn, C., Solomon, A. and Stuart, K. (2007) 'Who's Afraid of Rachel Corrie?' *Theater*, 37: 55–65.
Carnicke, S. M. (2010) 'Stanislavsky's System' in Hodge, A. (ed.) *Actor Training* (2nd edn) (London: Routledge) 1–25.
—— (2010) 'The Knebel Technique' in Hodge, A. (ed.) *Actor Training* (2 ndedn) (London: Routledge), 99–116.
Casey, M. (2009) '*Ngapartji Ngapartji*: Telling Aboriginal Australian Stories' in Forsyth, A. and Megson, C. (eds) *Get Real: Documentary Theatre Past and Present* (Basingstoke: Palgrave Macmillan) 122–39.
Chambers, C. (2009) 'History in the Driving Seat: Unity Theatre and the Embrace of the "Real"' in Forsyth, A. and Megson, C. (eds) *Get Real: Documentary Theatre Past and Present* (Basingstoke: Palgrave Macmillan) 38–54.
Chazen, D. (2009) Telephone interview with author (16 January).
Cheeseman, P. (1977) *Fight for Shelton Bar* (London: Eyre Methuen).
Chekhov, M. (1985) *Lessons for the Professional Actor* (New York: Performing Arts Journal Publications).
—— (2002) *To the Actor: On the Technique of Acting* (London: Routledge).
—— (2005) *The Path of the Actor* (London: Routledge).
Chung, C. (2008) Telephone interview with author (7 March).
Churchill, C. (1989) *Cloud Nine* (London: Nick Hern Books).
—— (1991) *Mad Forest* (London: Nick Hern Books).
—— (1996) *Plays One* (London: Methuen).

—— (1999) *Plays Two* (London: Methuen).

Clapp, S. (2007) Review of *Called to Account, Observer* (29 April).

Clyde, J. (2009) Telephone interview with author (27 May).

Coger, L. I. (1964) 'Stanislavski Changes his Mind', *Tulane Drama Review*, 9, 1. 63–8.

Coles, E. (2008) Telephone interview with author (14 October).

Conciliation Resources (2010) *Conciliation Resources Website*, www.c-r.org, accessed 10 July 2010.

Corrie, C. (2005) 'Rachel was Bulldozed to Death, But Her Words are a Spur to Action', *Guardian* (8 October).

Corrie, R. (2008) *Let Me Stand Alone: The Journals of Rachel Corrie* (London: Granta Press).

Craig, S. (ed.) (1980) *Dreams and Deconstructions: Alternative Theatre in Britain* (Derbyshire: Amber Lane Press).

Cullen, J. (2008) Telephone interview with author (4 June).

Davis, W. (2007) *Art and Politics: Psychoanalysis, Ideology, Theatre* (Pluto Press: London).

Davy, C. (ed.) (1938) *Footnotes to the Film* (London: Readers Union).

Dawson, G. F. (1999) *Documentary Theatre in the United States* (Connecticut: Greenwood Press).

Deavere Smith, A. (1993) *Fires in the Mirror* (New York: Anchor Books).

—— (1994) *Twilight Los Angeles, 1992 (*New York: Anchor Books).

Derbyshire, H. and Hodson, L. (2008) 'Performing Injustice: Human Rights and Verbatim Theatre', *Law and Humanities*, 2, 2: 191–211.

Devine, H. (2006) *Looking Back – Playwrights at the Royal Court* (London: Faber).

Diver, C. (2010) Question and answer session with cast members of *Hush* at the 'Acting with Facts' Conference, Reading (3 September).

Dodds, M. (2005) Interview for the Royal Court Theatre's 'Educational Resources' to accompany *My Name is Rachel Corrie*, www.inplaceofwar. net/web_db/artifacts/0001/185/Educationpack%20Rachel%20Corrie.pdf (no longer accessible).

—— (2006a) Interview for Official London Theatre (30 March), www.officiall ondontheatre.co.uk/news/latest-news/article/item71603/megan-dodds, accessed 17 June 2011.

—— (2006b) Interview with Caroline Bishop, *London Theatre Guide* (31 March), rachelswords.org/2006/03/31/ltg-the-big-interview-with-megan -dodds, accessed 17 June 2011.

—— (2011) Telephone interview with author (19 June).

Doty, G. A. and Harbin, B. J. (eds) (1990) *Inside the Royal Court Theatre, 1956–1981: Artists Talk* (Louisiana: Louisiana University Press).

Double, O. and Wilson, M. (2006) 'Brecht and Cabaret' in P. Thomson and G. Sacks (eds) *The Cambridge Companion to Bertolt Brecht* (2nd edn) Cambridge: Cambridge University Press).

Drury, K. (2009) Telephone interview with author (8 January).

Dunbar, A. (2000) *Rita, Sue and Bob Too* (London: Methuen).

Eddershaw, M. (2006) 'Actors on Brecht' in Sacks, G. and Thompson, P. (eds) *The Cambridge Companion to Bertolt Brecht* (2nd edn) (Cambridge: Cambridge University Press) 278–96.

Edgar, D. (2001) *The Prisoner's Dilemma* (London: Nick Hern Books).

—— (2008) 'Doc and Dram', *Guardian* (27 September).

Edney, B. (2009) Telephone interview with author (9 January).

El Lozy, M. (2008) 'Palestine Uncovered in *My Name is Rachel Corrie*', *Alif: Journal of Comparative Poetics*, 28: 102–26.

Elworthy, S. (2005) *Hearts and Minds: Human Security Approaches to Political Violence* (London: Demos).

—— (2008) Telephone interview with author (22 December).

Elworthy, S., Cerletti, F. and Roddick, A. (eds) (2004) *Unarmed Heroes: The Courage to Go Beyond Violence* (London: Clairview Books).

Elworthy, S. and Rifkind, G. (eds) (2006) *Making Terrorism History* (London: Rider).

Ettridge, C. (2008) Interview with author, Leeds (23 May).

Escolme, B. (2010) 'Being Good: Actors' Testimonies as Archive and the Cultural Construction of Success in Performance', *Shakespeare Bulletin*, 28, 1: 77–91.

Evans, L. (2007) Review of *Called to Account, The Spectator* (5 May).

Farber, Y. (2008) *Theatre as Witness: Three Testimonial Plays from South Africa* (London: Oberon).

Favorini, A. (ed.) (1995) *Voicings: Ten Plays from the Documentary Theater* (Hopewell, NJ: Echo Press).

Feinberg, A. (1986) 'The Appeal of the Executive: Adolf Eichmann on the Stage', *Monatshefte*, 78, 2: 203–14.

Féral, J. (1987) 'Alienation Theory in Multimedia Performance' trans. Ron Bermingham, *Theatre Journal*, 39, 4, 'Distancing Brecht': 461–72.

Filewod, A. (2009) 'The Documentary Body: Theatre Workshop to Banner Theatre' in Forsyth, A. and Megson, C. (eds) *Get Real: Documentary Theatre Past and Present* (Basingstoke: Palgrave Macmillan): 55–73.

Filewod, A. and Watt, D. (2001) *Workers' Playtime: Theatre and the Labour Movement Since 1970* (Strawberry Hills: Currency Press).

Findlater, R. (ed.) (1981) *At the Royal Court: 25 Years of the English Stage Company* (New York: Grove Press).

Fletcher, D. (2007) Telephone interview with author (25 July).

Forrest, T. (2008) 'Mobilizing the Public Sphere: Schlingensief's Reality Theatre', *Contemporary Theatre Review*, 18, 1: 90–8.

Forsyth, A. (2009) 'Performing Trauma: Race Riots and Beyond in the Work of Anna Deavere Smith' in Forsyth, A. and Megson, C. (eds) *Get Real: Documentary Theatre Past and Present* (Basingstoke: Palgrave Macmillan), 140–50.

Forsyth, A. and Megson, C. (eds) (2009) *Get Real: Documentary Theatre Past and Present* (Basingstoke: Palgrave Macmillan).

Franklin, C. and Lyons, L. (2004) 'Bodies of Evidence and the Intricate Machines of Untruth', *Biography*, 27, 1 (Winter): 5–22.

Freed, D. (1970) *Inquest* (New York: Hill & Wang).

Freedberg, D. (1989) *The Power of Images* (Chicago: University of Chicago Press).

Freeman, S. (2006) 'Writing the History of an Alternative-Theatre Company: Mythology and the Last Years of Joint Stock', *Theatre Survey*, 47: 51–72.

Fricker, K. (2008) Review of *The Girlfriend Experience*, *Variety* (25 September).

Fry, S., Pinter, H. and Slovo, G. (2006) 'In Defence of a Play', Letter to the *New York Times* (22 March).

Fuchs, A. (1990) *Playing the Market: The Market Theatre Johannesburg, 1976–86* (New York: Harwood Academic Publishers).

Gaskill, W. (1988) *A Sense of Direction* (London: Faber & Faber).

Gilroy, S. (2008) *Motherland* (London: Oberon).

Ginman, J. (2003) 'Out of Joint: Max Stafford-Clark and "the Temper of Our Time"', *Contemporary Theatre Review*, 13, 3: 23–6.

Gomm, R. (2008) *Social Research Methodology* (Basingstoke: Palgrave Macmillan).

Gorchakov, N. (1954). *Stanislavsky Directs*, trans. Miriam Goldina (New York: Funk & Wagnalls).

Gordon, M. (1987) *The Stanislavsky Technique: Russia* (New York: Applause Theatre Books).

Gray, P. and Munk, E. (1966) 'A Living World: An Interview with Peter Weiss', *Tulane Drama Review*, 11, 1: 106–14.

Gupta, T. (2005) *Gladiator Games* (London: Oberon).

Haberl, F. P. (1969) 'Peter Weiss's Documentary Theater', *Books Abroad*, 43, 3: 359–62.

Haedrick, C. (2011) 'A Journey for Rachel: Taking My Name is Rachel Corrie From Corvallis, Oregon to Antioch, Turkey', *The Western States Theatre Review*, 17: 45–9.

Hammond, W. and Steward, D. (eds) (2009) *Verbatim: Verbatim: Contemporary Documentary Theatre* (London: Oberon).

Hanson, A. (2008) Telephone interview with author (9 July).

Hardiman, T. (2009) Telephone interview with author (12 March).

Hare, D. (1971) *Slag* (London: Faber).

—— (1974) *Fanshen* (London: Faber & Faber).

—— (1986) *The Asian Plays: Fanshen, Saigon and A Map of the World* (Boston, MA: Faber).

—— (2003) *The Permanent Way* (London: Faber & Faber).

—— (2004) *Stuff Happens* (London: Faber & Faber).

Harker, B. (2009) 'Mediating the 1930s: Documentary and Politics in Theatre Union's *Last Edition* (1940)' in Forsyth, A. and Megson, C. (eds) *Get Real: Documentary Theatre Past and Present* (Basingstoke: Palgrave Macmillan) 24–37.

Hayman, R. (1979) *British Theatre Since 1955: A Reassessment* (Oxford: Oxford University Press).

Heddon, D. (2007) *Autobiography and Performance* (Basingstoke: Palgrave Macmillan).

—— (2009) 'To Absent Friends: Ethics in the Field of Auto/biography' in Haedicke, S. C., Heddon, D., Oz, A. and Westlake, E. J. (eds) *Political Performances* (New York: Rodopi) 113–31.

Hemming, S. (2006) Review of *My Name is Rachel Corrie*, *Financial Times* (4 April).

Hesford, W. S. (2010) 'Staging Terror' in Martin, C. (ed.) *Dramaturgy of the Real on the World Stage* (Basingstoke: Palgrave Macmillan) 45–60.

Hill-Gibbins, J. (2010) Interview with author, London (16 April).

Hodge, A. (ed.) (2010) *Actor Training* (2nd edn) (London: Routledge).

Holmes, J. (2007) *Fallujah: Eyewitness Testimony from Iraq's Besieged City* (London: Constable).

Houchin, J. (2008) 'Bodily Fear: Recent American Performance Controversies', *Theater*, 38, 3: 5–21.

Hoyland, W. (2009) Telephone interview with author (20 January).

Hughes, J. (2007) 'Theatre, Performance and the "War on Terror": Ethical and Political Questions arising from British Theatrical Responses to War and Terrorism', *Contemporary Theatre Review*, 17, 2: 149–64.

Hutchinson, L. (2008) Telephone interview with author (4 March).

Hutchinson, Y. (2009) 'Verbatim Theatre in South Africa: "Living History in a Person's Performance"' in Forsyth, A. and Megson, C. (eds) *Get Real: Documentary Theatre Past and Present* (Basingstoke: Palgrave Macmillan) 209–23.

Innes, C. (1992) *Modern British Drama 1890–1990* (Cambridge: Cambridge University Press).

—— (2007) 'Towards a Post-millennial Mainstream? Documents of the Times', *Modern Drama*, 50, 3: 435–52.

Irmer, T. (2006) 'A Search for New Realities – Documentary Theatre in Germany', *Tulane Drama Review*, 50, 3: 16–28.

Itzin, C. (ed.) (1971) 'Production Casebook No.1, *The Staffordshire Rebels*', *Theatre Quarterly*, 1: 86–102.

—— (1980) *Stages in the Revolution* (London: Eyre Methuen).

Jeffers, A. (2009) 'Looking for Esrafil: Witnessing "Refugitive" Bodies in *I've Got Something to Show You*' in Forsyth, A. and Megson, C. (eds) *Get Real: Documentary Theatre Past and Present* (Basingstoke: Palgrave Macmillan) 91–106.

Jones, A. (2008) Review of *The Girlfriend Experience*, *Independent* (25 September).

Jones, D. R. (1986) *Great Directors at Work* (Berkeley: University of California Press).

de Jongh, N. (2007) Review of *Called to Account*, *Evening Standard* (24 April).

—— (2008) Review of *The Girlfriend Experience, Evening Standard* (24 September).

Jordan, S. (2003) 'Making of a Martyr', *Observer* (23 March).

Kalb, J. (2001) 'Documentary Solo Performance: The Politics of the Mirrored Self', *Theater*, 31, 3: 13–29.

Kaufman, M. (1998) *Gross Indecency: The Three Trials of Oscar Wilde* (London: Methuen).

—— (2001) *The Laramie Project* (New York: Vintage Books).

Kent, N. (2005a) *Srebrenica* (London: Oberon Books).

—— (2005b) *Tribunals at the Tricycle*, interview with Terry Stoller, http://www.hotreview.org/articles/tribunalsatthet.htm, accessed 27 February 2008.

—— (2007) Interview with Matthew Amer (18 April), www.officiallondon theatre.co.uk/news, accessed 12 May 2009.

Kent, N. and Norton-Taylor, R. (2007) 'Blair in the Dock', Interview with Mark Brown, *Socialist Review* (May), www.socialistreview.org.uk/article. php? articlenumber=9954, accessed 9 May 2009.

Kipphardt, H. (1967) *In the Matter of J. Robert Oppenheimer* (London: Methuen).

Krasner, D. (2010) 'Strasberg, Adler and Meisner: Method Acting' in Hodge, A. (ed.) *Actor Training* (2nd edn) (London: Routledge) 144–63.

Kritzer, A. H. (2008) *Political Theatre in Post-Thatcher Britain: New Writing 1995–2005* (Basingstoke: Palgrave Macmillan).

Kuhn, T. and Giles, S. (eds) (2003) *Brecht on Art and Politics* (London: Methuen).

Kustow, M. (2000a) 'Horror That May Not Shock', *Evening Standard* (September).

—— (2000b) *theatre@risk* (London: Methuen).

Kvale, S. (1996) *InterViews: An Introduction to Qualitative Research Interviewing* (London: Sage).

Lambert, M. (1989) 'The Max Factor: Recent Productions at the Royal Court', *Theatre Ireland*, 17 (March): 36–7.

Lane, D. (2010) 'A Dramaturg's Perspective: Looking to the Future of Script development', *Studies in Theatre and Performance*, 30, 1 (March): 127–42.

Lappiny, Y. (2005) Review of *My Name is Rachel Corrie, Jewish Theatre News* (8 May), www.jewish-theatre.com/visitor/article_display.aspx?articleID=1342, accessed 2 January 2012.

Lewenstein, O. (1994) *Kicking Against the Pricks: A Theatre Producer Looks Back* (London: Nick Hern Books).

Lewis, B. (1993) 'The Circle of Confusion: A Conversation with Anna Deavere Smith', *Kenyon Review*, 15, 4: 54–64.

Ley-Piscator, M. (1967) *The Piscator Experiment: The Political Theatre* (Carbondale and Edwardsville: Southern Illinois University Press).

Lindenberger, H. (1975) *Historical Drama: The Relation of Literature and Reality* (Chicago and London: University of Chicago Press).

Lipovetsky, M. and Beumers, B. (2008) 'Reality Performance: Documentary Trends in Post-Soviet Russian Theatre', *Contemporary Theatre Review*, 18, 3: 293–306.

Little, R. and McLaughlin, E. (2007) *The Royal Court Theatre Inside Out* (London: Oberon).

Littlewood, J. (1965) *Oh, What a Lovely War!* (London: Methuen).

Logan, B. (2005) Review of *My Name is Rachel Corrie*, *Time Out London* (20 April).

Lonergan, P. (2005) 'Speaking Out: The Tricycle Theatre's *Bloody Sunday* and Verbatim Theatre', *Irish Theatre Magazine*, 4, 23 (Summer).

Lowe, A. (2008) Interview with author, London (10 October).

Luckhurst, M. (2006) *Dramaturgy: A Revolution in Theatre* (Cambridge, Cambridge University Press).

—— (2008) 'Verbatim Theatre, Media Relations and Ethics' in Luckhurst, M. and Holdsworth, N. (eds) *A Concise Companion to Contemporary British and Irish Drama* (Oxford: Blackwell) 200–22.

Luckhurst, M. and Veltman, C. (eds) (2001) *On Acting: Interviews with Actors* (London: Faber & Faber).

McGinn, C. (2008) Review of *The Girlfriend Experience*, *Time Out* (29 September).

McGrath, J. (1974) *The Cheviot, the Stag, and the Black, Black Oil* (London: Methuen).

McKinley, J. (2006) 'Play About Demonstrator's Death is Delayed', *New York Times* (28 February).

MacPherson, W. (1999) *The Stephen Lawrence Inquiry: Report of an Inquiry* (February), www.archive.official-documents.co.uk/document/cm42/4 4262/4262.htm.

Margolis, E. and Renaud, L. T. (eds) (2009) *The Politics of American Acting Training* (New York and London: Routledge).

Market Theatre (2010) *Market Theatre Website*, www.markettheatre.co.za, accessed 10 July 2010.

Martin, C. (1993) 'Anna Deavere Smith: The Word Becomes You. An Interview', *Tulane Drama Review*, 37, 4: 45–62.

—— (2006) 'Bodies of Evidence', *Tulane Drama Review*, 50, 3: 8–15.

—— (2009) 'Living Simulations: The Use of Media in Documentary in the UK, Lebanon and Israel' in Forsyth, A. and Megson, C. (eds) *Get Real: Documentary Theatre Past and Present* (Basingstoke: Palgrave Macmillan) 74–90.

—— (ed.) (2010) *Dramaturgy of the Real on the World Stage* (Basingstoke: Palgrave Macmillan).

Mason, G. (1977) 'Documentary Drama from the Revue to the Tribunal', *Modern Drama*, 20: 263–77.

Matrix Chambers (2009) *Matrix: Who we are: Philippe Sands*, www.matrixlaw. co.uk/WhoWeAre_Members_PhilippeSandsQC.aspx, accessed 18 August 2009.

Megson, C. (2004) '"The Spectacle is Everywhere"': Tracing the Situationist Legacy in British Playwriting since 1968', *Contemporary Theatre Review*, 14, 2: 17–28.

—— (2005) '"This is All Theatre": Iraq Centre Stage', *Contemporary Theatre Review*, 15, 3: 369–71.

—— (2009) '*Half the Picture:* "A Certain Frisson" at the Tricycle Theatre' in Forsyth, A. and Megson, C. (eds) *Get Real: Documentary Theatre Past and Present* (Basingstoke: Palgrave Macmillan) 179–94.

Meisner, S. and Longwell, D. (1987) *Sanford Meisner on Acting* (New York: Vintage Original).

Melbourne Workers Theatre (MWT) (2012) MWT website, melbourne workerstheatre.com.au/about, accessed 20 January.

Melvin, M. (2006) *The Art of Theatre Workshop* (London: Oberon Books).

Merlin, B. (2001) *Beyond Stanislavski* (London: Nick Hern Books).

—— (2003) *Konstantin Stanislavsky* (London: Routledge).

—— (2007a) 'Acting Hare: *The Permanent Way*' in Boon, R. (ed.) *The Cambridge Companion to David Hare* (Cambridge: Cambridge University Press) 123–37.

—— (2007b) *The Complete Stanislavski Toolkit* (London: Nick Hern Books).

—— (2007c) 'The Permanent Way and the Impermanent Muse', *Contemporary Theatre Review*, 17, 1: 41–9.

Michaels, D. (2009) Telephone interview with author (17 March).

Michalski, J. (1966) 'German Drama and Theater in 1965', *Books Abroad*, 40, 2: 137–40.

Mitchell, G. (2001) *As the Beast Sleeps* (London: Nick Hern Books).

Mitter, S. (1992) *Systems of Rehearsal* (London: Routledge).

Moore, S. (1965) 'The Method of Physical Actions', *Tulane Drama Review*, 9, 4: 91–4.

Mumford, M. (2009) *Bertolt Brecht* (London: Routledge).

Myre, G. (2003) 'Israeli Army Bulldozer Kills American Protesting in Gaza', *New York Times* (17 March).

New York Theatre Workshop. (n.d.) 'History Of New York Theatre Workshop', nytw.org/history.asp, accessed 20 January 2012.

Nichols, B. (1991) *Representing Reality* (Indiana: Indiana University Press).

Nicola, J. B. (2002) *Playing the Audience* (New York: Applause Theatre Books).

Norton-Taylor, R. (1988) *Blacklist: The Inside Story of Political Vetting* (London: Hogarth).

—— (1990) *In Defence of the Realm? The Case for Accountable Security and Intelligence Services* (London: Civil Liberties Trust).

—— (1995) *Truth is a Difficult Concept: Inside the Scott Inquiry* (London: Guardian Books).

—— (1997) *Nuremberg – The War Crimes Trial* (London, Nick Hern Books).

—— (1999) *The Colour of Justice* (London: Oberon Books).

—— (2002) 'Don't Trust Bush or Blair on Iraq', *Guardian* (21 August).

—— (2003) *Justifying War: Scenes from the Hutton Enquiry* (London: Oberon Books).

—— (2005a) *Bloody Sunday: Scenes from the Saville Inquiry* (London: Oberon Books).

—— (2005b) 'Revealed: The Rush to War', *Guardian* (23 February).

—— (2006) 'Blair–Bush Deal Before Iraq War Revealed in Secret Memo', *Guardian* (3 February).

—— (2007a) 'Blair in the Dock', *Guardian* (16 April).

—— (2007b) *Called to Account: The Indictment of Anthony Charles Lynton Blair for the Crime of Aggression Against Iraq – A Hearing* (London: Oberon Books).

—— (2007c) 'The Colour of Evidence', *Guardian* (8 November).

—— (2011) *Tactical Questioning: Scenes from the Baha Mousa Inquiry* (London: Oberon Books).

Nussbaum, L. (1981) 'The German Documentary Theatre of the Sixties: A Stereopsis of Contemporary History', *Modern Drama*, 4, 2: 237–55.

Oliver, R. (2009) Email correspondence with author (21 August).

—— (2009) Telephone interview with author (13 January).

Oxford Research Group (2008) *Oxford Research Group Website,* http://www.oxfordresearchgroup.org.uk/about_us/, accessed 12 June 2008.

Paget, D. (1987) '"Verbatim Theatre": Oral History and Documentary Techniques', *New Theatre Quarterly*, 3, 12: 317–36.

—— (1990) *True Stories? Documentary Drama on Radio, Screen and Stage* (Manchester and New York: Manchester University Press).

—— (2007) 'Acting with Facts: Actors Performing the Real in British Theatre and Television since 1990. A Preliminary Report on a New Research Project', *Studies in Documentary Film*, 1, 2: 165–76.

—— (2009) 'The "Broken Tradition" of Documentary Theatre and its Continued Powers of Endurance' in Forsyth, A. and Megson, C. (eds) *Get Real: Documentary Theatre Past and Present* (Basingstoke: Palgrave Macmillan) 224–38.

Parham, S. (1976) 'Editing Hochhuth for the Stage: A Look at the Major Productions of "The Deputy"', *Educational Theatre Journal*, 28, 3 (October): 347–53.

Patterson, M. (1976) *German Theatre Today* (London: Pitman Publishing).

Peace Direct (2008) *Peace Direct Website – Our Values,* www.peacedirect.org/peace-direct/our-values.html, accessed 12 June 2008.

Peacock, K. (1999) *Thatcher's Theatre* (Westport: Greenwood Press).

Pearl, R. and Frum, D. (2003) *An End to Evil: How to Win the War on Terror* (London: Random House).

Pentabus Theatre (2009) *Past Productions: Strawberry Fields,* www.pentabus.
co.uk/index.php/past-productions/strawberry-fields, accessed 6 July 2009.
Perry, R. C. (1969) 'Historical Authenticity and Dramatic Form: Hochhuth's
"Der Stellvertreter" and Weiss's "Die Ermittlung"', *Modern Language
Review*, 64, 4: 828–39.
Peter, J. (2007) Review of *Called to Account, Sunday Times* (29 April).
Philips, A. (2003) 'Woman Killed by Bulldozer', *Daily Telegraph*
(17 March).
Piscator, E. (1980) *The Political Theatre*, trans. Hugh Rorrison (London: Eyre
Methuen).
Power, C. (2008) *Presence in Play: A Critique of Presence in the Theatre* (New
York: Rodopi).
Puga, A. E. (2008) *Memory, Allegory, and Testimony in South American
Theater: Upstaging Dictatorship* (London: Routledge).
Ravens, J. (2008) Interview with Derek Paget for 'Acting with Facts' Research
Project (29 July), www.reading.ac.uk/web/FILES/ftt/Jan_Ravens_29th_
July_2008.pdf, accessed 9 November 2012.
Rawi, R. (2009) Telephone interview with author (8 March).
Recorded Delivery Theatre Company (2010) *Recorded Delivery Website,*
www.recordeddelivery.net, accessed 10 July 2010.
Redgrave, V. (2006) 'The Second Death of Rachel Corrie: Censorship of the
Worst Kind', Open Letter to James Nicola (6 March), www.criticalconcern.
com/second_death_of_rachel_corrie.htm, accessed 3 May 2012.
Reinelt, J. (1994) *After Brecht: British Epic Theater* (Michigan: University of
Michigan Press).
—— (1994) 'Fanshen, Hare and Brecht' in Zeifman, H. (ed.) *David Hare: A
Casebook* (London: Routledge) 127–39.
—— (2004) '"Politics, Playwriting, Postmodernism": An Interview with David
Edgar', *Contemporary Theatre Review*, 14, 4: 42–53.
—— (2006) 'Towards a Poetics of Theatre and Public Events', *Tulane Drama
Review*, 50, 3 (Fall): 69–87.
—— (2007) 'The Limits of Censorship', *Theatre Research International*, 32,
1: 3–15.
Richie, R. (ed.) *The Joint Stock Book* (London: Methuen).
Rickman, A. (2011) Email correspondence with author (24 May).
Rickman, A. and Viner, K. (2005) *My Name is Rachel Corrie* (London: Nick
Hern Books).
Rimmer, S. (2009) Telephone interview with author (7 April).
Roach, J. (2007) *It* (Michigan: University of Michigan Press).
Roberts, P. (1999) *The Royal Court and the Modern Stage* (Cambridge:
Cambridge University Press).
Roberts, P. and Stafford-Clark, M. (2007) *Taking Stock: The Theatre of Max
Stafford-Clark* (London: Nick Hern Books).
Rotozaza (2009) *Rotozaza: ROMCOM,* www.rotozaza.co.uk/romcom,
accessed 18 January 2009.

—— (2010) *Rotozaza: Doublethink,* www.rotozaza.co.uk/doublethin k2.html, accessed 8 July 2010.

Rozik, E. (1999) 'The Corporeality of the Actor's Body: The Boundaries of Theatre and the Limitations of Semiotic Methodology', *Theatre Research International,* 24, 2: 198–211.

Russell, C. (2008) Telephone interview with author (16 June).

Ryman, C. (2008) Telephone interview with author (15 February).

Sacks, G. and Thompson, P. (eds) (2006) *The Cambridge Companion to Bertolt Brecht* (2nd edn) (Cambridge: Cambridge University Press).

Sands, P. (2006) *Lawless World: Making and Breaking of Global Rules* (London: Penguin).

Schall, E. (1986) 'An Interview with Ekkehard Schall', *Theater Magazine.*

—— (2000) *The Craft of Theatre* (London: Methuen).

—— (2004) 'Lessons of a Brechtian Actor', *Brecht Yearbook,* 28: 75–109.

Shakespeare, W. (1994) *A Midsummer Night's Dream* (London: Arden Shakespeare).

Shinn, C. (2008) 'Market Rules', *Index on Censorship,* 37, 4: 88–93.

Short, C. (2004) *An Honourable Deception? New Labour, Iraq and the Misuse of Power* (London: Free Press).

—— (2006) 'Open Resignation Letter to Jacqui Smith', news.bbc.co.uk/1/hi /uk_politics/6070156.stm, accessed 10 July 2012.

—— (2008) Telephone interview with author (30 May).

Shuttleworth, I. (2007) Review of *Called to Account, Financial Times* (25 April).

Sierz, A. (2005a) 'Beyond Timidity?: The State of British New Writing', *Journal of Performance and Art,* 27, 3: 55–61.

—— (ed.) (2005b) *Royal Court Special* (December), www.theatrevoice.com/ listen_now/player/?audioID=371ch 2008, accessed 10 May 2009.

—— (ed.) (2008) *Interview: Alecky Blythe* (September), www.theatrevoice. com/listen_ now/player/?audioID=609, accessed 10 May 2009.

Smith, L. (2009) 'Remembering the Past, "Growing Ourselves a Future": Community-Based Documentary Theatre in the East Palo Alto Project' in Forsyth, A. and Megson, C. (eds) *Get Real: Documentary Theatre Past and Present* (Basingstoke: Palgrave Macmillan) 107–21.

Soans, R. (2000) *A State Affair* (London: Methuen).

—— (2004) *The Arab-Israeli Cookbook* (London: Aurora Metro Press).

—— (2005) *Talking to Terrorists* (London: Oberon).

—— (2009) *Mixed Up North* (London: Oberon).

—— (2008) Telephone interview with author (15 June).

Soto-Morettini, D. (2005) 'Trouble in the House: David Hare's *Stuff Happens*', *Contemporary Theatre Review,* 15, 3: 309–19.

Spencer, C. (2004) 'Where Justice is Caged', *Daily Telegraph* (26 May).

—— (2005), Review of *My Name is Rachel Corrie, Daily Telegraph* (18 April).

—— (2007) 'Kangaroo Court Fails to Take Off', *Daily Telegraph* (24 April).

Stafford-Clark, M. (1989) *Letters to George* (London: Nick Hern Books).

—— (2004) *Interview with David Benedict* (January) www.theatrevoice.com /listen_now/player/?audioID=93, accessed 10 May 2009.

—— (2005) *Diary: March 2004–November 2005,* uncatalogued, British Library.

—— (2009) Interview with author, York (26 February).

Stand With Us (2003) 'All the Rachels' flyer printed by demonstrators www. standwithus.com/pdfs/flyers/RachelVictims.pdf, accessed 23 January 2013.

Stanislavski, C. (1958) *An Actor Prepares,* trans. Elizabeth Reynolds Hapgood (London: Geoffrey Bles).

—— (1961a) *Creating a Role,* trans. Elizabeth Reynolds Hapgood (London: Geoffrey Bles).

—— (1961b) *On the Art of the Stage,* trans. David Magarshack (London: Faber & Faber).

—— (1968) *Building a Character,* trans. Elizabeth Reynolds Hapgood (London: Methuen).

—— (1969) *Stanislavski's Legacy,* ed. and trans. Elisabeth Reynolds Hapgood (London: Methuen).

—— (1980) *My Life in Art,* trans. J. J. Robbins. (London: Methuen).

Stanislavski, K. (1990) *An Actor's Handbook,* trans. Elizabeth Reynolds Hapgood (London: Methuen).

—— (2008a) *An Actor's Work,* trans. Jean Benedetti (London: Routledge).

—— (2008b) *My Life in Art,* trans. Jean Benedetti (London: Routledge).

—— (2010) *An Actor's Work on a Role,* trans. Jean Benedetti (London: Routledge).

Stanley, S. K. (2005) 'Teaching the Politics of Identity in a Post-Identity Age: Anna Deavere Smith's "Twilight"', *MELUS,* 30, 2: 191–208.

Strasberg, L. (1988) *A Dream of Passion: The Development of the Method* (London: Bloomsbury).

Thompson, D. (2003) '"Is Race a Trope?"': Anna Deavere Smith and the Question of Racial Performativity', *African American Review,* 37, 1: 127–38.

Tian, M. (1997) '"Alienation-Effect" for Whom? Brecht's (Mis)interpretation of the Classical Chinese Theatre', *Asian Theatre Journal,* 14, 2 (Autumn): 200–22.

Ticker, B. (2004) 'Op-Ed: The Case Against Rachel Corrie', *Arutz Sheva 7* (30 May), www.israelnationalnews.com/Articles/Article.aspx/3735#.T_ F8sRee6fU, accessed 16 July 2012.

Time Magazine (1964) 'The Character Speaks Out' (20 November).

Toporkov, V. (1979) *Stanislavski in Rehearsal,* trans. Christine Edwards (New York: Theatre Arts Books).

Tricycle Theatre (2007) Programme for *Called to Account.*

—— (2010) *Tricycle Theatre Website,* www.tricycle.co.uk, accessed 10 July 2010.

Upton, C. (2009) 'The Performance of Truth and Justice in Northern Ireland: The Case of Bloody Sunday' in Forsyth, A. and Megson, C. (eds) *Get Real: Documentary Theatre Past and Present* (Basingstoke: Palgrave Macmillan) 179–94.

Valentine, A. (2007) *Parramatta Girls* (Sydney: Currency Press).

—— (2008) 'The Tune of the Spoken Voice', *Australian Writers Guild Magazine*, www.alanavalentine.com/media/australian-writers-guild-magaz ine.pdf, accessed 10 July 2012.

—— (2011) Interview on *Fresh Ink* website, www.freshink.com.au/programs/ interviews/alana-valentine, accessed 1 July 2012.

Victoria and Albert Museum (2009) *V&A Museum's Theatre Archive*, www. vam.ac.uk/vastatic/theatre/archives/thm-317f, accessed 3 July 2009.

Viner, K. (2011) Interview with author, London (14 April).

Walker, T. (2007) Review of *Called to Account, Sunday Telegraph* (29 April).

Wallenberg, C. (2008) 'Who's Afraid of "Rachel Corrie"?', *Boston Globe* (7 March).

Wardle, I. (1978) *The Theatres of George Devine* (London: Jonathan Cape).

Watson, J. (2008) Telephone interview with author (2 June).

Watt, D. (2003) 'The Maker and the Tool: Charles Parker, Documentary Performance, and the Search for a Popular Culture', *New Theatre Quarterly*, 19, 1: 41–66.

—— (2009) 'Local Knowledges, Memories, and Community: from Oral History to Performance' in Haedicke, S. C., Heddon, D., Oz, A. and Westlake, E. J. (eds) *Political Performances* (New York: Rodopi) 189–212.

Watt-Smith, T. (2012) Interview with author, London (12 March).

Weber, K. (1995) 'Brecht's "Street Scene" – On Broadway, of all Places? A Conversation with Anna Deavere Smith', *The Brecht Yearbook 20*: 50–64.

Weiss, P. (1966) *The Investigation: Oratorio in 11 Cantos* (London: Calder & Boyars).

—— (1971) 'The Material and the Models: Notes Towards a Definition of Documentary Theatre', trans. Heinz Bernard, *Theatre Quarterly*, 1, 1: 41–3.

Wengraf, T. (2001) *Qualitative Research Interviewing* (London: Sage).

Wertenbaker, T. (1989) *Our Country's Good* (London: Methuen).

Wheatley, T. (2007) Interview in London with author (8 May).

White, G. D. (2006) '"Quite a Profound Day": The Public Performance of Memory by Military Witnesses at the Bloody Sunday Tribunal', *Theatre Research International*, 31, 2: 174–87.

White, J. J. (2004) *Bertolt Brecht's Dramatic Theory* (London: Camden House).

Willett, J. (ed.) (1964) *Brecht on Theatre* (London: Methuen).

—— (1978) *The Theatre of Erwin Piscator* (London: Eyre Methuen).

Williams, H. (1966) *The Speakers* (London: Vintage Books).

Wilson, E. (2006) *Unprotected* (London: Josef Weinberger).

Woolf, D. (2006) *Beyond Belief* (unpublished play script).

Woolley, J. (2009) Telephone interview with author (17 March).

Wright, E. (1989) *Post-modern Brecht: A Re-representation* (London and New York: Routledge).

Wu, D. (2000) *Making Plays: Interviews with Contemporary British Dramatists and Directors* (New York: St Martin's Press).

Young, S. (2009) 'Playing with Documentary Theatre: *Aalst* and *Taking Care of Baby*', *New Theatre Quarterly*, 25, 1 (February): 72–87.

Zarrilli, P. (ed.) (2002) *Acting (Re)considered: A Theoretical and Practical Guide* (New York: Routledge).

Zuolin, H. (1982) 'A Supplement to Brecht's "Alienation Effects in Chinese Acting"' in Tatlow, A. and Wong, T. (eds) *Brecht and East Asian Theatre* (Hong Kong: Hong Kong University Press) 96–110.

Index

Printed in China